What Do We Expect from Our Government?

What Do We Expect from Our Government?

Edited by Beryl A. Radin and Joshua M. Chanin

LEXINGTON BOOKS
A division of
ROWMAN & LITTLEFIELD PUBLISHERS, INC.
Lanham • Boulder • New York • Toronto • Plymouth, UK

Published by Lexington Books
A division of Rowman & Littlefield Publishers, Inc.
A wholly owned subsidiary of The Rowman & Littlefield Publishing Group, Inc.
4501 Forbes Boulevard, Suite 200, Lanham, Maryland 20706
http://www.lexingtonbooks.com

Estover Road, Plymouth PL6 7PY, United Kingdom

British Library Cataloguing in Publication Information Available

Library of Congress Cataloging-in-Publication Data

What do we expect from our government? / edited by Beryl A. Radin and Joshua M. Chanin.
p. cm.
Includes bibliographical references and index.
ISBN 978-0-7391-4453-4 (cloth : alk. paper)
1. Government accountability—United States. 2. United States—Economic policy—2009- 3. United States—Social policy—1993- 4. Environmental policy—United States. 5. Terrorism—Government policy—United States. I. Radin, Beryl. II. Chanin, Joshua M.
JK421.W444 2010
320.60973—dc22 2010018270

∞™ The paper used in this publication meets the minimum requirements of American National Standard for Information Sciences—Permanence of Paper for Printed Library Materials, ANSI/NISO Z39.48-1992.

Printed in the United States of America

Table of Contents

Part Three: Focusing on Processes

Foreword

This outstanding collection of essays on critical public policy issues originated in a conference held at American University to celebrate the seventy-fifth anniversary of the founding of the School of Public Affairs (SPA). Seventy-five years ago we began the School of Public Affairs with just a handful of graduate students—federal employees who had come to Washington to staff the expanding government during the New Deal. Today we have some 2,000 students in thirteen degree programs, and over 15,000 living alumni.

As we thought about a theme for the conference, we wanted it to reflect the School's special character—our commitment to advancing knowledge through scholarship, and by so doing, to contribute to solving the great public policy problems of the day. Seventy-five years ago, President Franklin D. Roosevelt captured the idea perfectly when he came to American University and applauded our newly founded School for its mission of "practical idealism."

To reflect our enduring mission, we built the program for the conference around discussions of some of the most pressing issues we, as a nation, face today. Our approach to those issues was one that is a hallmark of the School of Public Affairs. We brought together scholars to present results of their research and practitioners—participants in the policy process—to reflect on how that research impacts their daily work. This cross-fertilization of scholarly knowledge and the practical wisdom of working professionals is a deeply powerful combination.

In asking, "What do we expect from our government?" we did *not* intend the obverse of President Kennedy's inaugural, "Ask not what your country can do for you . . ." As a school of public affairs, educating people for leadership in the public sphere, we have always believed in the honor of public service. Our students and alumni—and faculty—have long distinguished themselves by their contributions to the public good. They have never stopped asking what they could do for their country.

Rather, we wanted to put on the agenda a question that has become increasingly pointed in recent years, and that is very much on the agenda today: What should the role of government be? How should it work with the private sector and the non-profit sector to address the problems we face? President Lyndon Johnson's "Great Society" exemplified the faith of New Deal Democrats in an activist government, ready and able to take on major social and economic challenges. President Ronald Reagan, by contrast, saw such activism as intrusive. As he famously said in his first inaugural address, "Government is not the solution to our problems; government is the problem."

The Great Recession of 2008-2009 forced the federal government to take on staggering, unprecedented new responsibilities in the economy—an expansion of the role of government reminiscent of the 1930s. That expansion, together with President Barack Obama's ambitious legislative agenda of health care reform, financial regulation, and environmental protection, has once again provoked pointed debate about the proper role of government. As President Obama said in his 2010 State of the Union address, "These disagreements, about the role of government in our lives, about our national priorities and our national security, they've been taking place for over 200 years. They're the very essence of our democracy."

These essays cover a wide range of issues, all of which are urgent, and all of which are subject to ongoing debate about how government policy can and should address them. It is in the spirit of advancing that debate that we bring them together in this volume.

William M. LeoGrande, Dean
School of Public Affairs

Introduction: What Do We Expect from Our Government?

Joshua Chanin* and Beryl A. Radin+

As is clear from the extensive press accounts since the 2008 campaign and election, much has changed in the U.S. political environment since November 2008. While most of the press attention has been given to the actions and agendas of the new cast of characters in Washington, there are other impacts of this political shift that have not received as much emphasis. The election appears to have opened a window on a range of developments in the American policy and government world and has permeated multiple aspects of public and private activities. These changes have brought on a national soul searching that requires a rethinking of our views about the necessary role of government, the role of the private market, the impact of science, technology, and information, and, ultimately, our place in the world. At the least, there appears to be a shift away from the statement of President Bill Clinton in the 1996 State of the Union that "the era of big government is over."

The book attempts to provide a glimpse at this set of developments by focusing on a number of policies and processes. It is framed around the question, "What do we expect from our government?" and highlights changes in those specific areas as well as broader patterns that appear to emerge from those

* Ph.D. Student, School of Public Affairs, American University.

+ Scholar in Residence, School of Public Affairs, American University.

developments. The volume includes attention to a number of substantive policies (climate change, immigration, and terrorism) as well as governance processes (oversight, elections and campaigns, and regulation). In addition, it includes attention to broader issues such as national economic and fiscal policies and strategies for assuring equity and access in programs.

The book resulted from a series of papers and discussions that took place in March 2009, marking the 75th anniversary of the School of Public Affairs of Washington, D.C.'s American University. Papers were commissioned and written by individual scholars who were expert in specific areas. The papers were meant to frame a discussion on a range of policy issues and the conference itself provided the setting for discussion of those papers by panels of practitioners who were attempting to deal with the issues raised by the analyses. These practitioners included officials in both the executive and legislative branches as well as representatives from civil society organizations. The structure of the discussion provides a window on the relationship between research and practice and links between academic discussion and "real world" policy making.

The volume includes the commissioned papers as well as a summary of the discussion that followed the presentation of the written work. In addition, the book includes the plenary presentations made by well known individuals who focused on the broad question that framed the day and a half conference: "What do we expect from our government?" These include former GAO Comptroller General David Walker and former Clinton administration HHS official Peter Edelman.

The celebration of the School of Public Affairs anniversary provided an opportunity to examine the historical developments of one institution that has sought to develop both teaching and research work that is relevant to the changing needs of the American polity. The School of Public Affairs was the first school in the D.C. area focused on training of individuals who would go into the public service. It was created in 1934 with the support of then President Franklin D. Roosevelt; as a result the historical lens provides an interesting perspective on the theme of the book and the conference. One is struck by the similar political, social, and economic contexts of 1934 and the events of today. Various pundits have commented on the parallels between FDR's election and that of Obama. FDR's grandson, James Roosevelt, Jr., provided one of the pieces in the volume that emphasizes the historical framework and parallels.

Organization of the Book

The book is organized around three distinct but interrelated parts, each examining the central issues and themes relevant to a discussion of citizen expectations of government. Part 1 attempts to orient the reader by placing the early part of President Obama's first term in both policy and historical context.

Part 2 uses the contextual discussion as a springboard to examining three specific areas of public policy: climate change; terrorism; and immigration, each of particular resonance today. Part Three takes the reader through an analysis of three areas of governmental process: legislative oversight; campaigns and elections; and regulation. The hope is that the reader will be able to use the thoughts and arguments of experts and high-level practitioners as a means to think seriously about their expectations of and desires for the U.S. government as we move in to the second year of Obama's presidency and into the second decade of the 21st century.

Though references to earlier eras of war, economic strife, and dramatic political change appear throughout the book, none draws the parallel more directly or more poignantly than James Roosevelt, Jr.'s piece, which appears in Chapter 1. Roosevelt, the grandson of the 32nd President of the United States, acknowledges the seriousness of modern conditions, noting an eerie similarity between the joblessness and hunger of today and the desperation felt by many in the 1930s. He does not dwell on pain and strife, however. Roosevelt urges the reader to recognize "the importance of raising hope, instilling courage, and infusing the belief that people can change their circumstances."

Roosevelt, like his grandfather before him, and President Obama today, emphasizes not just the centrality of hope and energy, but the necessity of action, among individuals, publicly oriented educational institutions, and through a capable, willing federal government. In his view, the solution to today's problems—like those of 1934—are found in a vigorous, publicly minded citizenry working in concert with a government geared toward "a practical approach to practical problems."

In chapter 2, David M. Walker, President and CEO of the Peter G. Peterson Foundation and former Comptroller General of the United States, takes a much different approach to public spiritedness and to our expectations for our government. Walker begins by describing setting a set of principles that the American government should embody. His ideal type espouses a commitment to higher values, including those established in the constitution; competent, results-based systems constructed to serve the less fortunate with integrity and equality; innovative, bold solutions to enduring problems, regardless of political pressure or short-term convenience; and stewardship of resources—economic, environmental, and otherwise—with an eye toward long term prosperity and health.

To Walker, the reality of today looks nothing like this. His criticisms of the current political and institutional arrangements—the failures of which he ties directly to the country's struggling economy—run both wide and deep and demand systematic "transform[ation] of our policy, operational, and political processes." To overcome this systemic inertia, Walker calls for a series of reforms to be made by constitutional amendment, the only process he believes capable of circumventing the entrenched parochial interests and myopic thinking that have "broken Washington." The one constant running through his reform proposals is the desire to grant authority to technocratic experts as a means of avoiding political processes. Though his piece may be viewed as a polemic, it offers a sobering examination of the country's fundamental financial, political, and, as a direct result, social well-being.

Like Walker, Peter B. Edelman, a Georgetown University Professor of Law and Co-Chair of the Center for American Progress's Task Force on Poverty, uses a specific policy issue—poverty reduction—as a vehicle for addressing a much broader set of themes, including the nature of public service in America, the role of higher education in policy advocacy, and the necessity of research and public discourse on the structure and process of governance in the United States. In chapter 3, Edelman suggests that the 'business-as-usual' approach to poverty reduction—likely applicable to many, if not most, other contentious policy issues—simply has not worked. No ground is gained by rehashing old arguments about the proper size of government or in retreating to worn out ideological corners.

Instead, Edelman calls for a "coming together" to solve the country's most challenging issues. This is made possible through leadership from members of the executive and legislative branches, motivated by the 2008 election results and by the dire conditions facing the country. It is made possible through increased collaboration between relevant agencies at every level of government service delivery. It is made possible by process-oriented research geared toward improving the effectiveness and accountability of such initiatives and programs. Finally, and perhaps most importantly, Edelman suggests that it is possible through the empowerment of grass-roots organizations and community groups.

Part 2 of the volume moves from context and historical reference to an examination of our expectations for government in three specific policy areas: environmental protection, terrorism, and immigration. In chapter 4, American University professor and former EPA public servant Dan Fiorino conducts a broad review of the U.S. government's policy toward climate change and the impact of the recent economic crisis on that effort. Fiorino focuses on the nature of the problem, the political realities of environmental reform in the United States, and the several implications for private businesses and individual taxpayers of policies that aim to reduce greenhouse gases. The piece serves as both a primer on the climate change issue and an insightful real politic examination of the tensions presented by the 2008-2009 financial crisis for pro-environmental policy development.

Fiorino makes a convincing case that the future of climate change policy remains unwritten. He notes that despite the advancements made by leaders in the private sector, the policy making community has not yet defined the terms of the debate. The long list of policy challenges, ranging from health care to Afghanistan complicate the matter, as does the fiscal conservatism borne by high unemployment, growing deficits, and budgetary shortfalls. Even in light of these challenges, Fiorino seems to believe that the key to environmental sustainability may lie at the intersection of practical capitalism and public sector idealism. With this in mind, Fiorino closes with a warning, "If public policy stalls, business firms and investors will not know where to go. The political struggle to define the climate debate will determine the outcome."

Terrorism policy tends not to be imperiled by the types of economic arguments used to challenge climate change policy. There are no industries or trade groups that see robust anti-terror policy as an existential threat. As University of Maryland professor Gary LaFree argues in chapter 5, terrorism scholars to grapple with the role of evidence-based research and the importance of broad ideological participation in policy-making debates. To that end, LaFree's essay uses a new data set on terrorist attacks, the Global Terrorism Database, as a vehicle for challenging ten common misconceptions about terrorism. His conclusion is clear: terrorism policy would benefit greatly from a consistent dose of rationality. For instance, LaFree's review of the data suggests that there is no such thing as the ubiquitous, ultra-violent "super terrorist," impervious to government action and unburdened by operational mistakes or the usual limits on criminal behavior. Basing policy on such myths and the fears they engender can be a costly approach, both instrumentally and psychologically. Instead, LaFree calls for more systematic research and a dedication among policy makers and scholars to the use of all available information in crafting sensible counter-terrorism policy.

Though LaFree does not claim so directly, his data driven approach to busting 'myths' can be a powerful tool against terrorism itself, which "tries to exploit lack of knowledge to provoke emotional over reaction." This style of research is also an antidote to the "politics of fear," where governments take advantage of this very same public ignorance and fear. In the face of data and objective facts, the use of exaggeration, misconception, and stereotypes to achieve political or policy ends becomes much more difficult. LaFree challenges the reader to grapple not only with the value of data-driven policy and the need to revisit central assumptions about effective counter-terrorism strategy, but to consider carefully the political will necessary to follow his simple, but radical prescriptions.

In chapter 6, New York University sociologist Guillermina Jasso gives a primer on the current system of migration to the United States. She offers a detailed description of the varied procedures, rules, and particularities that define the system, identifies inequities and inconsistencies in that system, and offers a set of initiatives that would enhance the quality of experience for immigrants and yield tangible benefits for the U.S. government. Jasso's proposed reforms are built around three distinct principles: information; integrity; and inventiveness. In addressing the first, she calls on state and federal agencies to commit to data collection and dissemination. Doing so would enhance transparency and facilitate an evidence-based approach to immigration.

Jasso continues by arguing that returning to the system principles of equal justice and procedural fairness—what she terms 'integrity'—would produce substantial benefits. Finally, she reminds policy makers that immigration reform will require creativity and inventiveness, particularly given today's unfavorable political and economic conditions.

Jasso's essay touches on several of the volume's prevailing thematic issues, including the proper role for the academy and the value of systematic research efforts to immigration policy. She raises tough questions about the proper balance between an efficient policy and one that provides equitable treatment to all, and forces the reader to think through the varied institutional challenges immigration presents to the United States.

Part 3 steps away from substantive policy and into a discussion of three process-related issues: legislative oversight; campaigns and elections; and government regulation. Each issue is inextricably tied to the ability of our government to meet expectations, and certainly makes for no less interesting or important debate.

Chapter 7 addresses congressional oversight. Walter Oleszek's essay uses an historical lens to examine the current political moment in time, and presents a view of congressional oversight as a central, if not underused, tool in a representative's bailiwick. After all, there are few other mechanisms for holding the executive accountable, particularly in lower-visibility program areas. Beyond the check on executive authority, Oleszek, a staff member of the Congressional Research Service, sees oversight as a means to enhancing policy transparency; promoting public information; protecting Congress's institutional legitimacy; and improving existing law. In an era of unprecedented executive power and rapid federal spending growth, an assertive congressional "watchdog" is needed today as ever before.

Despite the need for an active congressional oversight, Oleszek makes clear that other legislative, electoral, and financial imperatives stand in the way. Members of congress may not have the time, the resources, or the incentive to vigorously examine the executive implementation of policy. This is all the more true in an age of unified Democratic control, where congressional leaders are less willing to challenge the actions of an executive led by a Democratic president. Oleszek's essay provides an updated look at institutional and operational questions that have challenged the American leaders since the country's founding.

In chapter 8, Oakland University professor David Dulio divides his look at our expectations for elections in to two categories: those related to the electoral process and those related to ability of election winners to govern effectively. In terms of the electoral process, Dulio argues that Americans are primarily desirous of free and fair elections—for voters, candidates, parties, and with respect to campaign finance. Further, he suggests that we want competitive, informative, and ethical races. After reviewing the literature and data on each of these issues, Dulio concludes that few, if any of our election cycle needs are being met. Though American elections have progressed since the founding era, voter intimidation, partisan redistricting, and the concentrated influence of wealthy private donors, among many other problems, continue to plague the process.

Dulio paints a much sunnier picture of our expectations for governance "after election day." Americans want—and tend to get—responsive, representative, and legitimate national politicians. Though threatened somewhat by the consistent reliance on pork-barrel spending and extraordinary events like *Bush v. Gore* (2000), Dulio argues that for the most part, voters have reason to be content with the composition and continued operation of the American democracy. He believes that the 200 plus years of peaceful government transition is an important indicator of our government's overall health. Though this is a positive sign, is that the best indicator of our government's "health"? Given the ongoing public debates over reform to our financial, health care, and environmental institutions, one wonders whether the government's ability to manage key areas of policy is nearly as robust.

In chapter 9, Rick Melberth, Director of Regulatory Policy at OMB Watch, argues the necessity of substantial reinvestment in the regulatory state as a way to address these and other challenges facing the Obama Administration and the 111th Congress. Melberth traces the decline of the federal regulatory infrastructure to Ronald Reagan, who famously declared, "government is not the solution to our problem; government is the problem." Melberth sees active federal social and economic regulation as the key to protecting the public from foodborne illness, financial collapse, environmental degradation, and industrial accidents, among countless other potential dangers facing the American public.

There are substantial challenges to strengthening the existing regulatory framework. Institutional conflicts over control of the process complicate the matter, as do persistent questions about the proper size, scope, and target of regulatory ends, to say nothing of the budgetary shortages brought on by the economic crisis. In the face of these difficulties, Melberth offers a set of prescriptions for reform and urges the new leadership to make good on its promise of transparency and increased public participation.

Book Themes

Roosevelt's use of 1934 as a reference point helps bring more sharply in focus a range of issues—both of process and policy substance—that are central to any discussion about the role of government and in particular the government's relationship with the academic, social, and political communities in its midst. These include:

1. The role of research in public sector decision-making. *What are the limits of traditional research? Where are the most pressing data challenges?*

What are our expectations about information? Who produces and uses it? What value for evidence-based policy?

Issues of climate change, immigration, and terrorism each present interesting substantive vantages from which to consider the role of data, information, and scientific evidence in public policy making. As this volume's discussion makes clear, both academicians and practitioners seem to agree on the importance of systematic, data-driven research to sound public policy. In the immigration context, Guillermina Jasso suggests that such an approach must begin with robust data collection and dissemination efforts by the federal government. Jasso urges the Obama administration to change key survey instruments—beginning with the U.S. Census—in order to enhance transparency and to facilitate useful analysis.

Gary LaFree takes a similar stance in his piece on terrorism policy, which uses data from the Global Terrorism Database, an open source database that houses information on international terrorism incidents dating to 1970, to debunk a set of commonly held 'myths' about terrorism. He concludes, "Objective research on terrorism is especially critical because policy in this area is likely to be driven by—even more than with common acts of violence—by exceptional cases. . . . Social science research can help."

Conversely, in some instances, data-driven research is superseded by economic considerations. In the environmental policy context, Dan Fiorino notes that despite the consensus among scientists that human actions are affecting the global climate, the findings have been largely ignored: "The years 2001-2009 were largely wasted in terms of national policy on climate…The [Bush] administration was unwilling to risk the economic well-being of the fossil fuel industry and other sectors, such as automobiles, that depended on it."

2. The role of the academy. *What is the role of educational institutions? Should it focus on training people for public service? Do we highlight leadership roles? How does it encourage dialogues between the academy and the public sector? Is its main role its research function? What about its role as a convener?*

To many of the authors, the academy serves a function well beyond its research initiatives. In addition to studying public programs and the governance process more generally, the volume's authors see the need for an academy geared toward educating citizens inspired by a better America.

To Peter Edelman, the intellectual resources of academic institutions are best used to promote aggressive policy ends. He argues specifically that American colleges and universities "should focus research and teaching on improving the efficacy of government in contributing to the amelioration of poverty in the United States." In his essay on regulation, Rick Melberth makes "a plea for our educational institutions to do their part in recognizing and teaching the importance of government's role in protecting the public." James Roosevelt sees the nation's educational institutions as best equipped to provide the Obama Administration's new "public servants with the education, dedication, and belief in greater good to become what President Roosevelt called a trained and loyal army willing to sacrifice for the good of a common discipline."

3. The relationship between economic imperatives and scientific information. *How do we balance these two essential areas? Who makes these decisions? How do we deal with interdependencies between public and private sectors? How are civil society/nonprofit organizations involved?*

To some, the economic imperatives brought on by the global financial crisis of 2008-2009 have dampened excitement over Obama's election and forced the country to grapple with public resource shortages and the realities of a prolonged recession. Themes of economic shortage and sacrifice—no matter whether related to the availability of scientific information, investment in robust accountability mechanisms, or otherwise—underpin almost every entry in this volume. To David Walker, for example, the country's fundamental economic conditions demand a wholesale shift in approach. He advocates reforming entitlement programs, constraining spending, raising taxes, and kicking our addiction to debt in the name of "promoting responsibility and accountability today in order to create prosperity tomorrow."

The economic downturn has created budget shortfalls at all levels of government. This has necessitated a shift in priorities, and in many cases resulted in fewer research dollars, particularly in those areas not directly related to job creation. Many of the book's entries see these conditions as an opportunity to correct long-standing problems. Walter Oleszek views the downturn as a justification for "sustained effort by the legislative and executive branches to try to make government operate more efficiently, including the elimination of unnecessary federal programs and agencies." Further, Rick Melberth uses a quote by President Obama to position the bad economic climate as an opportunity for fixing a broken financial regulatory system, "to ensure that a crisis of this magnitude never happens again . . . [i]t is time to put in place tough, new common-sense rules of the road so that our financial market rewards drive and innovation, and punishes short-cuts and abuse."

4. Dealing with uncertainty and change. *How do we deal with shifting parameters of issues? How do we factor in globalization? What are the limits of ideology? Should we assume conflict between players? What is the impact of new technology? Should we assume that complexity of decision making will increase?*

Uncertainty and change characterize the process of public policy making and the substantive policy that results. This uncertainty affects the government's ability to meet public expectations, and raises a host of questions about the future. Though no firm answers were forthcoming, many of the volume's pieces emphasize the need for public accountability, transparency, and creativity in a time when newly elected members of the government attempt to address a host of fluid policy issues. In extolling the virtues of "good governance," James Roosevelt reminds readers that "[c]hallenging times are frankly the most fertile ground for . . . creative thinking." Rick Melberth echoes that sentiment when he states, "[o]ur current challenges provide opportunities to start again and experiment with new approaches to rebuild the regulatory architecture of government".

5. Including a range of perspectives. *Are there boundaries to openness and transparency? How do we take citizenship seriously? How do we come to closure on decisions? Do issues "belong" to institutions? How do we balance values of efficiency, equity, and effectiveness? What do we expect from ourselves?*

Many of the essays in this volume highlight the importance of diverse approaches to governance and public policy. David Walker reminisces about the era when "individuals [came] out of their real jobs in the real world [to serve in government], whether it be as farmers or lawyers or businesspersons or physicians or professors," and laments the loss of such experiential diversity among our political class. Walter Oleszek suggests that President Obama's use of the term 'post-partisan' "might reflect a more pragmatic approach to lawmaking [where] good ideas are to be evaluated on their merits regardless of someone's ideology or which party offers them." Peter Edelman emphasizes the importance of a broad range of policy actors and institutions in addressing poverty in the U.S.:

> Government is only one of the relevant actors in reducing poverty. Speaking very broadly in delineating the role of government and the responsibility of the rest of us, we need a series of "both-ands." We need both public policy and private action. We need public policy at all levels of government. We need private action, both civic and one-on-one, civic in the sense of all the different sectors—business, labor, philanthropic, educational, faith-based, and so on—and individual in the sense of one-on-one volunteering and helping others.

6. Reexamining existing institutions. *Do we need to reinvent some institutional processes? What is the role of the traditional silos? Are there venues to deal with issues crossing jurisdictional boundaries? Where do we look for new approaches and models? How do we encourage inventiveness?*

Each piece in this volume examines in one way or another the operation of government institutions. Many, like Rick Melberth and David Walker, believe that circumstances demand wholesale institutional reform. Walker, for his part, seems to believe that neither of the political branches is capable of making the types of tough decisions America's current fiscal situation calls for. Neither is capable of raising taxes or cutting popular programs; neither will voluntarily institute term limits or stop using earmarks. Rather than work through the traditional policy making processes—a process he suggests may be broken—to approach the type of fiscal discipline and budgetary accountability the country needs, Walker proposes several constitutional amendments. It is no coincidence that Walker reminds readers of the fact that amending the constitution requires only "three-quarters of the states [to] call for a constitutional convention and Congress is out of it," a prospect he believes "would send the fear of God in Washington."

Though less far reaching than Walker's argument, Peter Edelman also advocates a set of procedural and organizational reforms designed to correct what he believes are significant problems in the current policy making infrastructure. Specifically, Edelman argues that several existing policy silos, including education, employment, health, and criminal justice services, to name a few, complicate service delivery to disconnected youth. To combat this problem, Edelman urges the invention of "an administrative structure, an implementation structure, that involves all these items . . . involved in the conceptualization and delivery of the requisite federal funding" to address the problem.

Guillermina Jasso, like many of the other authors writing for this volume, recommends institutional reforms that would shift the policy emphasis or focus of a specific agency or program. In a very granular example, Jasso argues for changes to specific census questions that she believes making both population description and immigration-related research more difficult: "Thus, the current year-of-entry questionnaire item [which asks immigrants to disclose the year they entered the United States], besides containing ambiguities that damage data quality, also has the potential to arouse fear among the foreign-born of being placed in legal jeopardy. It might be prudent for the Census Bureau to consider removing the question or undertaking a major revision."

7. Reopening classic questions. *Are the questions asked today new or variations on classic questions (e.g., conflict between a democracy and a republic)? Do current problems stem from our political structure and thus could be anticipated? Can the U.S. political system deal with complex and technical issues? Do we require reform of those institutions?*

Many of the pieces in this volume raise directly—or at least implicitly—questions debated by government officials, scholars, and citizens of every American generation. Some scholars grapple with questions related to government size, scope, and orientation. David Dulio, for example, considers the proper role of an elected official in the American system of representative government: "The questions of representation and leadership are again ones with which the Framers struggled. In the late 1780s, the Federalists and Anti-Federalists engaged in a debate that dates back to Edmund Burke—should elections produce delegates or trustees?" Similarly, Walter Oleszek argues that the classic dispute between Jefferson and Hamilton is alive and well today, and is especially salient in the debates over federal efforts to address the challenges presented by the economic crisis. Though James Roosevelt, Jr. acknowledges that debates over government size remain heated, he argues that they miss the point: "the question we ask today is not whether our government is too big or too small but whether it works."

Some authors examine questions of institutional role and the relationship between branches of government in addressing public concerns. In the context of regulatory policy, for instance, Rick Melberth raises several questions regarding control of the regulatory process: "Is there a need for Congress to reassert itself in regulatory matters? In what ways can Congress reassert its role or at least the continued expansion of presidential control?"

A third example is evident in the work of other scholars who, like Dan Fiorino, address the complex relationship between private enterprise and public policy making. In so doing, Fiorino argues that:

> [a] major task in designing public policies is defining the role of business in responding to the problem and adapting to the effects of climate change. The issue of climate change affects business in two ways. The first is the effect that policies for stabilization of greenhouse gas emissions will have on costs, products and operators. . . . The second kind of effect on business is the need for adaptation to the physical effects of climate change.

Conclusion

In 1934, President Franklin Delano Roosevelt declared to an audience of American University students, "Among the universities, American is yet young. But you have a great future—a great opportunity for initiative, for constructive thinking, for practical idealism, and for national service." At that point in American history, such unqualified optimism was rare: Over twenty percent of the country remained out of work and there appeared no near end to the Great Depression.

As American University's School of Public Affairs (SPA) celebrated its 75th Anniversary in March, 2009, the country faced a remarkably similar set of challenges. Like Roosevelt, a newly elected president, Barack Obama, had swept into office on the promise of a course correction driven by deep changes to the approach of policy making and governance. Though hopeful, Americans were not naïve to the challenges ahead.

With both historical and modern day context at the fore, scholars and practitioners involved in the two-day conference to celebrate SPA's anniversary debated the question, "What do we expect from our government?" From poverty, terrorism, and immigration to campaigns and legislative oversight, participants debated questions of substantive policy and procedural nuance.

We hope this volume captures the excitement and challenge of these debates and serves to reprise the discussion in a way that illuminates the gravity of the moment.

Part One:

The Policy and Historical Context

Chapter 1

The FDR Legacy: Yesterday and Today

James Roosevelt, Jr.*

It's clear that the work of the School of Public Affairs has never been more relevant to the work of the nation. I'm sure that you think, as I do, that there are amazing parallels between the events of today and those when my grandfather spoke at the founding of the school in 1934. That time of great fiscal strife and the corresponding resolve among the American people and their new president to change government in order to make it more effective for all resonates with the same clarity of tone and purpose today as it did then.

In 1934 there was an intense public interest and discussion about the role of government as the country was facing an unprecedented financial collapse. From Wall Street to Main Street storefronts citizens were focused not only on economic issues, but in some cases on basic survival. When I was preparing this speech I was thinking of that as a little bit of a contrast with today. Then I looked at the picture of the tent city on the front page of today's *New York Times*, in Sacramento, California, one of several in other cities in California.

In those days it wasn't only the big cities that were affected, and it isn't today. The future of small towns and family farms hung in the balance. Thanks to the powerful photographs of Dorothea Lange and Walker Evans, searing images of farmers and migrant workers are forever embedded in our hearts and in our national conscience. People across the land were hungry for new leadership to solve the national crises, and hungry in the most basic sense. We recall bread-

---

* President and Chief Executive Officer of Tufts Health Plan; Co-chair of the Rules and Bylaws Committee of the Democratic National Committee.

lines and think again—and you can walk down not far from here to the FDR memorial and see the haunting images of gaunt and desperate families.

But Americans in 1934 were seeking not only resolution to their immediate problems but they also wanted a reframing of the country's financial structure in order to address the root causes of these problems. And they, like us, sought long-term solutions. They needed, as much as anything else, hope. Just one year earlier, in 1933, my grandfather had delivered his inaugural speech containing the phrase, "The only thing we have to fear is fear itself." For most people the speech has fallen by the wayside, while that phrase has become embedded in the American lexicon.

My grandfather understood the importance of raising hope, instilling courage, and infusing the belief that people can change their circumstances. What most of us don't know today is that there was another, more instructive theme in that speech that resonated so forcefully at the time that it overshadowed the famous line that we know today. What galvanized those who read his words or heard him as they gathered around their radios was the theme of action. He said, "This nation is asking for action and action now. There are many ways in which it can be helped, but it can never be helped by merely talking about it. We must act. We must act quickly."

This is where the students and faculty of today come in. The American people are once again looking to their government for strong leadership and action. The administration now in place is ready to take that action and is seeking public servants with the education, dedication, and belief in the greater good to become what President Roosevelt called a trained and loyal army willing to sacrifice for the good of a common discipline.

I was struck by a paragraph in an article in the January 26 issue of *The Nation* magazine, in an article written by Tony Badger, the Paul Mellon professor of American history at Cambridge University in England, and the master of Clare College there. This paragraph particularly struck me.

> Finally in 1933 Roosevelt brought to Washington a remarkable group of public servants to staff New Deal agencies. Intellectuals, lawyers, economists, farm specialists, and social workers. Notable women with social policy experience who entered senior levels of government in large numbers for the first time. They have been scorned by right wing historians as impractical theorists, dogooders who had never met a payroll and who were driven by intense antibusiness prejudice. Actually they provided a model of disinterested public service that was socially concerned and competent. Let us hope Obama can instill the same zeal for public service in the young people who so energized his campaign and the whole political process.

Those were the first students of this school. Those are the people this school was founded for. So I thought that acknowledgement by a British historian was particularly relevant today.

I can think of no message that surpasses what my grandfather said seventy-five years ago to another audience here at American University. He told them, as I would tell you today, "You have a great future, a great opportunity for initiative, for constructive thinking, for practical idealism, and for national service. Government needs not only the sociological and economic point of view, but it also needs the practical assistance of men and women who represent the academic, business, and professional elements in all our communities." That's a direct quote from that speech seventy-five years ago.

The efforts of 1934 saw fear kept in check by purpose, and despair succumb to determination. Though generations removed, we are the same Americans who are called to build a new democracy. As it was true in 1934, today I believe we have entered a time of inclusion and great expectation for what national service and civil servants can achieve for our country and in the lives of ordinary Americans. As President Obama said in his inaugural address, the question we ask today is not whether our government is too big or too small but whether it works. Whether it helps families find jobs at a decent wage, care they can afford, a retirement that is dignified.

It is to the alumni and the students of American University that President Obama must look to put that commitment to the public good into action, to make government work for all its citizens. Governing requires a professional, committed, and diverse civil workforce so that all Americans are represented. But there is another subtle, yet important point worth mentioning. You may think it's so obvious as to be assumed, but you cannot assume this. You must believe it as a principle, and that is, governing well requires a belief in the effectiveness of good governance.

I don't believe that I've overstated by saying that the School of Public Affairs fosters this philosophy. To govern well means to be actively engaged. It means appointing professional managers, encouraging new public employees, and actively advancing the profession of civil service, while thinking creatively. Challenging times are frankly the most fertile ground for this sort of creative thinking.

President Obama challenged public employees in his inaugural address to greater transparency and wise use of public dollars. Is not that the definition of public administration, the pursuit of the public good by enhancing civil society and social justice? This is common sense. It is a practical approach to practical problems. And it will restore the vital trust between the people and their government.

Whether pursuing a career in politics, or working for an NGO, for a non-profit (as I do), or a public agency or institution, public service is a career that embraces practical idealism. In 2009, as in 1934, the environment is rich for those who believe that working in government is a way to advance our nation, achieve lofty ideals, contribute to a greater good, and experience a career that offers personal satisfaction. It can be no less a calling than that to teach, or to heal, or administer to others.

As my grandfather said in 1934, "These dark days, my friends, will be worth all they cost us if they teach us that our true destiny is not to be ministered unto, but to minister to ourselves and to our fellow men." That is what I think a public affairs program and the public affairs program here at American University is all about, and I congratulate all of you on this 75th anniversary of the founding of the School of Public Affairs.

Chapter 2

The Economic Crisis: How Can We Deal with It?

David M. Walker*

When I looked at the issue of what do we expect from our government, I thought of six things. First, *commitment*. Secondly, *competency*. Thirdly, *caring*. Fourthly, *integrity*. Fifthly, *innovation*. And last, but certainly not least, *stewardship*.

And when I say commitment, what type of commitment am I speaking about? First, *commitment* to the Constitution of the United States. I carry a copy in my briefcase. I have a copy on my desk at work. I have a copy on my desk at home. And quite frankly, I think we ought to give an annual exam to elected and appointed officials on the Constitution because it is pretty clear to me that some people need a refresher course. Secondly, a commitment to the greater good, the collective best interest of all, rather than the narrow interest of a few.

Competency—focusing on results, focusing on things that will generate value, that will mitigate risk, that will avoid crises. Dealing with economy, efficiency, effectiveness, ethics, and equity.

Caring—Caring for those who are less fortunate in our society. Caring for those who fought for our independence and many who died. Caring for those who will come after us. And caring, obviously, in the case of elected officials, for their constituents, while recognizing that sometimes you have to do what you think is right rather than what is necessarily popular. But you need to stay in touch with your constituents and carefully consider what they have to say.

Integrity—truth, the whole truth and nothing but the truth. Leading by example, practicing what you preach, making sure that actions match words. Fairly simple concepts, but ones that frankly aren't always followed. Recognizing that

* President and CEO of the Peter G. Peterson Foundation, former Comptroller General of the United States and head of the U.S. Government Accountability Office (GAO).

the law represents the floor of acceptable behavior and that ethics and morality represent a higher calling. And our objective is not to crawl on the floor, but to reach for the ceiling. Recognizing that in the final analysis, it is not necessarily doing what is popular; it is doing what is right. That is what leadership is all about.

Innovation—finding new ways to address old problems. Helping others to see the way forward. Recognizing that in many cases, and clearly such as the case today, we need dramatic, fundamental transformational change, not incrementalism. We are on a burning platform and we need to recognize that reality.

And last, but certainly not least, *stewardship*. Recognizing that as leaders, no matter what our role might be and what sector of the economy we might be in that it is not just about generating positive results today; it is not just trying to leave things better off when we leave than when we came, whether it is a position or this earth; it is about leaving things better positioned for the future. That is what stewardship is. And it is a long and proud tradition of many generations of Americans.

And what about the American dream? In my personal opinion, the American dream is not owning a home (although I do and many Americans do). I believe that the American dream is really about two things. There is an individual element and there is a collective element.

The individual element is for every individual to be able to achieve their full God-given potential, to have the opportunity to be all that they can be. Secondly, to recognize our collective responsibility to be able to leave things better off and better positioned for future generations. And candidly, this country had a long and proud tradition of doing that, but it is now at risk because we have strayed from the principles and values that made us great.

If we look at the Constitution, for example, we will find that we have strayed from many of the principles and values in the Constitution, which our founders fought and died for. If we look, for example, at the composition of government, we will find that all of the express and enumerated responsibilities envisioned by the founding fathers for the federal government are in the 39 percent of the federal budget that is deemed to be discretionary spending and is getting squeezed with increasing frequency as we move ahead.

If we look at our political process, we will see that rather than having individuals come out of their real jobs in the real world, whether it be as farmers or lawyers, business persons, physicians, professors, or whatever it might be, that all too frequently today, we see individuals who want to be professional politicians. They view their position as a job and they want to make a career out of it. As a result, there is an increasing disconnect between the real world and those who are representing their constituents out in the real world.

If we look from a national security standpoint, we will find that Washington cautioned us not to involve ourselves in foreign conflicts. And yet for the first time in the history of the United States, we engaged in a preemptive war, a war that was not declared by the Congress. And quite frankly, war has not been declared since World War II. So that is a matter of concern.

If we look at the issue of thrift, this country was founded on thrift. If you didn't pay your bills at the beginning of the republic, you went to prison. Savings represented the seed corn needed to create a better future. And today, unfortunately, bankruptcy no longer has a taint. And in fact, it is a strategy for some companies and for some individuals, and our savings rates are very low. And for the federal government, they are negative—big time.

Now, we face a number of sustainability challenges—fiscal, environment, health care, taxes, immigration, international relations, education—and if I have said it already, I am going to say it again—health care. Our current policies and practices in these and other areas are unsustainable in their present form. We need to make significant course corrections. And we need to do it sooner rather than later.

From a fiscal standpoint, we have gone from large and growing surpluses at the turn of the millennium to record current deficits, and projected trillion-dollar-plus deficits based on reasonable assumptions for a number of years in the future. We have gone from a creditor nation to a debtor nation. We have gone from where the United States had no foreign lenders at the end of World War II, to where over half of our public debt is held by foreign lenders. Over 70 percent of our new debt is purchased by foreign lenders because we are not saving enough. And our foreign lenders are now publicly stating their concerns about our creditworthiness that the world may need to move to a global currency rather than continued reliance on the dollar.

These are market-based warning signals that are being shot across the bow of our ship of state. It is important that we heed them. The simple fact of the matter is that we are in a recession. It is a global recession. But we will come out of it. But this is not a typical business-cycle recession. There are other factors that are at play: the financial institutions' credit crunch, the burst of the housing bubble and a number of ripple effects that occurred related thereto. Clearly, we need to take steps to turn the economy around. Clearly, we need to take steps in order to address these various crises. And by doing so, it is going to cost money. And therefore, the fact that our deficit and debt levels are escalating dramatically in the short term, it may be a matter of concern, but they are understandable under the circumstances. And we will just have to accept that.

At the same point in time, when you end up running deficits and accumulating debt levels as large as we are, we have to make sure that people don't get numb to the numbers. Specifically, when you start running deficits, which the latest Congressional Budget Office (CBO) estimates at $1.85 trillion, $1,850 billion dollars, there is a tendency for people to say, gee, what is a few hundred billion more? It is just not that much money. And while yes, we need a stimulus program. Stimulus spending should be timely, targeted and temporary. And while yes, the government needs to be able to meet certain legitimate needs, an

8.3 percent increase in the base of discretionary spending, including a 10 percent increase in the legislative branch, is outrageous. It does not pass a "straight face test" in these tough times. This is in the base of federal spending that will be with us forever and not part of the stimulus. And there are thousands of earmarks, some of which clearly are politically motivated rather than economically merited.

We need to recognize that yes, financial institutions and certain other entities might need assistance. But we need to have clearly defined objectives about what are we trying to achieve. We need to have criteria established as to who is going to get the money and who is not going to get the money. We need to have conditions that are known up front as to what you can and cannot with the money. And the failure to have those three things can lead to a situation like TARP, the Troubled Asset Relief Program, where we spent $350 billion and we have to ask what did we get for it. And the answer that we get is well, it would have been worse had we not done it.

Well, you can't prove a negative. And so therefore, we really don't know. We need to learn lessons from that experience. Yes, we need to reform our health care system. Yes, we need to engage in some transformational changes with regard to energy. Yes, we need to address some of the challenges that exist with regard to education and infrastructure. At the same point in time, we also have to recognize that we cannot spend and borrow our way to prosperity. And the simple fact of the matter is that while the United States does not have an express credit card limit, there is a credit card limit. And that limit will be determined by China and our foreign lenders when they decide that they need to start charging a higher risk premium because of our inability to get our financial house in order. And we are already hearing some rumblings of that now.

We are stoking inflation with fiscal policy after we turn the corner, and we are stoking inflation with monetary policy. The Federal Reserve has tripled its balance sheet in the last two years. How does it do that? It prints money. The Federal Reserve is engaging in a number of actions designed to help us in the short term deal with certain crises, but it is also increasing our risk over time. The Federal Reserve has now announced that it is going to buy huge amounts of federal government debt. Why? Because there may not be as much appetite for that debt in the market. And by having a captive purchaser of that debt on a scale much greater than the Social Security surplus, it serves to hold down interest rates in the short term. But you cannot change market forces over time.

We must recognize the reality that the United States' financial condition is deteriorating and that the American people are ahead of their elected officials. We conducted a statistically valid research study by Peter Hart and Bill McInturff. And here are the findings. This is what the American people think.

The number one thing they are concerned about is the need to turn the economy around. Surprisingly, the number two thing that they are concerned about is escalating deficit and debt levels and our increased reliance on foreign lenders. Americans understand what can happen when you take on too much debt. And they know that the too-big-to-fail concept has been proven wrong over and over again.

They rated this issue—escalating deficits and debt and increased reliance on foreign lenders—significantly ahead of healthcare reform, significantly ahead of global warming, significantly ahead of middle-class tax cuts, significantly ahead of Iraq and Afghanistan, significantly ahead of another nation who might have adverse interests to us getting a nuclear weapon. These are all important issues, as well. But everything in the world is relative.

They believe that Washington is broken—at least the elected officials' part of Washington is broken. They believe that by 90 percent—nine to one—that we need to start making tough choices to put our own financial house in order, and the sooner the better. They believe that the regular order in Washington—you know, the normal legislative process—is dysfunctional. And they believe that we need a fiscal future commission where everything is on the table, that will engage the American people in ways they have never been engaged on these public-policy issues, that will leverage the internet in ways it has never been leveraged before for a public-policy issue, that will be able to make a range of recommendations on budget controls, Social Security, healthcare, taxes and other needed reforms with guaranteed hearings and an up-or-down vote in Congress with limited amendments.

They believe we need that and they are right. And hopefully, what we will see in the not-too-distant future is that we not just take steps to try to turn the economy around in the short term and to deal with our immediate crises. Those are necessary. But that we also recognize the reality that we need to put a process in place, such that once the economy does start turning the corner, such that once that we do get past the immediate crises that we will be able to have our elected officials start making some tough choices on a range of issues that we have known that we have had for a long time—large, known and growing problems, but we have been kicking the can down the road far too long.

We need to transform our policy, operational and political processes. In many cases, it can be done administratively. In others, it will require changes in law. In some, it will require constitutional amendments.

But here is the bottom line. We are a great country. We have faced great challenges in the past. And when the first three words in the Constitution came alive, we the people, we have always risen to meet the challenge successfully. Yes, we can re-impose tough budget controls in order to make sure that we put ourselves in a more prudent and sustainable fiscal path. Yes, we can reform the Social Security system to make it solvent, sustainable, secure, and more savings-oriented. It is a critically important program. Yes, we can reform our healthcare system to reduce cost growth and to be able to make sure it doesn't bankrupt our country, while at the same point in time, making sure that all Americans have basic and essential care that is affordable and sustainable over time and yet, avoids taxpayer-funded heroic measures and subsidizing middle- and upper-income individuals for voluntary programs.

Yes, we can end up reforming our tax system to make it more streamlined, more simplified, more competitive to deal with the tax gap, to help make sure that it generates adequate revenues to pay our current bills and deliver on the promises we intend to keep. Yes, we can re-baseline government to separate the wheat from the chaff between which programs and tax policies are generating positive results, which ones are focused on the future rather than perpetuating the past. Yes, we can do these and many other things, including regulatory reforms to be able to make sure that we can try to reduce the possibility that the type of disruptions and crises that we have seen lately will happen in the future.

At the same point in time, we cannot achieve all of these things with the business as usual, status quo, do-nothing mentality in Washington, D.C. We desperately need presidential leadership on these issues. We desperately need some bipartisan support from the Congress. And more importantly than anything else, we desperately need the first three words in the Constitution to come alive, we the people.

We the people are responsible and accountable for what does or does not happen in the capital, around this country. We the people owe it to our founding fathers. We the people owe it to our children and our grandchildren. We the people owe it to future generations yet unborn in order to effectively discharge our stewardship responsibility and to make sure that the United States' future will be better than its past. And if we do take these choices, that will be true. Our greatest years will be ahead of us. And if we don't, then our greatest years may be behind us.

I think we might need to think about some constitutional amendments over time in two areas—financial and political. And I will just mention a few for consideration.

On the financial front, I think if the federal government is going to spend money on something, it needs to have a national purpose. One of the biggest problems I have with earmarks is that many do not have any national purpose at all. They are local issues. Many earmarks circumvent the competitive betting process. Both practices are unacceptable. Now, earmarks don't represent a tremendous amount of money as it relates to our fiscal challenge (typically about 1 percent of annual spending) but they corrupt the process and undercut credibility.

Secondly, I think we need to think about whether or not there ought to be a limit as to how much in total contributions can be received from people who can't vote for a particular candidate. We should make sure that a vast majority of campaign funds are coming from people who actually can vote for a candidate? Novel concept, all right.

We have to keep in mind that 10,000 baby boomers are retiring every day for the next twenty years—10,000 a day for the next twenty years. And the way that we keep our books from a budget standpoint is cash flow, cash basis, not accrual basis, so that will have an impact.

So on the political side, I think the redistricting process is a major problem and that we need to take that out of the hands of state legislatures, where politicians protect politicians. They protect parties. They protect incumbents.

Thirdly, I think we need to think about what might need to be done such that if somebody wants to be a professional politician, you can do so, but you can't stay in the same job more than a stated period of time; e.g., twelve to eighteen years, whatever. Now, many states have term limits too short which can be counterproductive. But the idea that you can be a career official in the same job, I think, is a problem because it doesn't facilitate dramatic and fundamental reform.

But there is a lot we can do without constitutional amendments. And we are trying to do that. Keep in mind there are two ways to get constitutional amendments. One is the old-fashioned way: two-thirds of the House, two-thirds of the Senate, and then three-quarters of the states ratify it. Then there is Plan B: cut the Congress out all together, three-quarters of the states call for a constitutional convention and Congress is out of it. That would send the fear of God in Washington.

And one of the things that might have to be tested in a constitutional convention is whether the states can authorize their delegates to only vote on a short list of issues because one of the concerns about a constitutional convention is what issues might be proposed and whether or not Pandora's Box might be opened. That is a legitimate concern. Therefore, why not try to orchestrate an effort that says we authorize you to go to a constitutional convention on issues A, B, C, and D—or subject matters. It hasn't been tested. And the question is, could that be done?

We must also dispel some common myths. First, we cannot grow our way out of the problem because mathematically, we would need double-digit real GDP growth every year for decades to do it. That hasn't happened and it isn't going to happen in the future.

Second, we can't inflate our way out of the problem because, while inflation would reduce the burden of the $11 trillion in current debt, our real problem is not the current $11 trillion in debt. Our real problem is the $45 trillion in off-balance sheet obligations for Medicare, Social Security, etc., that grow faster than the economy. They grow faster than inflation.

And so we are going to have to make tough choices. One of the things that happened after World War II is we were over 50 percent of the global economy because Europe was in ashes, Japan was in ashes. We were it. And as a result, we had tremendous economic growth. We didn't have the kind of competition that we have now. And as a result, we were able to lessen our load by growing the economy, in addition to paying down some debt, but by growing the economy.

Realistically, we have to say to ourselves that when we get out of this current economic downturn, two things need to happen. Number one, we need to have somewhat higher savings rates. And we are starting to see somewhat higher savings because Americans now know what a rainy day is. They didn't necessarily know what it was before, but now they do. Somewhat higher savings means somewhat less consumption. Therefore, we are going to have somewhat less economic growth than otherwise might be the case, but maybe more sustainable economic growth.

And so as a result, I think, you know, there is no escaping the fact that we are going to have to reform entitlement programs, reprioritize, and constrain spending. And we are going to have to have more revenues, too. Taxes are going to have to go up. And one of the concerns that I have is the longer we wait to achieve the so-called grand bargain that President Obama says he wants to do, the longer we wait to do that, the higher taxes are going to go. Why? Two reasons: math and demographics/politics. It is not rocket science.

My contention is that the President needs to focus his energies and efforts on a shorter list of issues in the short term. And secondly, the President and the Congress need to pass a law that will create a fiscal future commission that will have some members of Congress, one or two people from the administration and some non-government officials on it that will end up taking this issue, go to the people, educate the people, engage the people, make a range of recommendations that will force an up-or-down vote. We are not going to get there through the regular order. We just won't get there. We now have a dysfunctional democracy.

I think we have a broader societal problem. Starting in the 1980s (and this is not a political statement; this is a factual statement) America and too many Americans became addicted to debt. And our savings rate started declining dramatically. That was a very different cultural change for this country. We now have a situation where we have a combination of three maladies: myopia (near sightedness); tunnel vision (one issue at a time); and self-centeredness (everybody wants everything, they want it now and they don't want to pay for it).

Look at what is going on with regard to government now. We want this, we want this, we want this, and we will just charge the credit card, all right? So I think, you know, we have a societal challenge, all right? Another issue that is going on is right now 40 percent of Americans don't pay any income tax at all. They pay payroll taxes, but the payroll taxes don't pay for the programs that they are funding. We are headed to where 50 percent of Americans won't pay income taxes. Income taxes are what fund the role and function of the federal government the founding fathers envisioned.

And so we have a number of different issues to deal with. In my view, government needs to focus its energies and efforts to help those who need help and to make sure that it doesn't end up creating programs and policies that are overreaching and therefore unsustainable. And let me give you two examples. They may be controversial, but that is okay. Let me give you two examples that deal with healthcare.

Medicare—there are three Medicare programs: Medicare Part A (I was a trustee)—is mandatory, funded with a payroll tax, hospital insurance. It already has a negative cash flow. All of the bonds are going to be exhausted within ten years. All of the bonds will be exhausted, so we are not going to be able to pay all the bills within ten years. Medicare Part B and D—voluntary programs, not mandatory, not funded with a payroll tax, funded with two things—a premium and general revenues. On average, the premium pays for 25 percent of the cost of the program. Well, now, if you are near poor, it makes sense to have a 75 percent subsidy. If you are middle and upper income, it makes no sense to have a 75 percent taxpayer subsidy for a voluntary program that is being debt financed and we are passing the burden on to our children and grandchildren.

On the tax side, we lose a trillion a year because of tax preferences, deductions, exemptions, inclusion. That is backdoor spending. The tax preference for healthcare, the fact that probably none of us in this room pay income tax or payroll tax on employer provided and paid health insurance—$250 billion a year, fastest growing tax preference in the code. Now, what does that mean? That means if you are a CEO for a private-sector company with a gold-plated plan and the highest marginal tax rates, the taxpayers subsidize your health care big time.

If you are near poor working in small business, part of the 47 million who don't have health insurance, you get no federal subsidy whatsoever. And is that equitable? Does that make sense? Is that sustainable? That is current policy. It is a situation where rather than government saying look, there is a societal need. We have a role to be able to try to meet that societal need. But there is a difference between providing opportunity and engaging in programs that basically provide middle- and upper-class welfare and put them in a situation where they are fundamentally unsustainable, to where those who are in need are left more at risk over time because the programs are not sustainable in their present form.

And so we have to start making some of these tough choices and we need to do it sooner rather than later. We are trying to promote responsibility and accountability today in order to create more opportunity tomorrow. And what we are trying to do is to educate and engage the American public. We are trying to partner with others to develop sensible solutions and to bring pressure on Congress to act and to hold it accountable if it fails to act to try to address some of these challenges.

The Peterson Foundation has several groups that we are spending a disproportionate amount of time on: young people, business/professional/community leaders, new and traditional media and key opinion leaders and policy-makers. Those are four key groups. We are using very non-traditional means: movies, the internet as well as more traditional means—advertising, funding research and things of that nature in order to try to pull all of these things together.

The way I articulate it is we are not a think tank; we are an action tank. In many cases, it is not that there aren't enough ideas out there about what needs to be done. It is a matter of pulling them all together, coming up with sensible solutions, building coalitions, helping to engage the public in order to actually get things done because that is the problem—getting things done.

If we want to keep America great and the American dream alive, we need to turn our economy around, address our immediate crises and we need to be able to start making some tough decisions that we have been kicking the can down the road far too long. We do need to make some targeted investments. But we also have to make sure that we are putting our own financial house in order. And we need to do both.

We need to achieve a grand bargain. That means budget process reform, Social Security, health care, taxes, among other things. By definition, a grand bargain means you are looking at it in a comprehensive and integrated manner and that there are tradeoffs. It is not a piecemeal kind of thing. Secondly, the President has also said that we need to understand which programs are working and which ones aren't and separate the wheat from the chaff. He is right. I would add tax policies. You know, people keep on forgetting about tax policies and all of the backdoor spending. You have got to do that, too. So he is right about that.

Chapter 3

Worrying about Equity Issues: The Case of Youth Policy and Poverty

Peter B. Edelman*

I want to speak with you this evening about poverty, but in a particular way. My topic is not the substantive policies that would reduce American poverty, but rather some of the structural barriers that reduce the efficacy of what governmental actors try to do, particularly the federal government. My suggestion will be that this School and others like it should focus research and teaching on improving the efficacy of government in contributing to the amelioration of poverty in the United States.

Let me begin with the obvious. Government is only one of the relevant actors in reducing poverty. Speaking very broadly in delineating the role of government and the responsibility of the rest of us, we need a series of "both-ands." We need both public policy and private action. We need public policy at all levels of government. We need private action, both civic and one-on-one, civic in the sense of all the different sectors—business, labor, philanthropic, educational, faith-based, and so on—and individual in the sense of one-to-one volunteering and helping others.

* Professor of Law, Georgetown University; Co-Director, Joint Degree in Law and Public Policy; Faculty Director, Center on Poverty, Inequality, and Public Policy. Former Assistant Secretary for Planning and Evaluation, U.S. Department of Health and Human Services (HHS).

We heard a great deal about volunteering over these last few decades as basically the sole answer that, added to people taking responsibility for themselves, would solve the problems. That was simplistic and one can hope we have turned a corner that leads us away from that kind of thinking. At the same time, we do need responsibility outside of government, both communal and individual. The community must take responsibility to help in many different ways, but also individuals do need to take responsibility for themselves and their children. One way to say it would be to say that the community (including public policy) and the individual need to meet one another halfway. The broader society has a responsibility to see that opportunities exist. Only the individual can walk through the door.

Let's dig a little deeper as to who should do what, including who does what best and—importantly—how we can assure that what is done is done effectively and well. I think that's an issue of particular concern when we're having a conversation at a School of Public Affairs. There are some paradoxes here. What government can probably do best in the area of dealing with poverty is to write checks to individuals. But if writing checks is the totality of our policy, we will have a very incomplete and, I would suggest, a very bad policy.

When we look at why people are poor and near-poor we find that many people are working as hard as they can and can't make ends meet. It is actually kind of astonishing when you think about it—we have arranged our economy so that (and we are not the only industrial or post-industrial society that has done this) the lower end of the labor market is so damaged that large numbers of people are forced to take low wage jobs. While they may not be poor in the technical sense of what we call poverty in this country, they nonetheless can't make ends meet and it is not because of any fault on their part. It is the consequence of what has happened to our labor market.

So we have many people who are working as hard as they can and can't pay all their bills, and we have others who can't find work or aren't in a position to work. The latter includes disability, but not only disability. All of these people need money, and that is an appropriate role for government. There is some dispute about the details but we certainly have the ability to do it, with responsibility mainly at the national level along with some contribution at the state and local level.

Writing checks to people or to programs and institutions that deliver a service to people adds up to a substantial list. It includes not just supplements for low wage workers, and safety net payments, but also money that helps with health care, housing, child care, and going to college, to name just a few. The thought arises that writing so many checks may be inefficient, although perhaps we do better politically if the assistance remains divided up into a larger number of smaller pots.

This idea of getting money or cash equivalents to people is a very big part of what we can expect from our government. Of course a big question, apropos of what I said about the labor market, is whether and how we can get employers to pay more to workers whose earnings are so low that they can't get by. And also there is a continuing argument about how much we should write checks, especially during times of prosperity, to people who are of working age and are not legally disabled. So there are many policy issues even about all of the areas that are encompassed under the category of writing a check.

The question of check-writing is only one aspect of the problem. It gets harder. In area after area there is the question of how to be sure that money we appropriate here in Washington gets into the best hands and is spent in the wisest possible way. Whether the money is for education or child care or housing production or something else, and whether Washington sends it to the state or local government or to some other recipient such as a nonprofit organization, we have never figured out how to assure maximum accountability for the money we spend.

We do have good reason to expect a role for our national government in dealing with these problems. But after all of these years, whether you want to go back to the New Frontier or the Great Society or to the New Deal, we still have huge questions about what is the best delivery system. I go into this detail because I think these are questions that scholars in public affairs should be examining, and that students should be learning about and thinking about as they go on out into the world.

There are block grants, formula grants, incentive grants, and competitive or categorical grants. There are big dilemmas: too few strings or too many. If you want to have few strings, if you want to go toward the block grant/formula grant end of the continuum, some local people may know better what to do. But I think we would all agree that many don't, and too many still have attitudes, especially about poor and minority people, that get in the way of doing the best to be helpful.

But can people in Washington do an unfailing job of picking winners? That is also a problem. There is no easy answer, except we need to keep working on realistic guidelines and outcome measures and non-back-breaking accountability oversight to go with formula money, and evaluation to go especially with anything that is experimental or involves a demonstration of some kind.

It has been refreshing over the course of the last months to meet with people who have come into the new administration and are actually searching for answers to those kinds of questions. They are not only asking about substance—what we should be pursuing and what are the best answers based on our knowledge—but also about the best structures for the flow of funds to go from here to there and how to evaluate the results of the spending.

The new Center on Poverty and Inequality at Georgetown, in which I am involved, hosted a meeting recently that was attended by senior staff from the White House, OMB, the Senate, and the House. The government officials asked what research supports proposals that were made. That was absolutely astonishing! I am not sure I ever heard that even in the 1960s, or under Carter or Clinton.

That is not to say that any of those people has a vote in Congress, but nonetheless, in terms of the advice that they're going to give President Obama, or in the case of the people from Capitol Hill, their bosses, it was amazing to observe the interaction that took place.

I think many of you have a role to play here. We need policy research, obviously on substance but maybe that's in other disciplines and other places in any university. And some of you here are experts in substantive areas, of course. But we need policy research on delivery systems and evaluation. We're still stuck in some unsatisfactory paradigms of how to evaluate some kinds of initiatives. We find that the best we can say, given the kind of vocabulary and conceptualization that we have, is that something that we're quite sure is making a difference is only promising because it was impossible to design an evaluation with an experimental group and a control group.

We need talented people to go into government to administer programs of all kinds—not only substantive experts but also people who will get into the nuts and bolts of how to run programs.

A huge case in point is occurring right now. When we give the Department of Education money in the tens of billions of dollars, or even $4 billion to the Department of Labor to put into the Workforce Investment Act system and get on out to the local level, we hold your breath because we are not completely sure that we have the mechanisms either to specify the outcomes that we want, or to hold them accountable even if we had them, and to be sure even what has been done with the money. What I say couldn't be more pertinent at this moment in history.

I want to use disconnected youth, both pre- and post-disconnection, if you will, as a case study. By pre-disconnection I mean young people who are still in high school and are at high risk of dropping out and not finding their way back. Disconnected actually is a kind of term of art in labor, economics, referring to someone who has been both out of school and out of work for a year or more.

This is a very big problem. We all know this. We are continuing to lose large numbers of young people, especially young people of color, to adult lives of going in and out of prison, or just being disconnected from the labor market and everything else in a more general way. Clearly there is no one answer, no easy answer. We need all those "both-ands" that I mentioned before in terms of public and private and all the rest.

Start with the national policy. You want to spend some billions of dollars, probably in the low billions. There's actually $1 billion right now for youth in the Workforce Investment Act, Title I, Chapters four and six. Just about everybody says it is being spent rather badly, if they even know how it's being spent. The word stepchild, not a pun, comes up repeatedly as we talk to people around the country about how youth are viewed by the workforce investment boards, the employment and training agencies at the local level.

People complain all the time about silos—that the young people in question need a coherent package of help and support, and instead are confronted by fragmented institutions and agencies and funding streams that don't relate to them as whole human beings. Some of the responsibility rests in the field of education, high schools and community colleges both. Employment and training agencies are in the picture somewhere. Various nonprofit organizations have various roles. Some of the young people get enmeshed in the child welfare system and, later on, in the juvenile and criminal justice systems.

We need to invent an administrative structure, an implementation structure that involves all these items, that gets Labor and Education and HHS and Justice and HUD and the Corporation for National and Community Service, and probably some others, involved in the conceptualization and the delivery of the requisite federal funding. I do insist that federal funding to help deal with this problem is imperative.

We need collaboration among the relevant agencies to help on all of this, to help write the legislation, write the funding guidelines, write the request for proposals, and judge them insofar as competitive grants are concerned, and create the specifications for evaluation. Those are tall orders.

Many of you have been in the federal government. Many of you study the federal government. How do you get departments to talk to each other? How do you get them to cooperate? Each of them has a different committee on the Hill. At least in the area of education and labor there is the same parent committee. But for lots of reasons there is turf and a general unwillingness to go at this.

We get interagency councils all the time. That is not the answer. They meet with each other and they have a talk. Maybe it starts out as a Cabinet-level thing, but nothing happens. So the Cabinet member doesn't come to the next meeting. Pretty soon the next one is the deputy. The deputy says, oh, that's not for me. I've got something better to do. Pretty soon you're down to the fifth level person. So that's not where it's at.

There needs to be someone who makes people come together. It has to be leadership from the White House. We also need people on the Hill who are willing to legislate in this way. And we need policy research to help think through what these mechanisms are and should be and how to make them happen.

Even more important is what happens on the community end. How do we use a federal policy to leverage local collaboration? Again our competence and our capacity are vastly underdeveloped. How do we create the templates and the incentives and the requirements to get communities to create the necessary partnerships for planning, implementation, outcome measurement, and evaluation?

How do we get the schools and community colleges and employers and the nonprofit community and the public officials, and everybody who needs to be there—the unions—to be at a serious table? You can create various councils and so on, and if they don't have some clout and some substantive responsibility and role, what happens is that the people who have real power and can make something happen stop showing up.

My impression is that we have not done the research and scholarship that we need to do on these hard structural questions, particularly about issues that cut across traditional substantive lines. Of course the issue I'm discussing is just one of them. The whole question of what happens to children zero to five as we start trying to think more holistically about putting together Head Start and child care and pre-K into a whole system at the community level is another very good example. What can the federal government do to incentivize that, or to carrot it, to stick it, to use a variety of things to get people to come together at the local level?

The child and the family now in Head Start end up being the pawns in that discussion. Head Start is only part of a day, it's only part of a year, and yet if you want to get the child care people and the Head Start people to sit down and talk to each other, you find more than a little politics that gets in the way. You want to get homeless children educated? You need to have a conversation that involves HUD and the housing people and the school people. If you want to deal with child nutrition in the schools, then you need to have a conversation that involves the Department of Agriculture and the Department of Health and Human Services, and again the Department of Education.

So the list of challenges now, with an administration that wants to get things done, is very long and very important. Getting the help of researchers and scholars and people who are students of the way government works is very important.

We have had a sterile debate for decades. Big government versus no government is essentially what it has been. Or a more sophisticated version of the no government side has been federal government for defense and some entitlements (and entitlements are under attack) and state and local government for prisons and schools, done badly. And private responsibility for everything else.

I hope we are at a point where we can end the sterile debate. But if we want to accomplish that, you and I have a big role to play. It is the job of this school and others like it to do the research and turn out the graduates who will make a difference in proving that government can do the part of the job that we want it to do.

I was inspired just today, sitting in the Old Executive Office Building with some young people whom President Obama has brought into government and, equally impressive, the young career people who were also there. Everyone there was very bright and committed to figuring out better ways to help the young people whom we are losing in such large numbers now. We need to get more graduates of schools like this one and its counterparts around the country to be interested in making government work better for people who need help most urgently.

So as you enter the next seventy five years of existence of this wonderful school, my challenge to you would be this—to help Americans have the confidence that their government can be effective in pressing toward the full social and economic and racial inclusion of everyone, and that it can play that role because there are able and caring people who want to be a part of government to work toward those ends.

Public service is vital, and if people truly believe that, it will become a fact that Americans can truly expect their government to do what it is needed to do because it will be run by people who can deliver the goods. Not big government, not no government, but good government. Not a new idea, but nonetheless one that is absolutely and totally vital, and one that has been lost in the fog of ideological debate over the past forty years. We have a chance right now. Let's all help to make sure we don't blow it.

Part Two:

Policy Debates

Chapter 4

Climate Change, the Economic Crisis, and Prospects for the Future

Daniel J. Fiorino*

The last few years may be described as unsettling, at best. The long-term and growing evidence of the effects of global climate change accelerated, with new signs of glaciers melting, species threatened, weather patterns disrupted, agricultural output jeopardized, and economic livelihoods uncertain. At the same time, in 2008, signs of an impending recession turned into a full-scale, global financial crisis that invoked comparisons to the Great Depression of the 1930s. Clearly, 2008 was not a year for those who valued serenity. Are these two sets of changes—the first long term and physical, the second more immediate, economic, and social—connected in some way? Does the response of government and firms to one affect their ability to deal with the other? What does the global

---

* Executive in Residence, School of Public Affairs, American University; Former Director, National Environmental Performance Track, U.S. Environmental Protection Agency.

financial crisis and the ensuing economic uncertainty and recession mean for our ability to respond to the threat of climate change?

This chapter presents a broad look at the problem of climate change and some implications of the recent economic crisis for addressing it. For some people, economic turmoil and uncertainty should cause us to delay action in response to evidence of climate change. For others, the economic crisis only makes the case for action more compelling and the potential benefits more attractive. The first part of the article presents a brief outline of the climate issue, the political context, and policy options. The purpose is to provide a basis for discussing the links between the climate issue and the economic crisis later. The second part considers the effects of the economic crisis on business and the implications for climate policies. It concludes that whoever succeeds in framing the economy-environment debate with respect to climate will determine the policy outcomes not only for climate, but environmental sustainability more generally.

The Problem and the International Setting

Climate change differs from more conventional environmental issues, such as air and water pollution, toxics dispersal, waste management, and ecosystem losses in many key respects. First, it is difficult to establish that a long-term process of changing climate is underway and that human activity is a cause. Climate change is a long-term problem that is knowable largely through the use of complex mathematical models. The existence of the problem and its effects are not easily observed and predicted, although that is changing to some degree. Second, the causes are spread throughout the economy and society. In the older set of pollution problems, it was usually possible to identify some industry or sector of the economy (e.g., the steel or chemical industries) as the villain and mobilize action to restrict their behavior in the name of the public good. With the climate issue, it is not as easy to isolate the sources of the problem. Virtually every group in society and nearly every sector of the economy contribute to climate changes.

Third, the perceived relationship between the costs and benefits of taking action are separated in time. Especially for opponents of action, real costs must be absorbed now in exchange for uncertain and hard to measure benefits that extend well into the future. This perceived combination of certain, immediate costs and uncertain, long-term benefits make it difficult to mobilize political support. Fourth, the climate problem, its causes, and the effects are unequivocally global. No one country can solve this problem on its own. Some nations, seeking to benefit economically, will be tempted to free ride on the actions of others. Inaction by a few major players (China or the United States, for example) will undermine action elsewhere. The climate issue requires collective action on a broad scale within a global governance system that may not be up to the challenge.

Although the science behind it is complex, the basic model for explaining climate change is fairly straightforward.[1] Some of the sunlight striking the earth is absorbed and converted into heat, and some is released back into space. The presence of carbon dioxide and other greenhouse gases in the atmosphere increases the amount of sunlight that is absorbed and converted into heat, thus having a warming effect. Some level of global warming is essential to life as we know it. Without the natural heat-trapping effects of greenhouse gases, global temperatures would on average be some sixty degrees Fahrenheit higher than they have been historically. The problem arises from what is known as the "enhanced greenhouse effect." As CO2 and other gases accumulate in the atmosphere due to human activity, as they have since the start of industrialization, more heat is absorbed rather than released and global temperatures rise. Changes in average temperatures have been linked directly with increased levels of CO2 and other gases in the atmosphere, largely due to increased use of coal and other fossil fuels. Of the three main greenhouse gases, CO2 has increased about 35 percent; methane by 155 percent; and nitrous oxide by about 18 percent since pre-industrial levels, dating to about 1850. The scientific consensus is clear; a review of 900 climate-related articles in scientific journals a few years ago found none concluding that human actions did not affect the global climate (Oreskes, 2004).

This warming process sets off a variety of changes. Thomas Friedman describes it more as a process of global "weirding" than warming because of the range of effects (Friedman, 2007). Among them are rising sea levels, due to melting glaciers and the thermal expansion of the seas as they expand; melting polar ice, of which there is increasingly clear evidence; the loss of glaciers and snow pack, which means lost water supplies in many parts of the world; more extreme weather events, such as more intense hurricanes due to warmer ocean temperatures and droughts and flooding due to changes in precipitation patterns; a range of human health effects, including the spread of infectious diseases such as malaria and cholera; and threats to ecosystems, such as coral reefs and many species. These effects are no longer just the product of scientific predictions. Loss of polar ice, melting glaciers, threats to polar bears and intense weather have drawn public concern.[2]

The seven largest contributors of greenhouse gases are China, the United States, the European Union (EU), Russia, Japan, India, and Canada. Their greenhouse gas intensity (emissions relative to income or per capita) varies greatly. For example, the U.S. emits about ten tons per capita, Japan about nine, India just over one. In emission intensity per dollar of national income, the U.S. fares better than the world average and is much more efficient than China or India. Still, the U.S. accounts for nearly a fourth of global emissions, with less than a fifth of the population. If current trends continue, China's emissions are likely to double and India's to increase by some 80 percent by 2025.

The climate issue rose steadily on the global policy agenda in the last two decades. Two aspects of this issue, already mentioned above, have made it far more challenging than an older set of environmental issues. One is the lack of clear effects that are felt directly. Until fairly recently, climate change did not present immediate effects that make it salient to the public. The long-range predictions of expert models are too abstract and uncertain to be easily grasped. To the extent that climate change has drawn attention, it appears to be due to observable effects, such as melting ice caps, threatened species (e.g., polar bears), and evidence of extreme weather. The second aspect is that it requires global action where there is no sovereign. No international political regime exists with the authority to aggregate interests, resolve conflicts, formulate solutions, and apply legal coercion. Opportunities for free riders abound. The challenges to collective action are formidable in what surely is the largest collective action problem in history.

The lead global institution is the United Nations Environment Programme (UNEP) and specifically the Intergovernmental Panel on Climate Change (IPCC), created in 1988 under the auspices of UNEP and the World Meteorological Organization (WMO). The 2,000-member IPCC's self-described purpose is "to provide the world with a clear scientific view of climate change and its potential environmental and socio-economic consequences."[3] From the start, the IPCC focused on three activities: assess and report on the scientific basis for and consensus on climate change; assess the environmental and socio-economic consequences; and formulate response strategies.

Serious international efforts to address climate change began with the UN Framework on Climate Change, negotiated at the 1992 Earth Summit in Rio de Janeiro. Its stated goal was to stabilize emissions at levels preventing "dangerous interference" with world climate systems. Signatory countries, including the U.S., agreed to non-binding goals that collectively would lead to stabilizing emissions at 1990 levels by 2000. This goal was translated into country goals and incorporated the principle of "common but differentiated responsibilities." Accepting their role in climate change, the developed nations agreed to take the lead and help developing ones address the problem. A series of interim negotiations considered such issues as which countries should be asked to set binding targets for emission reductions and what those targets should be. A crucial distinction in these discussions was that made between Annex I (developed) and Annex II (developing and transitional) nations. The Framework Convention provided that only Annex I nations would be required to set targets in the initial agreement, based on their historical contributions to the problem. The U.S. Senate ratified the Convention in 1992.[4]

These efforts set the stage for negotiation of the Kyoto Protocol in 1997. It was clear by then that the good intentions of the earlier agreements were insufficient. At the same time, evidence of the extent and consequences of climate change was growing. The overall goal adopted was a 5.2 percent cut below 1990 emissions by the 2008-2012 time frame. This goal was translated into country targets. The U.S. target called for a 7 percent reduction; for the EU it was 8 percent; the goal for Japan was set at 6 percent.

The Protocol gave Annex I nations five options for meeting their targets. They could establish policies that would lead to lower emissions; enhance carbon sinks, such as forests; participate in emissions trading agreements with other countries; use joint the implementation option, which allows developed countries to earn credit for projects that lower developing country emissions; and use "clean development mechanisms" that transfer energy-efficient technologies to developing countries and reduce emissions. In what proved to be a fatal flaw from the U.S. political perspective, China led a group of developing nations in opposing a last-ditch effort to include obligations for emission cuts.

To the dismay of the international community, the U.S. refused to ratify Kyoto. The show-stopper issue for the Senate, which had to ratify it by the constitutionally-required two-thirds majority, was the lack of binding targets for Annex II nations. The main stated objections were economic. Opponents argued that binding targets would impose costs on the economy and undermine the nation's economic competitiveness relative to China and other nations not facing such obligations. The political sentiment in the U.S. became clear in 1997, when the Senate voted 95-0 to direct the Clinton administration not to sign any agreement that did not include action from the developing countries. Although the U.S. did sign the Kyoto Protocol in 1998, it was never submitted for Senate ratification. President Bush shelved Kyoto upon taking office in 2001. Kyoto is no longer the issue in climate discussions anymore; it was a transitional agreement. The question now that people are asking is what happens after Kyoto?

Climate Politics in the United States

The United States has been viewed a global outlier on the climate issue. As the largest economy in the world, and source of nearly one-quarter of global CO2 emissions, other nations would expect the U.S. to be a leader. However, it was one of only two industrial nations that did not ratify Kyoto (the other was Australia) and has not adopted limits on greenhouse gases. To isolate the U.S. even further, Australia ratified Kyoto in 2008.

The years 2001-2009 were largely wasted in terms of national climate policy. George W. Bush had talked about climate during the 2000 presidential campaign, but dropped talk of any substantive action once he was in office. The administration was unwilling to risk the economic well-being of the fossil fuel industry and other sectors, such as automobiles, that depended on it. Not all of the fault for U.S. inaction can be laid at the feet of the Bush administration, however. Although the Clinton administration was more inclined to accept climate risks as real and favor action, it too had failed to develop political support for approving Kyoto, developing a national legal framework for reducing emissions, or creating a coherent policy to promote clean energy technologies.

Climate opponents in the 1990s and early 2000s based their case on two kinds of arguments—scientific and economic. The scientific one was that the rate of climate change over the long-term and the extent of its consequences are too uncertain. It is too risky, they argue to base fundamental policy choices with huge economic and social impacts on evidence that falls short of being definitive. Historically, climate patterns have been cyclical and observed trends at this point may simply be a part of such a cycle. In brief, human action may not be the cause of the observed changes, and the effects any change may prove to be manageable. The second argument is that the transition to a de-carbonized economy could be extremely costly and limit growth. Fossil fuels, especially coal, are ample and relatively inexpensive and are a mainstay of the economy. A particular concern is that having the U.S. adopt limits while such countries as China and India do not, would put U.S. firms at a competitive disadvantage. Some critics even see a kind of ideological plot behind climate advocacy; columnist Charles Krauthammer (2008) wrote in the *Washington Post* that climate action proponents were "advocating radical economic and social regulation" and using environmentalism to achieve political goals that advocates of socialism had failed to attain in the past. More recently, opponents of action have also argued that it will be cheaper in the long run to adapt to changing climate over time than to invest in aggressive efforts to reduce emissions (see, e.g., Goklany, 2008).

Proponents of action on climate had clear responses to both arguments. Although the precise rate and magnitude of change are difficult to predict, there is a scientific consensus that climate changes were underway and would grow in significance in the next several decades. The IPCC issued ever-stronger reports regarding the extent and consequences of these changes. With respect to the economic issue, proponents cited several studies that expected the effects of greenhouse reduction policies to have only a marginal effect on long-term growth. Going further, they argued that stabilizing emissions would produce substantial economic benefits through energy conservation, development of new technologies, international security and stability, and cleaner air.

One study that drew particular attention and reframed the policy debate was the report of British economist Sir Nicholas Stern. Commissioned by the Chancellor of the Exchequer, the *Stern Review* (2008) provides a comprehensive assessment of the likely costs and benefits of action to stabilize emissions. It finds that the scientific evidence points to serious, irreversible impacts from a "business as usual" (BAU) path. Not taking action (the BAU scenario) would lead to more than a tripling of emissions by 2050 and involve a 50 percent risk of a five degree centigrade average temperature increase. The costs of such a change would be substantial. Using conservative assumptions about the extent and effects of such a change, the *Review* predicted a loss of 5-10 percent in global consumption per head "now and forever" (x). Using less conservative but, the report asserts, more realistic assumptions based on recent evidence, a BAU scenario would lead to losses in the range of 5-20 percent of lost consumption per capita. Losses are likely to be in the upper part of that range. Costs of extreme weather alone could amount to 5-10 percent of world GDP annually by 2050. These impacts would be unevenly distributed; poorer countries would suffer most because of their dependence on agriculture; more variable climates; greater physical vulnerability, and a lack of economic resources for adaptation.

The costs of stabilizing emissions depend on the target to be achieved and when action is taken. One incontrovertible conclusion is that the longer the delay, the higher the costs and more limited the options (and higher the damages and costs of adapting). As for a target, the *Stern Review* assumes that we would aim to stabilize emissions in the range of 450 to 550 parts per million by 2050, the point at which most experts agree that some of the worst impacts could be minimized. To achieve the 550 target, emissions would have to peak in the next 10-20 years then fall at an annual rate of 1 to 3 percent. At a 450 target, they would have to peak in ten years and fall annually at a rate of more than 5 percent. The most likely costs of meeting the higher target would amount to about one percent of global GDP by 2050, within a cost range of -1 percent (a net gain) and 3.5 percent. These costs will "rise significantly as mitigation efforts become more ambitious or sudden" (xv). The *Review* concludes that "Weak action in the next 10-20 years would put stabilization even at 550 ppm CO2e beyond reach."[5] In sum, "the benefits of strong, early actions considerably outweigh the costs" (ii). Even given these modest costs, carbon reduction presents opportunities, from costs savings due to conservation and energy efficiency, cuts in inefficient energy subsidies (which amount to about $250 billion globally a year), and potential markets for low-carbon products that could amount to $500 billion by 2050.

The *Stern Review* has drawn a great deal of commentary, positive and negative. The most common criticism has been its use of a low discount rate in valuing the future benefits of acting to mitigate emissions and the effects of change (see, e.g., Nordhaus, 2007, at 201-202). A low discount rate has the effect of increasing the value of benefits in the future. Others have defended the methods and assumptions, including the discount rate (e.g., Dietz et. al., 2007, 121-68). Even among many of the technical (as opposed to the political) critics, the *Review*'s conclusions generally are accepted as being consistent with much of the thinking on the need for strong action (e.g., Pooley, 2009).

Several legislative actions have been proposed in the United States Congress. The one that came closest to passing before 2009 was the Lieberman-Warner Climate Security Act of 2008 (S.2191).[6] Any climate legislation adopted is likely to reflect its approach. The core of the bill is an allowance trading system in which participants may buy, sell, exchange, or transfer allowances (each allowance represents a ton of CO2). It creates a declining cap on emissions, beginning at 5,775 million metric tons of carbon dioxide equivalent in 2012 (from a total of just over 6,000 million in 2007),[7] to 3,860 in 2030 and 1,732 in 2050, about a 70 percent decline from covered sources by 2050. About 20 percent of these allowances would be auctioned initially; this percentage would increase over time. The remaining allowances would be given to emitters, states, and others. The bill includes emergency off-ramps to increase the availability of allowances if prices are too high; gives credit for prior reductions; and provides assistance to workers, carbon-intensive industries, and consumers. Funds from the carbon auctions would cover these costs as well as pay for energy-efficiency grants to local government, adaptation programs, deficit reduction, and other activities. In a June 2008 vote, the bill failed to gain the 60 votes needed to gain cloture and block a filibuster, and it was shelved (BNA Environmental Reporter, 2008).

Despite the inaction at the federal level, many state and local governments have taken an active stance on the climate issue. California in particular has been a leader on climate policy, as it historically has been on air pollution generally. Michele Betsill and Barry Rabe (2009, 201-225; also Rabe 2004) observe that California "is laying claim not only to national but rather world leadership on climate change." Passed in 2006, the state's Global Warming Solutions Act commits it to steady reductions over the next several decades, with a target of a 50 percent reduction to be achieved by 2050. California also is taking the lead in creating a western cap and trade program with Washington, New Mexico, Oregon, Arizona, and even Canadian and Mexican provinces and states. In the northeastern states, New York launched in 2005 the Regional Greenhouse Gas Initiative (RGGI). As of 2008, a clear majority of states had adopted at least one executive order calling for emissions reductions; nearly all states had begun to create greenhouse gas inventories (the first step toward creating a cap and trade system); a dozen states had adopted public goals for reductions by set deadlines; half had adopted Renewable Portfolio Standards for utilities; and over a dozen were involved in establishing regional cap and trade zones for utilities (Betsill and Rabe: 205).

Local governments also have taken initiative. Influential mayors have created networks for galvanizing action and sharing information. The most notable example is Seattle Mayor Greg Nickles' launch of the U.S. Conference of Mayors Climate Protection Agreement in 2005, which calls upon mayors to commit to a goal of a 7 percent reduction in greenhouse gases below 1990 levels by 2012. Mayors from some 600 cities have signed on.[8] Mayors have made a case locally based not only on the adverse effects on many cities of a changing climate, but on the corollary benefits of better air quality, cost savings, and a better quality of life made possible with balanced energy policies. Many of these climate initiatives may be viewed as part of an urban sustainability or "Smart Growth" agenda and relate not just to energy but to local waste management, land use, development, and transportation policies. Combined with state action, these local initiatives have prepared the ground for a more active national policy (on urban sustainability see Portney, 1999).

A major event in the evolution of U.S. climate policy came in the 2007 Supreme Court decision in *Massachusetts vs. EPA* (2007). The issue was whether or not carbon dioxide and other greenhouse gases should be considered an air pollutant, similar to ozone, lead, or nitrogen oxides, and if new vehicle emissions should be regulated under the Clean Air Act. Along with several other states, Massachusetts claimed that the federal government should be regulating CO2. Reversing a lower court, the Supreme Court held, in a 5-4 vote, not only that EPA had the authority but an obligation to regulate greenhouse gas emissions unless it could determine that they did not contribute to climate change. As important as the ruling was legally, it was also significant symbolically, because the Court accepted the evidence regarding human-induced climate change and the harm it will cause. In response, EPA issued an Advance Notice of Proposed

Rulemaking with options for regulating greenhouse gases under its Clean Air Act authority in July 2008.

The landscape for climate politics in the U.S. changed dramatically in January 2009. In marked contrast from the position of his predecessor, President Barack Obama committed to "placing the United States at the forefront of the international climate effort and raising hopes that an effective international accord might be possible" (Rosenthal, 2009). The President endorsed the concept of a national cap and trade program. The administration even decided to forecast projected revenues from such a program in the 2010 budget (BNA Environmental Reporter, 2009).

In June 2009, the House of Representatives followed up on the President's intent and passed The American Clean Energy and Security Act of 2009, coauthored by Representatives Henry Waxman of California and Edward Markey of Massachusetts (Broder, 2009a; 2009b). The bill establishes a cap and trade program with a goal of 17 percent in cuts by 2020 (from a 2005 baseline) and more than 80 percent by 2050, so it is more aggressive than the Lieberman-Warner bill that was stymied in the Senate in 2008. It also directs that states create Renewable Portfolio Standards and set new energy efficiency standards for buildings, lighting, and industrial facilities. The bill drew criticism from some climate action advocates for handing out 85 percent of the allowances initially and auctioning only 15 percent, although the percentage that would be auctioned increases over time. That the bill passed on a 219-212 vote along largely party lines suggests how close and partisan an issue climate action and cap and trade in particular have become. The prospects for the Senate, "where political divisions and regional differences are even more stark" are uncertain, although Senators John Kerry and Barbara Boxer introduced a Clean Energy Jobs and American Power Act in September 2009.

EPA also has changed its position substantially under the new administration. In April 2009, following up on the decision of the Supreme Court in *Massachusetts vs. EPA* two years earlier, EPA issued its proposed "endangerment" finding that emissions of CO2 and five other greenhouse gases "threaten the public health and welfare of current and future generations."[9] This proposal does not set standards but paves the way for issuing them under the Clean Air Act. EPA also determined that motor vehicle emissions contribute to concentrations of these pollutants and to the threat of climate change. In June 2009, EPA reversed the previous administration's denial of a waiver for California under the Clean Air Act. EPA granted the waiver; this allowed the state to set greenhouse gas emission standards for motor vehicles that are more stringent than federal ones. The turnabout from Bush administration policies thus was well underway by the summer of 2009.

The U.S. currently emits about seven billion metric tons of CO2 equivalents annually. The two largest sources of emissions are electricity generation (32 percent) and transportation (28 percent), followed by industrial (20 percent), commercial (7 percent), agricultural (7 percent), and residential (6 percent) sources (Pew Center, 2009). Whatever the path that U.S. policy takes from this point, it will likely combine four kinds of policies for reducing emissions from these sources.[10] The first set of policies is to *reduce demand for energy-intensive goods and services.* This could include less driving, more mass transit, and more energy conservation, among others. A second set is policies to *increase energy efficiency*, such as with more energy-efficient appliances, tighter fuel economy standards, or low-carbon fuel standards. The third set involves *action on non-energy issues*, such as reducing deforestation or promoting low-tillage agriculture. The fourth and most critical set of options would aim for a *transition to low-carbon (including no-carbon) technologies*, such as wind, biomass, solar, nuclear, or vehicle options like hydrogen fuel cell and plug-in hybrids. A long-term strategy must be fashioned out of some combination of these categories. More specific policy instruments, such as a cap and trade program, tax incentives, technology research, subsidies, and regulation could be applied in the context of these broad policy options.

Climate Change and Business

A major task in designing policies is defining the business role in responding to the problem and adapting to the effects of climate change. The issue of climate change affects business in two ways. The first is the effect that policies for stabilization of greenhouse gas emissions will have on costs, products, and operations. The inevitable result of limiting greenhouse gas emissions will be to increase the price of carbon. This will have widespread implications for the economy—affecting some sectors more than others. The second kind of effect on business is the need for adaptation to the physical effects of climate change. The first is more important in the near and mid-term, especially the next few decades, as the U.S. economy moves from carbon-based to alternative energy sources. The second is more important in the middle- and long-term, because the consequences of a changing climate will need to be absorbed over the next decades and beyond. These two issues—stabilization and adaptation—are a useful way of thinking about climate change and business.

Much of the industrialized world already has begun to adopt policies for mitigating emissions, as have many state and local governments in the U.S. The federal government soon will follow. The effect of carbon mitigation policies will be to increase costs for many kinds of firms, especially in manufacturing sectors. The extent of these costs will depend on two factors: the carbon-intensity of manufacturing processes and the degree to which firms can pass those costs on to customers. A recent study by Resources for the Future found that higher prices for carbon-based fuels would most directly affect (aside from fossil fuel producers themselves) petroleum refining, chemicals and plastics, cement, primary metals, and non-metallic metals. These effects would be felt mostly in the short-term. As firms in these sectors are able to switch to new fuel sources in the mid-term, and make capital investments in alternative energy sources for the longer-term, these effects fade. The non-manufacturing sector will experience more diverse effects. The service sector, the most rapidly-growing segment of the U.S. economy, would experience limited effects in terms of reduced output (Ho, et. al., 2008).

Another set of firms will worry more about the physical effects of climate change and what it means for their business. Of course, all firms will face some common risks, including property damage, disruptions in their value chain, or delays in electricity, transportation, and other vital services. Some will face even higher risks and uncertainties. The insurance industry is an obvious example. Extreme weather events and sea level rise will lead to more property damage. A recent report concludes, for example, that climate change "is increasing the potential for property damage at a rate of between two and four percent a year" (Allianz Group and World Wildlife Fund, 2005). Increased health risks, changes in rainfall patterns, and disruptions to business operations will increase the size and volume of claims on insurers. Consider some of the effects of climate change on different economic sectors (Sussman and Freed, 2008: 7-9):

- Vehicle manufacturers will need to cope with disruptions in their supply chain, design products that tolerate new extremes of climate, and adapt manufacturing processes (such as in drying time for paint).
- The construction industry will need to adapt to higher insurance costs, the need for new building design standards, disruptions in supplies, and changing weather conditions.
- The food and beverage sector will face a greater risk of animal infections, availability of water and other raw materials.

Given these risks and uncertainties, it is clear that the private sector has a great deal at stake in the evolution of climate policy in the coming years. Three questions are briefly considered here. First, to what extent are firms now concerned about climate change and taking actions to prepare for it? Second, why are firms taking steps to reduce emissions and move to new technologies absent national, mandatory limits? Third, what does this mean for public policy?

In the conventional model of environmental protection, profit-making firms resist any expansion of environmental regulatory controls because it will require expenditures that do not contribute to the bottom line. That model has defined public policy for decades. It was based on the assumption that environmental and financial success present a nearly inevitable zero sum. That assumption is challenged by a visible and measurable "greening of industry" that has been occurring in recent decades, largely among a subset of leading firms. Firms like Xerox, Johnson & Johnson, BP, Baxter, and many others have adopted explicit strategies of setting ambitious environmental goals, reporting publicly on their progress, adopting corporate environmental management systems, redesigning products, and defining standards for their suppliers in ways that go well beyond regulation. For such firms, regulatory standards are a starting point, not an end goal. These behaviors constitute a greening process that has been underway the last few decades. Climate policy is yet another illustration of corporate greening.

Two collective industry initiatives illustrate how firms are organizing to press for national action that will assign a price to carbon. One is the U.S. Climate Action Partnership (USCAP), an association of some two dozen firms (such as DuPont, Caterpillar, PepsiCo, General Electric and Rio Tinto) and several NGOs (including the Natural Resources Defense Council and Environmental Defense Fund). USCAP has urged the federal government to pass legislation requiring significant cuts in emissions. The group most recently has called for cuts of 10-15 percent of 2005 levels by 2012; 40 percent by 2030; and 80 percent by 2050, from a baseline year of 2005. It also recommends that the U.S. adopt a cap and trade system that allocates some emissions and auctions others; ample use of offsets (ways of earning credit for allowances not otherwise included in the cap); emission credits for firms that already have taken action; rules and incentives to promote CCS (Carbon Capture and Storage) technology and implementation; and new technologies in energy, transportation, and buildings (United States Climate Action Partnership, 2009).

The other initiative is Business for Innovative Climate & Energy Policy (BICEP), sponsored by CERES (formerly the Coalition for Environmentally Responsible Economies). Distinguishing itself from the USCAP, the BICEP plan claims that it "calls for stronger, more holistic climate and energy policies." BICEP recommends larger emission cuts (25 percent by 2020 and 80 percent by 2050, but starting with an 1990 baseline rather than the USCAP baseline of 1990) in greenhouse gases; an auctioning of all carbon allowances; a national renewable electricity standard of 20 percent by 2020 and 30 percent by 2030; and limits on construction of new coal-fired power plants to those having carbon capture and storage capability, as well as requiring CSS in all existing coal plants by 2030. In contrast to the USCAP, BICEP recommends that all carbon emission allowances be auctioned or sold, arguing that this will "more rapidly stimulate clean technologies such as energy efficiency and renewable energy and a shift away from carbon intensive technologies." Both BICEP and USCAP aim to signal "to investors and the rest of the financial community that new coal-fired power plants will carry financial risks due to higher operating costs associated with future carbon limits" ("BICEP Statement in Response to USCAP Blueprint," 2009).

Initiatives such as USCAP and BICEP illustrate the attitudes of leading firms and the strategic orientation they are taking for environmental issues. However altruistic their motives appear to be, their attitudes are based squarely on strategic business thinking. It is important to understand what is motivating these firms, because that enables us to design more effective and acceptable public policies. Briefly, these firms are calling for strong and certain action for several reasons: to reduce regulatory uncertainty; build credibility with elected officials, regulators, and the public; increase operational efficiency; minimize the physical risks of change; and create market opportunities for new products.

Regarding the first reason: why would business firms call for mandatory emissions limits? What conventional assumptions about private firms and regulation often miss is that firms often are less concerned about the *stringency* of regulations than the *uncertainty* associated with them. Successful business firms seek to reduce uncertainty, as Forrest Reinhardt and other students of greening suggest, and government rules present a major source of uncertainty (Reinhardt, 1999). A survey of thirty one major firms by the Pew Center on Climate Change (most were part of Pew's Business Environmental Leadership Council) found that 90 percent of the firms believed that regulation is imminent; 67 percent think the U.S. will adopt emission limits between 2010 and 2015 (Hoffman, 2006 at 1). Recognizing that regulation is inevitable, forward-thinking firms want to know what the rules will be so they can prepare.

A second way to reduce uncertainty is to play a credible role in policy making. An industry executive once said, about playing a constructive role in regulation, that it was better to have a seat at the table than be the main course. By urging clear, strong proposals for action, as both the USCAP and BICEP have done, the business community is in a position to be seen as constructive and is more able to influence the course of policy. The ultimate target for both is an 80 percent reduction in emissions by 2050, the same goal President Obama has called for and one that experts view as necessary to avoid the worst effects of climate change. Leading firms are promoting stringent goals but flexible means. A cap and trade system, in contrast to more conventional technology-based rules, is the leading option because business firms view it as most cost-effective and flexible. Similarly, proactive firms are urging that emission credits be awarded for reductions already achieved (i.e., early credits) before the rules take effect.

The third reason—increasing operational efficiency—seems obvious but is more complicated. Climate offers opportunities for the economy-environment "win-wins" that have been the holy grail of sustainability. Energy costs money and will cost more in the future. Conserving energy or finding cheaper ways to buy or generate it redounds directly to the bottom line. What is amazing in the current round of greening is that firms waited so long to pursue energy efficiency and the associated costs savings. Business firms, like other organizations, do not always act in ways that are the most rational economically. Organizational routines are difficult to change. Often production managers were not even aware of their energy costs. Investments for energy projects had to compete with other demands for capital within the firm. Concern with climate has empowered eco-efficiency advocates within firms and enabled them to bring information and investment capital to bear on energy initiatives. Indeed, when asked who in their firms were the main advocates and implementers of climate action, respondents in the Pew Center survey said that it was EHS staff, followed by CEOs and top corporate managers (Pew: 37-40). A commitment to climate strategy within the firm empowers change agents who seek and carry out these operational efficiencies. This is one way in which a voluntary program like EPA's Climate Leaders may promote eco-efficient behavior; joining the program and setting public goals gives internal company change agents more leverage.[11]

In addition to wanting to reduce uncertainty, these firms also recognize that the longer action is delayed, the less flexibility there will be and the higher the likely costs of stabilizing emissions and of developing and commercializing alternative technologies. This is a core lesson of the *Stern Review*: The more we delay, the more limited the options and higher the costs. USCAP states this in no uncertain terms: "Each year of delayed action to control emissions increases the risk of unavoidable consequences that could necessitate even steeper reductions in the future, with potentially greater economic cost and social disruption."

The fourth and fifth reasons are to minimize adaptation costs and create market opportunities for new products. As the above examples suggest, the costs and uncertainties of adaptation and those of stabilization do not necessarily affect the same business sectors. The physical effects of climate change have implications for a broad range of sectors. For some, such as insurance, these will be profound. This is why major insurers like Swiss Re and others are elevating climate issues to the top of their business strategy. Many firms also recognize that climate will present opportunities for new and innovative technologies. These range from companies like BP, which has committed to making renewable energy 10 percent of its business, to General Electric, which is developing clean energy technologies for gas and wind turbines, hybrid-electric trains, water recycling, and photovoltaic panels.

Based on these business and economic perspectives, one could conclude that public policy should be guided by the following considerations:

- A de-carbonization of the American economy is inevitable and should be undertaken quickly. The longer the United States fails to act domestically and to lead globally, the more limited the options and the higher the costs of stabilization and adaptation.
- Although certain sectors, particularly in manufacturing, will face near-term costs and reductions in output, these will diminish as firms are able to transition to a less carbon-intensive economy. An energy transition is unavoidable and is better undertaken sooner rather than later. The issue is not whether this transition will occur, but how quickly, in what terms, and toward what ultimate ends.
- Public policies that increase the price of carbon-based energy sources should aim to maximize flexibility for business while also establishing certainty about goals. Certain goals should be combined with flexible means. This is why firms are calling for emissions trading rather than an approach based on technology standards.
- Public policies should be developed in collaboration with business firms, in the context of stringent goals set in a legislative process. The economic implications are too profound to leave out this crucial set of stakeholders. Once Congress selects a target, some degree of collaboration is likely to lead to a better outcome, economically and environmentally.

Is Climate Action Doomed?

"Climate change legislation isn't dead. It's just taking a sobering detour"

Margaret Kriz, 2008

Economic troubles historically have pushed environmental concerns down on the political agenda. When people are worrying about the economy, they give less attention to the environment and may even perceive the two as being in competition. A recent public opinion survey suggests that this may now be the case with climate, given the financial crisis and severe economic slowdown. A Pew Research Center survey conducted in January 2009 found, not surprisingly, that the economy and jobs were the two top concerns on the public's mind. Among a list of twenty issues, the largest decline in public concern came on environmental protection, which fell from 56 percent to 41 percent over the last year as a priority. Global warming was ranked dead last among the twenty issues, with only 30 percent considering it a priority, compared to 85 percent and 82 percent for the economy and jobs, respectively (Pew b, 2009). For now, the economy appears to be pushing aside the environment generally and climate change specifically as priorities.

A quick survey of informed opinion reinforces this impression. "The global financial crisis is threatening efforts to fight climate change," observed the *Wall Street Journal* in October of 2008 (Power, 2008). The site *ebusiness.com* reported a European Union negotiator's observation that "The Germans are giving up and the Italians are getting ready to follow" (eBusiness, 2009). *Time* magazine reported in January 2009 that "financing for new wind farms and solar plants remains all but frozen, halting plans in the U.S. and Europe to expand clean power" (Walsh, 2009). An article in *UPI.com* observed in October 2008: "As concern over the economy increases, there is growing concern in the green energy industry that the current financial crisis will throw a wrench in efforts to tackle global climate change" ("Economic Woes Hit Green Energy," 2008).

For others, however, economic turbulence and uncertainty strengthen the arguments for action. Nicholas Stern (2006) argues that "The risk consequences of ignoring climate change will be very much bigger than the consequences of ignoring risk in the financial system." Inaction now, he asserted, "could cause economic pain equal to the Great Depression" (Pomfret, 2008). Bjorn Stigson (2008), Executive Director of the World Business Council for Sustainable Development, asserts that "The financial crisis allows us the opportunity to rethink the role of business and to push forward with the policies and developments necessary to move towards a low-carbon economy. It also highlights the need to work towards achieving widespread energy efficiency, which has the dual benefit of saving money and reducing greenhouse gas emissions." Achim Steiner, Executive Director of the United Nations Environment Programme (UNEP), argued at a Climate Conference in December 2008 that "Combating climate change is the stimulus package needed to power the planet out of its current malaise and set the stage for a 21st century green economy—one that prizes resource efficiency, innovation and decent employment in developed and developing societies alike" (Gray, 2008). Similarly, the *Insurance Journal* noted in a December 2008 article that "President-elect Barack Obama says that addressing climate change will also create jobs and help pull the U.S. economy out of recession."

Which is the stronger case? Is action on climate a threat to economic and financial recovery and likely to be pushed aside as priorities change, financing dries up, and governments and citizens turn to more immediate concerns? Or is the package of policies that make up a climate action program—conservation, energy efficiency, stimulating the "green" economy, and reduced dependence on fossil fuels—the key that will unlock the next generation of economic prosperity?

That economic conditions pose a threat to both a political consensus and a financial capacity to address climate change in the near term is undeniable. The economy has taken over as a dominant concern; governments are cutting budgets at all levels (except for the federal stimulus); private firms are cutting staff, scrambling for investment dollars, and coping with reduced demand. The challenges to concerted action on climate, public and private, are real. What may prove to be even more important, however, is how the economic situation and its relationship to climate are perceived.[12] Especially for interests that oppose serious action, such as the fossil fuel industry and sectors that depend on it, the economic situation in recent years presents yet another basis for arguing that limiting greenhouse gases would threaten growth and put U.S. firms at a competitive disadvantage in the global economy.

One could postulate two scenarios for how climate policy will unfold given the recent economic situation. Which scenario is borne out depends largely on who is more successful in framing the political debate. The argument underlying the scenario that impedes or derails action goes like this: The state of the economy is so serious and uncertain that our focus should be on jobs and growth above any other goals. Given the risk of lost growth due to climate action, we should postpone any major policy decisions at this point. Now is not the time to impose higher energy costs on manufacturers or increase electricity and fuel costs on consumers. Nor is it a time to create new financial mechanisms (such as a cap and trade system) when we doubt the effectiveness of existing markets and mechanisms, or to burden government with new financial obligations. Given the precarious state of credit markets, pressures for investments in clean energy and other technologies could constrain other investment. The prudent course would be to wait until economic growth indicators improve and markets stabilize. This, of course, could take several years.

The other scenario is based on a different argument. Here, the economic situation makes the case for action more rather than less compelling. Reflecting conclusions such as those in the *Stern Review*, it stresses that the costs of action would be marginal and will be overwhelmed by the benefits. Further, climate presents a series of economic opportunities in the form of energy efficiency; less reliance on oil imports; less support for oil-based dictatorships; better air quality; and clean energy jobs, products, and technologies. The huge increase in public investments that will be occurring in the next few years to stimulate the economy offers a particular opportunity for investments in green technology and jobs. The sooner business has clear signals, the more productive will be their investments and the lower the eventual costs of adapting to climate change.

The economic crisis serves as a gut check on the concept of sustainability and, more specifically, on climate as a sustainability issue. The sustainability concept asserts that economic and environmental values not only may be reconciled but may be mutually reinforcing, even synergistic. If advocates of action on climate cannot frame the issues in a way that makes their case, it is fair to say that the entire sustainability enterprise comes into doubt. The key now lies in the political realm. Most observers seem to agree with the assertion in one financial sector report that investors need "a clear regulatory framework on climate policy which they can adapt and base their business decisions." (Allianz and the World Wildlife Fund, 2005: 9). If public policy stalls, firms and investors will not know where to go. The political struggle to define the terms of the climate debate will determine the outcome.

Notes

1. For an overview, see Pew Center for Global Climate Change, "Climate Change 101: The Science and Its Impacts," 2009, www.pewclimate.org/ docUploads/Climate101-Science-Jan09.pdf (accessed January 29, 2010).

2. Rahendra Pachauri and Andy Reisinger, "Climate Change 2007: Synthesis Report," Fourth Assessment Report of the Intergovernmental Panel on Climate Change 2007, www.ipcc.ch/pdf/assessment-report/ar4/syr/ar4_syr.pdf (accessed January 29, 2009).

3. Intergovernmental Panel on Climate Change, "Organization," www.ipcc.ch/organization/organization.htm (accessed January 29, 2010).

4. For general reviews of the evolution of climate policy, see Lamont C. Hempel, "Climate Policy on the Installment Plan," in *Environmental Policy: New Directions for the Twenty-First Century, Environmental Policy: New Directions for the Twenty-First Century*, 6th ed., ed. Norman J. Vig and Michael E. Kraft (Washington, DC: CQ Press, 2006), 288-310; Judith Layzer, *The Environmental Case: Translating Values into Public Policy* (Washington, DC: CQ Press, 2006), 278-312.

5. CO2e refers to carbon dioxide equivalents, in which all greenhouse gases are converted to equal units in terms of their effects.

6. EPA's analysis of the Lieberman-Warner bill in March 2008 estimated, under a range of scenarios, that it would cost the U.S. economy between 0.9 and 3.8 percent of projected GDP by 2030. Most estimates of costs are in this range.

7. For a summary of emissions, see Energy Information Agency, "Emissions of Greenhouse Gases Report," U.S. Department of Energy, www.eia.doe.gov/oiaf/1605/ggrpt/pdf/0573(2007).pdf (accessed January 29, 2010).

8. United States Conference of Mayors, "U.S. Conference of Mayors Climate Protection Agreement," Mayors Climate Protection Center, http://usmayors.org/climateprotection/agreement.htm (accessed January 29, 2010).

9. United States Environmental Protection Agency, "Endangerment and Cause or Contribute Findings for Greenhouse Gases Under the Clean Air Act," Climate Change – Regulatory Initiatives 2009, http://epa.gov/climatechange/endangerment.html (accessed January 29, 2010).

10. These categories are adapted from a discussion in Nicholas Stern, *The Stern Review Report on the Economics of Climate Change* (Cambridge, UK: Cambridge University Press, 2006), xii.

11. The importance of these internal factors is suggested in the conclusions about "environmental management style" reached in Neil Gunningham, Robert Kagan, and Dorothy Thornton, *Shades of Green: Business, Regulation, and Environment* (Stanford, CA: Stanford University Press, 2003).

12. On public opinion regarding climate change, see Deborah Lynn Gruber and Christopher J. Bosso, "Past the Tipping Point? Public Discourse and the Role of the Environmental Movement in a Post-Bush Era," in *Environmental Policy: New Directions for the Twenty-First Century*, 7th ed., ed. Norman J. Vig and Michael E. Kraft, (Washington, DC: CQ Press, 2009), 51-74.

References

"Advance Notice of Proposed Rulemaking with Options for Regulating Greenhouse Gases Under its Clean Air Act Authority in July 2008." *Federal Register* 73, no. 44 (July 30, 2008): 354.

Allianz Group and World Wildlife Fund. *Climate Change and the Financial Sector: An Agenda for Action.* June 2005. www.wwf.org.uk/filelibrary/pdf/allianz_rep_0605.pdf.

Betsil, Michele M. and Barry G. Rabe. "Climate Change and Multi-level Governance: The Evolving State and Local Roles." Pp. 201–225 in *Toward Sustainable Communities: Transition and Transformations in Environmental Policy*, 2nd ed., edited by Daniel Mazmanian and Michael E. Kraft. Cambridge, MA: MIT Press, 2009.

Broder, John M. "Climate Bill Clears Hurdle, but Others Remain," *New York Times*, May 21, 2009.

Broder, John M. "House Passes Bill to Address Threat of Climate Change," *New York Times,* June 26, 2009.

Ceres."BICEP Statement in Response to USCAP Blueprint," *Business for Innovative Climate and Energy Policy.* 2009. www.ceres.org/ Page.aspx?pid=1016.

"Despite Financial Crisis, Climate Concerns Continue." *Insurance Journal.* December 29, 2008. www.insurancejournal.com/news/international/ 2008/12/29/96609.htm.

Dietz, Simon, Chris Hope, Nicholas Stern, and Dimitri Zenghelis. "Reflections on the Stern Review (1): A Robust Case for Strong Action to Reduce the Risks of Climate Change," *World Economics* 8, no. 1 (January–March 2007): 121–168.

"Economic Woes Hit Green Energy," October 13, 2008, available at www.upi.com/Energy_Resources.

Energy Information Agency. "Emissions of Greenhouse Gases Report." U.S. Department of Energy. www.eia.doe.gov/oiaf/1605/ggrpt/pdf/ 0573(2007).pdf (accessed January 29, 2010).

EUBusiness. "Financial Crisis Clouds EU's Climate Change Plans." October 2008. www.eubusiness.com/news-eu/1223777821.61 (accessed January 26, 2009).

Friedman, Thomas L. "The People We Have Been Waiting For," *New York Times*, December 2, 2007.

Gray, Louise. "Charities Claim Action on Climate Change Will Ease Financial Crisis." *Telegraph.* December 9, 2008. www.telegraph.co.uk/earth/environment/ climatechange/3691010/Charities-claim-action-on-climate-change-will-ease-financial-crisis.html.

Goklany, Indur M. *What to Do About Climate Change*. Washington, DC: Cato Institute, 2008.

Gruber, Deborah L., and Christopher J. Bosso. "Past the Tipping Point? Public Discourse and the Role of the Environmental Movement in a Post-Bush Era." Pp. 51–74 in *Environmental Policy: New Directions for the Twenty-First Century*, 7th ed., edited by Norman J. Vig and Michael E. Kraft. Washington, DC: CQ Press, 2009.

Gunningham, Neil, Robert Kagan, and Dorothy Thornton. *Shades of Green: Business, Regulation, and Environment.* Stanford, CA: Stanford University Press, 2003.

Hempel, Lamont C. "Climate Policy on the Installment Plan." Pp. 288–310 in *Environmental Policy: New Directions for the Twenty-First Century*, 6th ed. Edited by Norman J. Vig and Michael E. Kraft. Washington, DC: CQ Press, 2006.

Ho, Mun S., Richard Morgenstern, and Jhih-Shyang Shih. *Impact of Carbon Price Policies on U.S. Industry.* Washington, DC: Resources for the Future, 2008.

Hoffman, Andrew. *Getting Ahead of the Curve: Corporate Strategies That Address Climate Change.* Washington, DC: Pew Center for Global Climate Change, 2006.

Intergovernmental Panel on Climate Change. "Organization." www.ipcc.ch/organization/organization.htm (accessed January 29, 2010).

Krauthammer, Charles. "Lost Left Replaces Socialism with Environmentalism," *Washington Post*, June 2, 2008. For a less restrained view, see "The Climate Change Security Act? Reject the Ignorami," *Pittsburgh Tribune Review*, June 1, 2008.

Kriz, Margaret. "Financial Crisis Dims Chances for U.S. Climate Legislation," *environment360.* October 6, 2008. http://e360.yale.edu/content/ feature.msp?id=2070.

Layzer, Judith. *The Environmental Case: Translating Values into Public Policy.* Washington, DC: CQ Press, 2006.

Massachusetts vs. EPA, 549 U.S. 497 (2007).

Nordhaus, William D. "Critical Assumptions in the Stern Review on Climate Change." *Science* 317, (July 13, 2007): 201–202.

"Obama Budget Forecasts Revenues in 2012 from Cap-and-Trade Program," *BNA Environmental Reporter,* February 25, 2009.

Oreskes, Naomi. "Beyond the Ivory Tower: The Scientific Consensus on Climate Change." *Science* 306, (2004): 1686.

Pachauri, Rahendra, and Andy Reisinger. "Climate Change 2007: Synthesis Report." Fourth Assessment Report of the Intergovernmental Panel on Climate Change. 2007. www.ipcc.ch/pdf/assessment-report/ar4/syr/ar4_syr.pdf (accessed January 29, 2009).

Pew Center for Global Climate Change, "Climate Change 101: The Science and Its Impacts." 2009, www.pewclimate.org/docUploads/ Climate101-Science-Jan09.pdf (accessed January 29, 2010).

Pew Research Center b, "Economy, Jobs Trump All Other Policy Priorities in 2009." *Pew Research Center for the People and the Press.* 2009. http://people-press.org/reports/pdf/485.pdf.

Pomfret, James. "Risks of Global Warming Greater Than Financial Crisis: Stern." *Reuters.* October 28, 2008. www.reuters.com/article/ idUSTRE49Q19120081027.

Pooley, Eric. "How Much Would You Pay to Save the Planet? The American Press and the Economics of Climate Change." Discussion Paper, #D-49 Cambridge, MA: Joan Shorenstein Center on the Press, Politics, and Public Policy, January 2009.

Portney, Kent E. "Sustainability in American Cities: A Comprehensive Look at What Cities Are Doing and Why." Pp. 227–254 in *Toward Sustainable Communities,* edited by Daniel A. Mazmanian and Michael E. Kraft. Cambridge: Massachusetts Institute of Technology, 1999.

Power, Stephen. "Climate Effort Could Be Stalled by Credit Crisis," *Wall Street Journal*, October 16, 2008.

Rabe, Barry G. *Statehouse and Greenhouse: The Emerging Politics of American Climate Change Policy.* Washington, DC: Brookings, 2004. "Senate Climate Bill Goes Down to Defeat, Falling 12 Votes Short on Cloture Motion." *BNA Environmental Reporter.* June 6, 2008. DBLCHK.

Reinhardt, Forest. *Down to Earth: Applying Business Principles to Environmental Management.* Cambridge, MA: Harvard Business School Press, 1999.

Rosenthal, Elisabeth. "Obama's Backing Raises Hopes for Climate Pact," *New York Times*, March 1, 2009.

Stern, Nicholas. *The Stern Review Report on the Economics of Climate Change*. Cambridge, UK: Cambridge University Press, 2006.

Stigson, Bjorn. "Sustainable Development, the Financial Crisis, and Barack Obama." *Bjorn Stigson Blog*. http://president.wbcsd.org/2008/11/sustainable-development-the-financial-crisis-and-barack-obama.html.

Sussman, Frances G., and J. Randall Freed. *Adapting to Climate Change: A Business Approach*. Washington, DC: Pew Center for Global Climate Change, 2008.

United States Climate Action Partnership. "Summary Overview: USCAP Blueprint for Legislative Action." 2009. www.us-cap.org/ newsroom/blueprint-for-legislative-action/overview/ (accessed January 29, 2010).

United States Conference of Mayors. "U.S. Conference of Mayors Climate Protection Agreement." Mayors Climate Protection Center. http://usmayors.org/ climateprotection/agreement.htm (accessed January 29, 2010).

United States Environmental Protection Agency. "Endangerment and Cause or Contribute Findings for Greenhouse Gases Under the Clean Air Act." Climate Change – Regulatory Initiatives. 2009. http://epa.gov/_climatechange/endangerment.html (accessed January 29, 2010).

Walsh, Bryan. "Will Green Enterprises Survive the Economic Crisis?" *Time,* January 26, 2009.

Climate Change Panel Summary

Amanda M. Girth*

Presenter: *Daniel J. Fiorino*, Executive in Residence, School of Public Affairs, American University; Former Director, National Environmental Performance Track, U.S. Environmental Protection Agency

Discussants: *Terry F. Yosie*, President and Chief Executive Officer, World Environment Center

Barton W. Forsyth, Minority Deputy Chief of Staff and Chief Counsel, U.S. House Select Committee on Energy Independence and Global Warming

J. Clarence Davies, Senior Fellow, Resources for the Future

Moderator: *Robert F. Durant*, Professor of Public Administration and Policy, School of Public Affairs, American University

Introduction

Managing the change in global climate is among the most wicked and puzzling policy problems facing the United States today. Attempts to establish an appropriate policy response result in vastly diverging expectations of what we expect from our government. While the Democratic majorities in both chambers of Congress and the White House achieved in the 2008 election appeared to signal an environmental mandate, the swift economic downturn has potentially lowered the salience of the climate change issue. As such, environmental sustainability presents a key challenge for policymakers faced with balancing

* Ph.D. Student, School of Public Affairs, American University.

potentially disastrous climate change impacts with economic imperatives. The purpose of the climate change panel was to discuss the hard challenges, choices, and opportunities that reconciling these values present. Daniel J. Fiorino's "Climate Change, the Economic Crisis, and Prospects for the Future" served as a point of departure. Following his presentation, four leading experts responded to Fiorino's arguments, elaborated on them, and offered their own thoughts on this important topic.

Robert F. Durant

To frame the discussion, Robert F. Durant revisited 1934, the year the School of Public Affairs at American University was founded. He revealed many similarities between 1934 and 2009. For instance, the highest temperature deviation from normal ever recorded was in 1934. It was also the year that the "dust bowl tragedy" began and when 80 percent of Oklahomans left that state, dust storms plagued Chicago, and red snow fell in New England. While the 2009 economic crisis did not rival the societal devastation created by the Great Depression, there are parallels to the current economic crisis, including high unemployment, reliance on public works projects to provide jobs and economic stimulus, and the leadership of a president focused on getting the economy moving. President Franklin Delano Roosevelt also had a strong environmental program as a component of economic recovery under the leadership of his Interior Secretary Harold Ickes. Today, President Obama views the greening of the U.S. economy as a central bridge to the 21st century.

Upon visiting American University seventy five years ago to attend the inauguration of the University's president, President Roosevelt remarked, "American University is yet young, but you have a great future. You have a great opportunity for initiative, for constructive thinking, for practical idealism and for national service." Durant postulated that practical, constructive idealists are just as needed today to tackle the interrelated issues of climate change and the economy. To that end, the panel was specifically charged with addressing the connection between climate change and the economy. Durant offered two questions to shape this morning's discussion: "Is there really an environmental upside to an economic downside? Is there an economic upside to addressing climate change?"

Daniel J. Fiorino

To begin the presentation, Fiorino provided a general overview of the climate change issue. Then he discussed the role of the business community in the climate change debate, and closed with an assessment of the current financial crisis and its predicted effect on climate change. The central premise of his argument was that climate change should not be viewed as a primarily environmental problem, but rather "an economic, political, social, and governance issue. It's a sustainability issue."

The leading hypothesis in the science of climate change is that fossil fuels and other substances are leading to long-term changes in climate. These changes have significant effects on the future of agriculture, ecosystems, water, as well as other resources, leading to much broader political, demographic, and social consequences. The causes and consequences of climate change are spread across the U.S. and throughout the world. Climate change is unequivocally a global problem. Yet, it is at the global level where institutions are weakest.

The costs and benefits of addressing (or ignoring) climate change are also spread out over time, which is an important political consideration. Costs of mitigating climate change are borne now for the future benefit of proceeding generations. Due to the nature of the problem, climate change is also the biggest collective action problem in history; addressing the problem will require government and nongovernmental cooperation.

There are salient arguments both for and against taking immediate action to mitigate further changes in the global climate. To begin, those who argue against climate change action assert the science is not absolutely clear. Interestingly, this lack of consensus also tends to fall along partisan lines, as Republicans are less likely to agree with the absoluteness of the science, while Democrats are more likely to agree the science is "absolutely clear." The second argument against climate change stems from costs. Few argue with the notion that responding to climate change will create costs for numerous economic and commercial sectors. However, one school of thought suggests that no strong action should be taken now because adaptation may be less costly in the long run than immediate regulatory efforts to minimize greenhouse gases.

Alternatively, there are strong arguments for taking immediate action to curb climate change. First, proponents of this position contend the science is clear and that there is proof that the production and consumption of fossil fuels and carbon emissions have warmed the planet. Second, the effects on economic growth will be minimal, not economically crippling. Third, those who support climate change policy argue that adaptation may be either highly disruptive or not possible at all, which makes waiting a risky proposition. Finally, the corollary benefits of taking action are especially high in terms of improving economic efficiency, opening new markets, increasing the quality of life, and curbing of air pollution.

Fiorino noted that business firms are largely ahead of government on the issue of climate change. One might ask why businesses would be in front of the climate change issue—but businesses have compelling reasons for taking a leadership role on this issue. Primarily, many businesses seek to minimize uncertainty in order to promote stable pricing of both labor and capital. Uncertainty in current and future climate change policy makes this type of business strategy much more difficult. It is also advantageous for business to be ahead of government policymaking so that individual firms can leverage some degree of credibility with government officials (as policymaking commences), as well as with consumers. Minimizing carbon emissions can result in increased operational efficiency, which gives forward-leaning firms a market advantage —

and minimizes the long-term costs of adaptation associated with climate change. Finally, firms can create market opportunities to appeal to environmentally conscious consumers.

In closing, Fiorino surmised that the current economic crisis creates two possible scenarios. First, when people worry about economy, they worry less about environment because environmental action sacrifices growth. This pushes environmental policies aside on the policy agenda. Alternatively, taking action on climate change could both outweigh the future risk of non-action and bolster a new "green" economy. "Which argument wins out really depends on who's able to frame the political and economic debate."

Terry F. Yosie

Finding no fundamental disagreement with the underlying premises of Daniel Fiorino's presentation, Terry F. Yosie responded by outlining five areas of consideration that expand upon Fiorino's assertions.

First, he agreed with Fiorino that climate change should not be thought of as an environmental problem. Indeed, the less it is thought about as an environmental issue, the better the associated innovation will be, primarily because climate change is a manifestation of a much larger historical trend in international political economy. It is the result of the industrial revolution and capital and resource intensive businesses constructed around large hierarchal organizations. This process created much of the wealth of modern nations as well as pollution that spawned the creation of government regulation. According to Yosie, "climate change is both a manifestation of the golden goose and an exhibit of some of its worse habits. The challenge going forward is preserving the global house we live in and rebuilding the economic foundation."

Second, climate change poses a more serious problem than previously estimated. Evidence suggests that society will experience adverse effects sooner, while the benefits of policy change will take longer to manifest. International climate change negotiations and voluntary mitigation is necessary to reduce greenhouse gases, but it's also the time to begin to lay a parallel adaptation track "in order to simultaneously adapt to the climate change that is already occurring and, in my view, will accelerate." There is increasingly persuasive evidence that inland regions are being affected, not just coastal regions and small island nations. As a result, business operations will have to be modified due to weather-related conditions. Globally, businesses engage in "risk-reward ratio" analysis to weigh the balance between adaptation and mitigation of climate change. These efforts sometimes require a significant undertaking—especially for agricultural areas, urban areas, and the modification of business practices against the extremes of health risks, temperature, precipitation, and weather.

Third, climate change will create business opportunities through innovation. The current economic crisis will stimulate thinking to make business more competitive. Firms are rethinking business models across supply chains, considering new markets to marry profit potential with climate challenges. As

Fiorino suggested, these innovation policies should also coincide with government policy. There is a great opportunity to stimulate economic growth by introducing new technologies—hybrid cars, transportation technology, smart electricity grids, green buildings, and pro-environmental management of watersheds and ecosystems. One of the byproducts of innovation will undeniably be the death of some businesses, but also the birth of others. It is likely that firms may migrate to other industrial markets. The new intersection of business, public policy, climate change, technology and innovation will cause a reexamination of Peter Drucker's classic question "What business are you in?"

Fourth, consumers play a direct part in solving the climate change problem and need to be better informed regarding the problem and their role in solving it. To date, governing through the regulatory process has attempted to control pollution after the fact. Yet under a market-driven approach, consumers would play a greater role. Consumer focus varies based on the state of the economy and the effects of policy change on their lifestyle and values. Missing in the climate change debate is how consumers will be affected when controls are implemented. Will they be better off? Will quality of life improve? Will we see additional economic opportunities and expanded choices? Alternatively, what additional costs will be imposed and how will those costs impact living standards and lifestyles? These are all vital ingredients to addressing climate change. Leaders in government, businesses, environmental groups, and universities should better integrate this information for consumers.

Finally, Yosie argued that climate change solutions will reorient public policy, economic analysis and public values through a fundamental reexamination of public policy economics. Andy Grove, former chairman at Intel, describes a "strategic inflection point," the existential moment in a business's life when market conditions force a fundamental shift in its approach. Yosie suspected that we may be at a similar inflection point in the evolution of society's approach to climate change, a moment with the potential to generate secondary and tertiary consequences, the nature of which will depend on what specific action is taken. What emerged through the consideration of these five topics was not only the need for new technologies but also new forms of institutional design, collaboration opportunities, and a new set of consumer participation mechanisms necessary to affect climate change at the local, regional, and global level.

Barton W. Forsyth

Agreeing with Fiorino that the central problem in the climate change debate is sustainability, Barton W. Forsyth asserted that any solution to the problem has to be feasible for both environmental and economic reasons. In large part because public attention is short, and unless the solution is sustainable, the public will lose interest.

Forsyth expanded upon the political frames postulated by Fiorino, focusing on the cap and trade system currently under consideration by policymakers.

Forsyth characterized the proposed cap and trade program as essentially "a complicated regulatory method of price control," and argued that a more transparent and effective alternative would include a direct carbon tax borne by both consumers and producers. He concluded that even opponents of a carbon tax must acknowledge that such a tax would make carbon-intensive activities more expensive while promoting economic efficiencies and innovation in low-carbon technology.

Cap and trade policies assume distrust of the market, favoring instead a government-driven regulatory model. To Forsyth, this creates unnecessary implementation costs and operational inefficiencies. For instance, the sizeable and expensive bureaucracy necessary to maintain a national cap and trade policy would only grow larger over time, necessarily enduring at a considerable cost. A direct carbon tax would be more efficient, in part because it does not require creating a bureaucracy to manage the program, as taxation mechanisms are already in place. Further, the cap and trade program would create vast new political constituencies to leverage bureaucratic regulations to their advantage and open profit opportunities for businesses with political clout.

Forsyth contended that business innovation and market forces should be the predominant policy approach to addressing climate change issues. Businesses should be in front of government on environmental issues—and as previously mentioned by Fiorino—it is already happening. The economic crisis should also be used to stimulate new, cost-effective technologies geared toward promoting innovation and adaptation.

J. Clarence Davies

J. Clarence Davies concluded that Fiorino provided a calm, rational perspective in summarizing the climate change issue. Yet, he wondered about his decision to treat climate change as a test of sustainability. Sustainability can be thought of either substantively or politically. Substantively, climate change policies are evaluated by whether or not they encourage economic and environmental sustainability. Davies suggested that framing sustainability as a political issue, as Fiorino did, can lead to the possibility of framing it in terms of a populist-regulatory framework. Under that scenario, climate change might depend less on sustainability and "good companies" and more on anti-business and pro-regulatory attitudes, given the shift in attitudes evidenced by the 2008 elections.

There are also institutional and policy questions related to climate change that Fiorino did not address. For instance, questions remain about the implications of the Supreme Court's decision in *Massachusetts v. Environmental Protection Agency*, 549 U.S. 497 (2007), which granted to the EPA authority to regulate greenhouse gases via the Clean Air Act. There is broad agreement that the Court's holding will be used to encourage Congress to act on climate change, whether it is through a cap and trade system or another approach. Davies argues that the Clean Air Act and its focus on public health has historically been a problematic approach to setting regulatory standards. He believes that it would present similar problems for addressing climate change.

Of equal concern to Davies was the need for regulation and implementation on an international level. The U.S. has tried to push for a joint implementation model advocated by economists and lawyers but institutional considerations are not adequately considered by a cap and trade approach to climate change. Institutional mechanisms for an international cap and trade system do not exist now and are not likely to be feasible anytime soon.

Another of Davies's concerns with the current climate change debate was that it may be dominating the environmental agenda to the exclusion of other important issues. While climate change relates to other environmental issues, it is different, especially in scale, and positive carryover effects to other important environmental issues may not be that great. Toxins, water availability, land use, and endangered species are among the many other important issues on the environmental and natural resource agenda. President Obama has seemed to equate environmental issues with climate and energy issues to the neglect of others. The sole focus on climate change comes at a political cost to these other areas.

Finally, new technologies would also have an impact on how climate change issues are managed. For example, nanotechnology has advanced significantly over the last five years. All sides of the climate change debate could agree that climate change involves technological change. Yet Davies contended that the U.S. is not good at assessing the impact of new technologies or involving the public in such decisions. Furthermore, the current regulatory system is inadequate for dealing with new technologies. New regulatory approaches are required.

Questions from the Audience

Panelists fielded questions from the audience on topics ranging from disparities between poor and developing countries, the role of international institutions, alternative policy responses to climate change, framing climate change as a security concern, and consumer preferences. A brief synopsis of the questions and the discussion they raised follow.

Question: Winners and losers are produced as a result of climate change in terms of growing seasons, water, and consumption adjustments. How will we deal with these global "seeds of conflict"?

Answer: There is undoubtedly a conflict between poor and rich countries. Poor countries do not have the resources of their wealthy counterparts and they are highly dependent on agriculture and less able to adapt. Of further concern, economic globalization may produce "environmental" refugees, people displaced by food shortages, environmental catastrophes, or other related issues. Because such tragedies are increasing in both likelihood and intensity, policy designed to provide resilience to them is an emerging theme in the global debate, as is the drive to create greater flexibility in developing economies.

Question: On the topic of climate change, the World Bank and other international institutions appear to take more comfort in making grants to developing nations rather than looking internally at how they can be more sensitive to climate change issues. Is that a process at work not only internationally but also domestically?

Answer: There has been a more integrative approach that is more promising today than it was five years ago. There will be a shake-up in institutions, especially with the International Monetary Fund. One can argue that new institutions will have positive views on the ability to act on climate change and formulating policy. The World Bank gives loans/grants for infrastructure projects with little engagement with the private sector, but the business community has been making investments in emerging countries.

Question: Considering policy responses to mitigate carbons domestically—whether it is a cap and trade system or a carbon tax—is EPA the right organization to oversee the process? Does EPA have the capacity to deal with climate change?

Answer: As it stands, the carbon trading system would be under EPA (at least as it was proposed in the Warner-Lieberman bill). But this is totally different than what the EPA has done before. The real challenge at EPA is that the agency is highly fragmented; yet this is a process that requires considerable integration. There is a case to be made that a taxing structure is a better solution, but both debates remain a means to the same end. Alternatively, the key factor should be which scheme will encourage new technology.

Question: Is there merit in reframing the climate change issue as a security issue?

Answer: National security and the economy are the two issues that trump all others in recent years. The economic support of petrol dictators has resonance with policymakers, but invoking national security can be a slippery slope. For instance, would the U.S. be willing to go to war over climate change? These are direct issues that can arise by framing the issue as a national security concern.

Question: Mitigating climate change requires a change in consumer behavior, yet there is a lack of desire on the part of consumers to give up comforts. How—if at all—can these be reconciled?

Answer: This is reminiscent of the discussion on direct consumer taxation. One compelling way to change consumer behavior is not to appeal to their "moral good side," but through their pocketbooks. A hidden piece of the economic crisis and the recession is that people are rethinking consumption; evidence exists that consumers are pulling back in many respects. Cultural patterns of consumerism may reemerge more subdued than the pattern over the last 20 years, but evidence suggests that consumer values are stable over time. The question remains: Will consumer values change first or will the business community develop new products that create new markets?

Chapter 5

Countering Myths about Terrorism: Some Lessons Learned from the Global Terrorism Database

Gary LaFree*

There is a central irony in our approach to global terrorism: while effective policy against terrorism depends especially on hard data and objective analysis, the study of terrorism has lagged behind many other fields in the social and behavioral sciences. In their encyclopedic review of political terrorism, Schmid and Jongman (1988: 177) identified more than 6,000 published works but point out that much of the research is "impressionistic, superficial [and offers] . . . far-reaching generalizations on the basis of episodal evidence." More recently, Silke (2003) concludes that only three percent of articles in terrorism journals used inferential analysis compared to 86 percent in forensic psychology and 60 percent in criminology. Similarly, Lum, Kennedy, and Sherley's (2006: 8) Campbell systematic review of over 14,000 terrorism articles published between 1971 and 2003, found that only 3 percent were based on quantitative analysis. Thus, as a result of the lack of systematic empirical research, an area that is especially in need of clear-eyed, dispassionate facts is especially susceptible to half truths and myths. The purpose of this review is to use a newly available data set on

* Director, National Consortium for the Study of Terrorism and Responses to Terrorism (START); Professor of Criminology and Criminal Justice, University of Maryland, College Park.

terrorist attacks around the world since 1970 to challenge ten common myths about terrorism. I use myths here in the everyday sense of fictitious or unscientific conclusions.

In fairness to researchers, studying terrorism raises unique challenges. To begin with, terrorism represents a type of behavior that is especially difficult to define and measure. As PLO Chairman Arafat famously noted in a 1974 speech to the United Nations, "One man's terrorist is another man's freedom fighter." For example, while the United States regards Hamas as a Foreign Terrorist Organization (U.S. Department of State, 2007), many Palestinians regard it as a legitimate political party that recently won a major democratically held election. By contrast, while the Chinese regard the ethnic Uyghurs that have been detained by the United States at Guantanamo Bay as terrorists, much of the rest of the world appears to disagree (*Washington Post*, 2005). Indeed, many of the most prominent terrorist groups in the world (including Shining Path, ETA, the FMLN, the IRA, FARC, the ELN, and the PKK) often define themselves as freedom fighters. This fundamental characteristic of terrorism no doubt explains in part why international organizations such as the United Nations have not succeeded in adopting a universally-accepted definition (European Commission 2008: 3-4).

Defining terrorism is no less complex for researchers. Schmid and Jongman's review (1988: 5) found 109 different research definitions of terrorism. Indeed, the first chapter of many influential books on terrorism (e.g., Hoffman, 1998; Smelser, 2007) is devoted to exploring and defending competing definitions. But despite the considerable complexity, most commentators and experts agree on several key elements, captured in the operational definition we use here: *"the threatened or actual use of illegal force and violence by non-state actors to attain a political, economic, religious or social goal through fear, coercion or intimidation"* (LaFree and Dugan, 2007). Note that this operational definition excludes state terrorism and genocide, topics that are important and complex enough to warrant separate treatment.

Beyond the challenge of arriving at a defensible definition of terrorism is the considerable difficulty of collecting valid data on terrorism. Data on illegal violence has come traditionally from three sources, corresponding to the major social roles connected to criminal events: *"official" data* collected by legal agents, especially the police; *"victimization" data* collected from the general population of victims and non-victims; and *"self-report" data* collected from offenders (LaFree and Dugan 2004: 53-74). Victimization surveys have been of little use in the study of terrorism. Despite the attention it gets in the global media, terrorism is much rarer than more ordinary violent crime. This means that even with extremely large sample sizes, few individuals in most countries will have been victimized by terrorists. Moreover, because victims of terrorism are often chosen at random, they are unlikely to know perpetrators, making it impossible to produce details about offenders. And finally, in many cases, victims of terrorism are killed by their attackers—a problem in criminology research limited to the study of homicides.

Self-report data on terrorists have been more important than victimization data, but they also face serious limitations. Most active terrorists are unwilling to participate in interviews. And even if willing to participate, getting access to known terrorists for research purposes raises obvious challenges. As Merari (1991: 88) has put it, "The clandestine nature of terrorist organizations and the ways and means by which intelligence can be obtained will rarely enable data collection which meets commonly accepted academic standards."

Although government departments in some countries do collect official data on terrorism (e.g., the U.S. National Counter Terrorism Center), data collected by governments are suspicious either because they are influenced by political considerations or because many fear that they might be so influenced. Moreover, while vast amounts of detailed official data on common crimes are routinely produced by the various branches of the criminal justice system in most countries, this is rarely the case for terrorism. For example, the majority of offenders suspected of terrorism against the United States are not legally processed for terrorism, but rather for other related offenses, such as weapons violations and money laundering (Smith, Damphousse, Jackson and Sellers, 2002). In addition, much primary data are collected by intelligence agents (e.g., informers, communications intercepts) and are not available to researchers working in an unclassified environment.

In response to these data challenges, researchers have long relied on open source unclassified terrorist event data bases. Terrorism event databases generally use the electronic and print media to collect detailed information on the characteristics of terrorist attacks. LaFree and Dugan (2007) describe eight of these event databases, with varying coverage going back as far as 1968. Analyses based on event databases have provided important insights into a wide range of terrorism-related empirical questions. However, an important limitation of most event data bases is that they include only transnational events—those involving a national or a group of nationals from one country attacking targets in another country or attacking foreign targets in their home country. This is a potentially critical limitation because sources that have compared domestic and transnational terrorist attacks (Asal and Rethemeyer, 2007; Schmid, 2004; LaFree, Yang and Crenshaw, 2009) conclude that the former outnumber the latter by as much as seven to one.

Moreover, as Falkenrath (2001: 164) points out, dividing bureaucratic responsibility and legal authority according to a domestic-international distinction is "an artifact of a simpler, less globally interconnected era." Groups such as al Qaeda have global operations that cut across domestic and international lines. Others (e.g., the Abu Nidal Organization or the Kurdistan Workers' Party) operate in multiple countries and hence, engage in acts of both domestic and transnational terrorism. In short, excluding domestic terrorist attacks impedes a more sophisticated understanding of terrorism and may ultimately weaken counterterrorism efforts.

In this essay I present conclusions drawn from newly available data on 82,910 world-wide terrorist attacks from 1970 to 2007 from the Global Terrorism Database (GTD). The GTD is to my knowledge the most comprehensive open source data base on terrorist attacks assembled to date. Importantly, it is also the first unclassified event data base that traces domestic as well as transnational terrorism over a prolonged time period. In the rest of this essay I will rely on the GTD to evaluate ten myths about terrorism. These myths are centered on common misconceptions about the characteristics of terrorism, terrorist attacks, terrorist groups, and counter terrorist policies.

Myth 1: Terrorist attacks were rapidly increasing in the years leading up to 9/11.

The tragic events of September 11, 2001 had an immediate and dramatic impact on levels of public concern about terrorism in the United States and well beyond. Similarly, more recent attacks such as those in Madrid on March 11, 2004, in London on July 7, 2005 and in Mumbai on November 26-29, 2008 also raised concerns about terrorism among citizens, not only in the countries attacked but from observers around the world. Accordingly, many might assume that terrorist attacks and fatalities were up sharply in the years leading up to the twenty-first century. But the GTD shows that the patterns of terrorist attacks since 1970 are more complex than is commonly recognized. Figure 5.1 shows trends in total attacks and fatalities from 1970 to 2007.

According to figure 5.1, terrorist attacks reached their twentieth century zenith in 1992 (with over 5,100 attacks worldwide), but had substantially declined in the years leading up to the 9/11 attacks.[1] In fact, total attacks in 2000 (1,351) were at about the same level as total attacks in 1977 (1,307). Looking more broadly at overall trends, figure 5.1 shows that world-wide terrorist attacks through the mid-1970s were relatively infrequent, with fewer than 1,000 incidents each year. But from 1976 to 1979 the frequency of events nearly tripled. The number of terrorist attacks continued to increase until the 1992 peak, with smaller peaks in 1984, at almost 3,500 incidents, and 1989, with over 4,300 events. After the first major peak in 1992, the number of terrorist attacks declined until the end of the twentieth century, before rising steeply to a ten-year high of nearly 3,300 in 2007—four years after the start of the Iraq war. Still, total attacks in 2007 were 36 percent lower than total attacks for the 1992 peak.

Fatal attacks also declined in the years prior to the 9/11 attacks. In fact, fatal attacks in 2000 (580) were considerably lower than they had been more than two decades earlier, in 1979 (832). In general, the number of fatal attacks clearly followed the pattern of total attacks ($r = .93$), but at a substantially lower magnitude (averaging 947 fatal attacks per year compared to 2294 total attacks per year worldwide). Fatal attacks rose above 1,000 per year for the first time in 1980. After hovering close to 1,000 attacks annually for most of the 1980s, they more than doubled between 1985 and 1992. Like total attacks, fatal attacks declined somewhat after 1992, bottoming out in 1998 with 426 attacks and then rising again to a global peak of more than 2,100 fatal attacks in 2007. The peak in 2007 (2,111) was similar to the peak in 1992 (2,178).

Figure 5.1. Total and Fatal Terrorist Attacks, 1970-2007 (n = 82,910)

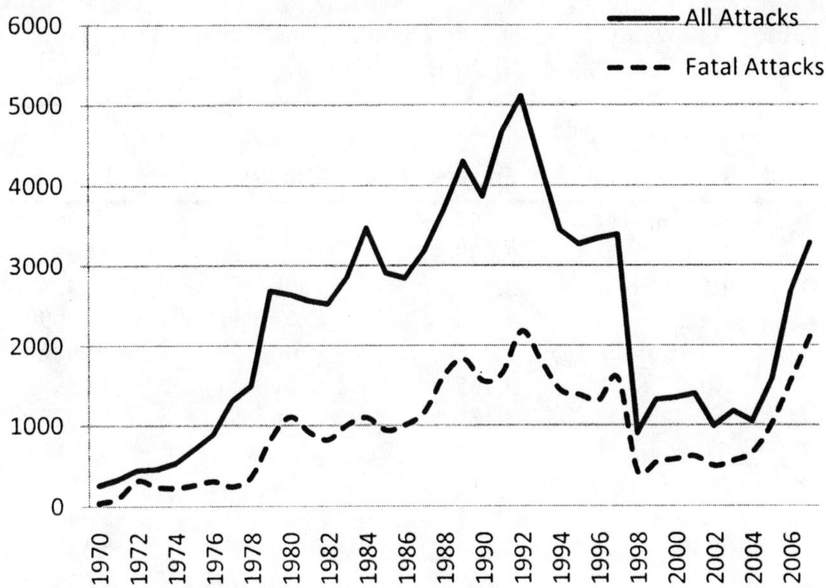

Source: Global Terrorism Database

In short, in the four years prior to 9/11 world-wide terrorist attacks and fatal attacks were at the lowest level they had been at for twenty years. However, both total and fatal attacks have increased considerably since then so that in 2007 total attacks were back to levels they had been at in the mid-1990s and total fatal attacks were approaching the peak year of 1992.

Myth 2: The U.S. is more frequently targeted by terrorists than any other country in the world.

The United States has long been perceived as being the target of an inordinate number of terrorist attacks. Thus, Neumayer and Plumper (2008: 2) argue that most foreign victims of terrorist attacks are U.S. citizens and the U.S. State Department recently claimed that one-third of all terrorist attacks worldwide are directed at the United States (Crenshaw, 2006: 8). However, because previous estimates of attacks against the U.S. have been based only on transnational terrorist attacks, they do not take into account the possibility that the groups that target the U.S. may be even more active in targeting their own countries.

In table 5.1 I present new data from the GTD showing the twenty most frequently attacked countries in the world, from 1970 to 2007. I also present a rank ordering of the twenty countries with the most terrorist fatalities for the same years.

Table 5.1. Twenty Top Ranking Countries in Terms of Total Terrorist Attacks and Fatalities, 1970-2007

	Most Frequently Attacked		Most Fatalities	
Rank	Country	Frequency	Country	Fatality Count
1	Colombia	6,767	Iraq	17,754
2	Peru	6,038	Sri Lanka	14,272
3	El Salvador	5,330	India	13,434
4	India	4,318	Colombia	13,009
5	Northern Ireland	3,762	Peru	12,822
6	Spain	3,165	El Salvador	12,496
7	Iraq	3,161	Nicaragua	11,324
8	Turkey	2,691	Algeria	8,545
9	Sri Lanka	2,611	Philippines	6,304
10	Pakistan	2,536	Pakistan	5,540
11	Philippines	2,490	Guatemala	5,135
12	Chile	2,287	Turkey	4,674
13	Israel	2,140	Burundi	4,084
14	Guatemala	2,023	Afghanistan	3,764
15	Nicaragua	1,986	United States	3,339
16	South Africa	1,921	Rwanda	3,200
17	Lebanon	1,913	Lebanon	3,093
18	Algeria	1,650	Russia	3,057
19	Italy	1,487	Angola	2,861
20	United States	1,362	Northern Ireland	2,842

Source: Global Terrorism Database

According to table 5.1, the United States ranks twentieth in terms of total attacks. The most frequently attacked country in the data set is Colombia with over 6,700 attacks. Note that the top three most frequently attacked countries are all Latin American and three other Latin American countries are in the top twenty (Chile, Guatemala and Nicaragua). Latin America had the largest number of terrorist attacks of any region of the world throughout the 1980s and the first half of the 1990s. Four Middle Eastern or Persian Gulf countries are in the top twenty (Iraq, Turkey, Israel and Lebanon) and four are in South Asia or Southeast Asia (India, Pakistan, Sri Lanka, Philippines). Western Europe contains three countries in the top twenty (Northern Ireland [treated here as a country],

Spain and Italy). South Africa and Algeria are the sole countries from Africa in the top twenty most frequently targeted countries.

Table 5.1 shows that at number fifteen, the United States ranks higher in terms of total fatalities than attacks. However, 90 percent (N=3,007) of total U.S. terrorism fatalities from 1970 to 2007 are accounted for by a single event—the four coordinated attacks on September 11, 2001. If these attacks are removed from the estimates, U.S. fatalities during the period spanned by the data would be similar to fatalities for Canada or Greece.

In a recent study, my colleagues and I (LaFree, Yang and Crenshaw, 2009) examined the attack patterns of fifty three foreign terrorist organizations that were identified by the U.S. Department of State and subsequently the National Counterterrorism Center as especially dangerous for the United States. In Figure 5.2, I show the proportion of attacks by these 53 groups against the U.S. homeland and U.S. targets in other countries compared to attacks on targets not connected to the United States. The results are striking. According to figure 5.2, between 1970 and 2004 more than 96 percent of the more than 16,000 terrorist attacks from these groups were directed at non-U.S. targets. Moreover, of the 3.4 percent of all attacks directed at the United States, only five attacks (less than 1 percent) were on the U.S. homeland. These include one attack by Farabundo Marti National Liberation Front (FMLN) on August 18, 1983 against the Washington, D.C. Navy Yard (Navy Regional Data Automation Center) with small explosives as well as the four attacks that occurred on September 11th, 2001.[2] Major targets for anti-U.S. attacks in other countries from these 53 groups included U.S. businesses (233), U.S. diplomats and embassies (106), and the U.S. military (96).[3] The rest of the attacks are widely scattered in terms of target selection and include U.S. educational institutions, journalists, non-governmental organizations, and tourists. The U.S. suffered proportionally more fatalities from attacks at the hands of these fifty three groups than their non-U.S. targets, with U.S.-directed attacks accounting for over 9 percent of total fatalities. But again, a very large proportion of these fatalities (76.3 percent) are accounted for by the 9/11 attack.

The fact that total attacks and fatalities by this set of designated anti-U.S. organizations is so lopsidedly against non-U.S. targets is consistent with the proposition that the decision of anti-U.S. terrorist groups to attack the U.S. is often strategic. Attacks on the U.S. may be useful for pragmatic as well as ideological reasons; attacks on Americans are highly visible and both acts of terrorism and the American response may well arouse popular emotions in an audience of importance to the terrorist organization. Also as Crenshaw (2001) suggests, the United States may become a preferred target if domestic challengers cannot succeed at home unless the scope of the conflict is expanded beyond local boundaries.

Figure 5.2. U.S. and Non-U.S. Attacks by 53 Foreign Terrorist Groups Identified as Threats to the United States

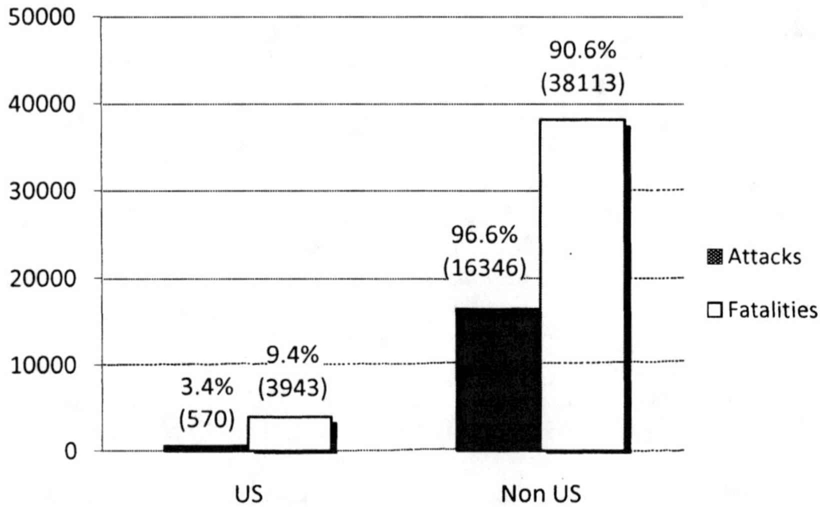

Source: LaFree, Yang and Crenshaw (2009)

Beyond these considerations, attacks on U.S. targets can be useful for directly influencing American policies—such as compelling the U.S. to withdraw from a military commitment that supports a local government. The bombing of the Marine Barracks in Lebanon in 1983 is a prominent example. Terrorism directed at the U.S. may also be a mechanism for drawing the U.S. into a local conflict, perhaps to pressure the government to make reforms or to undermine its legitimacy.

Regardless of the strategic intent behind attacks on the United States, or the virulence of anti-American ideology, our results show that the vast majority of terrorist attacks by foreign groups deemed dangerous to national security by the American government are in fact directed at non-U.S. targets. Local governments suffer the most. U.S. decision-makers might be well-advised to avoid parochialism and keep in mind the fact that even the most seriously threatening groups direct most of their activities elsewhere.

Myth 3: Terrorist attacks reach every corner of the world.

The ubiquity of modern communications systems means that individuals are now routinely bombarded by images of terrorist attacks from around the globe. This blanket coverage leaves the impression that no location on the planet is safe from terrorism. But in fact, our analysis of the GTD indicates that terrorist attacks are highly concentrated in geographic space. This concentration can be demonstrated at the national level by examining the proportion of all terrorist attacks that take place in those countries with the most terrorist activity. In table 5.2 we again present the top twenty countries in terms of terrorist attacks, but in this case we compare their cumulative percentage of total attacks to their share of all countries in the world.

According to table 5.2, the top twenty countries and territories in terms of terrorist attacks account for nearly 72 percent of all terrorist activities but less than 10 percent of all countries of the world. Two percent of the world's countries account for more than 27 percent of the world's terrorist attacks. Five percent of the world's countries account for half of the world's terrorist attacks.

Considerable concentration is also apparent if we examine terrorist attacks with smaller geospatial units. For example, in an analysis of known terrorist attacks in India from the GTD, Cutter (2005) found that the vast majority of all attacks were concentrated in just two regions: the Punjab and Kashmir region, on the border with Pakistan, and the area around Bangladesh. The vast majority of Indian territory suffered few terrorist attacks from 1970 until quite recently—which is one of the reasons why the recent attacks on Mumbai were so shocking. Similarly, in an analysis of the GTD for Germany, Behlendorf (2008) found considerable geospatial concentration of terrorist attacks at the province level. In short, terrorism, like more common crime, is highly concentrated across geographical units.

Myth 4: Terrorism is unrelated to traditional political grievances.

Because of the seeming irrationality of high profile al Qaeda attacks in recent years, it is easy to lose sight of the fact that a large number of terrorist attacks involve political disputes over territory. In table 5.3 we list the twenty most active terrorist groups in terms of attack frequencies and fatalities. This analysis is based on a study by LaFree and Dugan (2009) in which we analyzed both the GTD and an event database collected by the RAND Corporation. Notice how many of these groups are organized around disputes having to do with political control over territory. Although there are major differences in terms of their orientation, this explain in large part virtually all of the top twenty groups, including Shining Path, ETA, the IRA, FARC, Hamas, and the LTTE.

South Africa is an especially striking example of this phenomenon. Both pro- and anti-apartheid terrorist attacks in South Africa resulted in an enormous amount of political violence during much of the 1980s and early 1990s. However, in an analysis of terrorist attacks in South Africa using GTD data, Van Brakle and LaFree (2007) found that violence ended rapidly following the first democratic elections at the end of apartheid. In fact, a major reason why it is so difficult to develop a universal definition of terrorism is that it is often a method used to advance political goals on which nations and individuals disagree.

Table 5.2. Percentage of Total Attacks for the Twenty Most Frequently Attacked Countries, 1970-2007

Rank	Country	Cumulative % of All Attacks	Cumulative % of All Countries
1	Colombia	8.16	0.48
2	Peru	15.44	0.96
3	El Salvador	21.87	1.44
4	India	27.08	1.92
5	Northern Ireland	31.62	2.40
6	Spain	35.44	2.88
7	Iraq	39.25	3.37
8	Turkey	42.49	3.85
9	Sri Lanka	45.64	4.33
10	Pakistan	48.70	4.81
11	Philippines	51.71	5.29
12	Chile	54.46	5.77
13	Israel	57.05	6.25
14	Guatemala	59.49	6.73
15	Nicaragua	61.88	7.21
16	South Africa	64.20	7.69
17	Lebanon	66.51	8.17
18	Algeria	68.50	8.65
19	Italy	70.29	9.13
20	United States	71.93	9.62

Source: Global Terrorism Database

Myth 5: Most terrorist attacks involve disgruntled groups and individuals from one country carrying out attacks on civilians in other countries.

As noted above, because none of the open source terrorist event data bases before the GTD included domestic terrorist attacks over a long time period, we have lacked baseline information about how common domestic attacks were compared to transnational attacks. In the recent study by LaFree, Yang and Crenshaw (2009), we were able to use the GTD to examine the domestic and transnational attack patterns of the fifty three foreign organizations that were identified by the U.S. government as especially dangerous for the United States. Figure 5.3 shows that between 1970 and 2004, more than 93 percent of the non-U.S. attacks of these groups were domestic attacks. That is more than nine times out of ten, these groups operated at home against local targets.

These 53 groups are not a random sample of terrorist groups in the GTD. However, because they have been identified by the U.S. government as foreign groups that are especially dangerous to the U.S., we might assume that

Table 5.3. Twenty Most Active Terrorist Organizations in Terms of Attack Frequency and Fatalities, 1970-2006

	Most Frequent Perpetrators		Most Fatalities	
Rank	Organization	Frequency	Organization	Fatalities
1	Shining Path (SL)	2,817	Shining Path (SL)	6,057
2	Basque Fatherland and Freedom (ETA)	1,378	Liberation Tigers of Tamil Eelam (LTTE)	4,038
3	Farabundo Marti National Liberation Front (FMLN)	1,249	Al Qaeda	3,460
4	Irish Republican Army (IRA)	1,165	Hutus	3,222
5	Revolutionary Armed Forces of Colombia (FARC)	1,066	Mozambique National Resistance Movement (MNR)	2,247
6	National Liberation Army of Colombia (ELN)	784	Farabundo Marti National Liberation Front (FMLN)	1,856
7	Hamas (Islamic Resistance Movement)	608	Revolutionary Armed Forces of Colombia (FARC)	1,791
8	Liberation Tigers of Tamil Eelam (LTTE)	569	Tanzim Qa'idat al-Jihad fi Bilad al-Rafidayn	1,646
9	Manuel Rodriguez Patriotic Front (FPMR)	568	Nicaraguan Democratic Force (FDN)	1,342
10	Kurdish Workers Party (PKK)	535	National Union for the Total Independence of Angola (UNITA)	1,151
11	New People's Army (NPA)	472	New People's Army (NPA)	1,084
12	Corsican National Liberation Front (FLNC)	455	Kurdistan Workers' Party (PKK)	1,071
13	Taliban	438	Lord's Resistance (LRA)	1,060
14	Tupac Amaru Revolutionary Movement (MRTA)	412	Hizballah	899
15	Communist Party of Nepal-Maoists (CPN-M)	403	Taliban	876
16	M-19 (Movement of April 19)	321	Tutsi	858
17	Nicaraguan Democratic Force (FDN)	287	Armed Islamic Group (GIA)	807
18	People's Liberation Front (JVP)	274	Irish Republican Army (IRA)	728
19	Movement of the Revolutionary Left (MIR) (Chile)	257	National Liberation Army of Colombia (ELN)	646
20	al-Fatah	243	Hamas (Islamic Resistance Movement)	630

compared to a random sample, they would be especially likely to carry out transnational attacks. The fact that they do not has several important policy implications. First, it underscores the importance of proximity to terrorist targeting.

Even though these groups have ample interest in striking the United States, actually doing so is not an easy task. Anti-American objectives are not sufficient. Mounting an attack against the United States from primary bases outside the United States is extremely challenging. Clarke and Newman (2006: 154) conclude that: "Terrorists are constrained by geography. Like criminals, they will choose targets that are close to their operational base."

And second, the ratio of transnational to domestic attacks likely reflects challenges faced by attackers due to cultural and linguistic barriers. Foreign attackers typically encounter an environment in which they have an imperfect understanding of local language, culture, and daily life. This impediment may explain why recent research by Smith and Damphouuse (2009) shows that international terrorist attacks against the United States have a much longer planning time horizon than attacks by domestic groups. To overcome cultural and linguistic obstacles, foreign attackers will probably be more likely than domestic attackers to rely on immigrant communities or Diaspora within the target country. Similar reasoning leads Clarke and Newman (2006: 143) to conclude that "externally based terrorists will mount their attacks from locations that are as close as possible to the target." Put in another way, foreign terrorist groups need locals. Thus a recent report by the U.S. State Department (2008) stresses the importance to al Qaeda of local recruits, especially in the West. More generally, the results underscore both the atypicality and the lethal ingenuity of the 9/11 attacks. Al Qaeda was able to engineer 9/11 without using locals, but instead relied on specially trained and highly qualified foreign operatives. Thus far the ability to commandeer such assets has been exceedingly rare.

Myth 6: Most terrorist attacks rely on sophisticated weaponry.

Terrorism-related plots in the electronic and print media are often portrayed as incredibly complex operations relying on split second timing and intricate weaponry. These images no doubt encourage us to think that most terrorist strikes depend on sophisticated weaponry. In figure 5.4 we show the weapons used in terrorism attacks from the GTD from 1970 to 2007.

Contrary to the view of terrorism that we commonly get from the media, the vast majority of terrorist attacks rely on readily accessible weapons. According to figure 5.4, the most common weapons in the GTD data base were explosives and firearms. These two categories account for nearly eighty percent of all attacks. For the most part, the explosives used were readily available, especially dynamite, grenades, mortars and improvised devices placed inside vehicles ("car bombs"). Similarly, the most common firearms were also widely available, including especially automatic weapons, shot guns, and pistols. After explosives and firearms, incendiaries (fire or firebombs) account for nearly eight percent of the incidents. Melee attacks, which include assaults with weapons such as blunt objects, knives, and ropes, account for fewer than two percent of all attacks. Weapons included in the "other" category were diverse, including items such as sabotage equipment, vehicles (not vehicle-borne explosives), biological, radiological, and fake weapons. Among the more sophisticated weapon types were 523 attacks using remote-detonated devices, 213 attacks using chemical agents,

Figure 5.3. Total Transnational and Domestic Attacks by 52 Foreign Terrorist Groups Identified as Threats to the United States

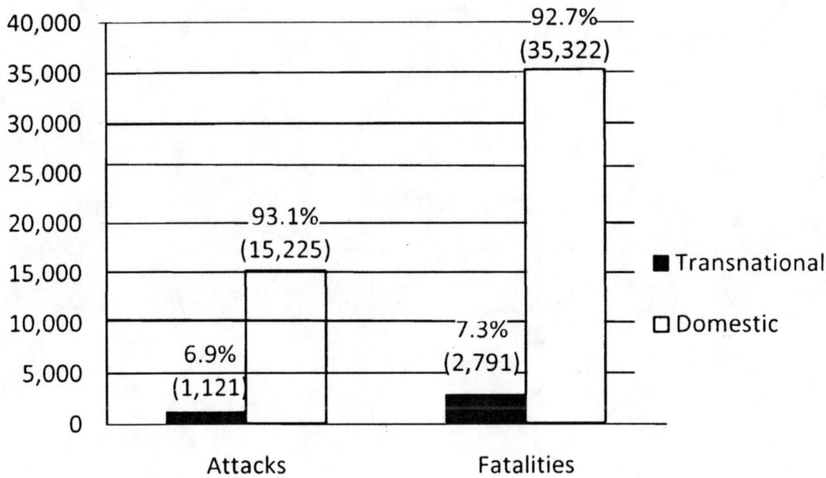

Source: LaFree, Yang and Crenshaw (2009)

Twenty-six attacks involving biological agents, and fifteen attacks involving radiological materials. Note that chemical agents were responsible for about one-quarter of one percent of all incidents and biological and radiological agents were each present in less than three-one hundredths of one percent of all attacks. The remote-detonated devices were usually left on the roadside or attached to vehicles. Sometimes, they were planted in packages and detonated at strategic locations. Chemical agents range from letters containing rat poison to tainted water supplies. Ten of the twenty-six biological weapons cases were the U.S. anthrax attacks of 2001—in which seven people died. Likewise, ten of the fifteen cases involving radiological materials were related to attacks in which an individual sent envelopes containing monazite to Japanese government officials, causing no injuries.

Terrorism is the tool of the poor and the weak. It is used precisely because the groups involved do not have a lot of sophisticated weaponry. If they did, they would probably use it in more conventional military ways. Typical terrorist attacks use readily available weapons. In contrast to high profile media reports, sophisticated weapons, including chemical, biological or radiological materials, are the rare exception.

Figure 5.4. Weapons Used in Terrorist Attacks, 1970-2007 (n = 82,910)

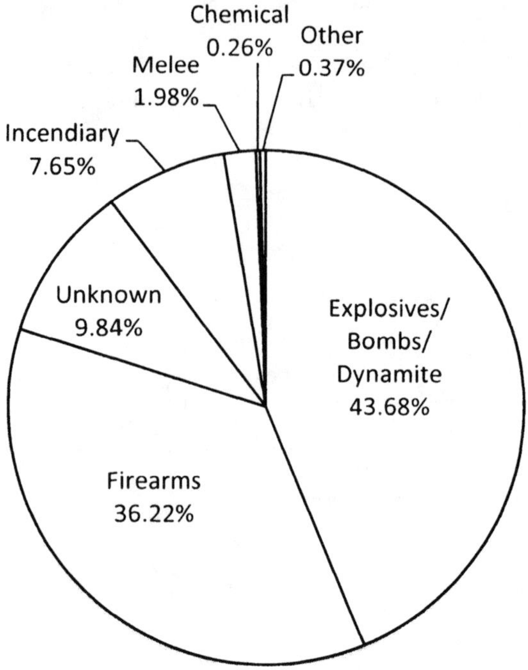

Source: Global Terrorism Database

Myth 7: Most terrorist attacks are incredibly lethal.

Again, because highly lethal terrorist strikes are the ones that grab the headlines, it is easy to suppose that most terrorist attacks are incredibly lethal. In figure 5.5 we examine total fatalities attributed to the 82,910 attacks in the GTD.

According to figure 5.5, more than half of all terrorist attacks since 1970 (where information was available) involved no fatalities. Many incidents are directed at property. Others attacks are aimed at civilians, but they fail. And in many other cases terrorist groups provide a warning to civilians before striking. This has been a common practice for ETA and the IRA and used to be a common practice for the Weather Underground. Thirty years ago these considerations led terrorism researcher Brian Jenkins (1975) to suggest that "terrorists want a lot of people watching, not a lot of people dead."

Of course, it is still the case that 45 percent of the attacks in the GTD (or more than 34,000 attacks) involved at least one fatality. Incidents that are especially worrisome are the 1.5 percent (or 1,138) that produced more than twenty five fatalities. And in fact, Jenkins (2007) has recently revisited his earlier statement and after reviewing the stated plans of terrorist groups operating in the early twenty-first century concluded that indeed "many of today's terrorists want a lot of people watching and a lot of people dead." But nevertheless, the majority of terrorist attacks since 1970 produced no fatalities.

Myth 8: Most terrorist organizations are long lasting and difficult to eradicate.

Given the persistence of high profile, long lasting groups like al Qaeda, the Tamil Tigers or the Irish Republican Army, there is also a common perception that most terrorist groups have long life spans. The GTD identifies more than 1,500 separate terrorist groups. We gauged their longevity by the amount of time from their first strike to their last. In figure 5.6 I show the average length of time these organizations have mounted attacks, based on a recently completed analysis of an earlier version of the GTD (LaFree, 2008).

According to figure 5.6, nearly 75 percent of the terrorist organizations identified in the GTD from 1970 to 1997 lasted for less than a year. These results suggest that most terrorist groups are like most business start ups—very likely to disappear during their first year of operation. Forming and maintaining groups is not all that easy, despite impressions to the contrary from the media. Why do we have the impression that terrorist groups are long lasting and difficult to eradicate? Probably because we hear so much about the groups that are successful. But for every al Qaeda and ETA, there are many more short lived, relatively unknown groups such as the Anti-Capitalist Brigades and the Revolutionary Flames.

Myth 9: To be effective against terrorism, governments must strike back rapidly and forcefully.

The belief that the credible threat of severe punishment deters crime and other objectionable behavior is as old as criminal law itself and has broad appeal to both policy makers and the public. Deterrence models generally assume that human beings are rational, self interested actors who seek to minimize personal cost while maximizing personal gain (Paternoster, 1987; Ross and LaFree, 1986). An important implication of such perspectives is that individual behavior can be altered by the threat and imposition of severe punishment. Deterrence models have been applied to a wide variety of criminal behavior, including drunk driving (Nagin and Paternoster, 1993), burglary (Wright and Decker, 1994), robbery (Wright and Decker, 1997), shoplifting (Piquero and Tibbetts, 1996), income tax evasion (Klepper and Nagin, 1989), drug selling (Jacobs, 1996) and white-collar crimes (Paternoster and Simpson, 1996; Simpson, Piquero and Paternoster, 1998). Deterrence models would seem to be especially appropriate for understanding terrorist violence, given that many terrorist attacks are carefully planned and appear to include at least some consideration for risks and rewards. Indeed deterrence-based thinking has dominated counter terrorist

Figure 5.5. Total Fatalities per Terrorist Attack, 1970-2007 (n = 82,910*)

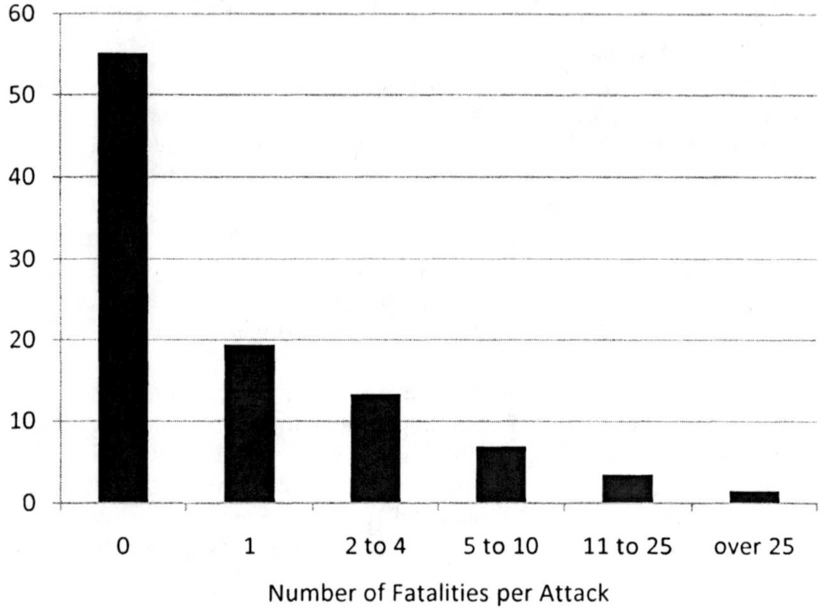

*Data on fatalities were missing in 8.1% of cases

Source: Global Terrorism Database

policies in most countries since the origins of modern terrorism in the late 1960s (Braithwaite, 2005; Collins, 2004; Frey and Luenchinger, 2002) and there is substantial research support for the argument that deterrence-based policies can reduce terrorist violence (Clarke and Newman, 2006; Dugan, LaFree and Piquero, 2005; Enders and Sandler, 2006).

However, research on terrorism (McCauley, 2006; Nevin, 2003) and more generally, research from criminology (Braithwaite, 2005; Pridemore and Freilich, 2007; Sherman, 1993) and psychology (Brehm and Brehm, 1981; Tyler, 1990) suggests that the threat and/or imposition of punishment does not always deter future acts of violence and may in some cases, actually increase violence. Thus, it is useful to contrast *deterrence effects* (i.e., the extent to which government threats or imposition of punishment reduces the future incidence of prohibited behavior) from *backlash effects* (i.e., the extent to which government threats or imposition of punishment increases the future incidence of prohibited behavior).

Researchers (Atran, 2003; Crenshaw, 2002; Higson-Smith, 2002) have long argued that terrorists frequently rely on the response of governments to mobilize the sympathies of would-be supporters. To the extent that government-based counter terrorist strategies outrage participants or energize a base of potential supporters, such strategies may result in a backlash that increases the likelihood of further terrorist strikes. Sharp (1973) refers to this phenomenon as "jujitsu politics"and McCauley (2006) points out that because of this principle, responses to terrorism can be more dangerous than terrorism itself. Thus, according to Benjamin and Simon (2005: 21), Osama bin Laden's decision to authorize the September 11 attacks was animated in large part by the belief that American retaliation would inevitably kill innocents and thereby demonstrate the extent of American hatred toward Muslims.

Figure 5.6. Years of Operation for Terrorist Groups, 1970-1997

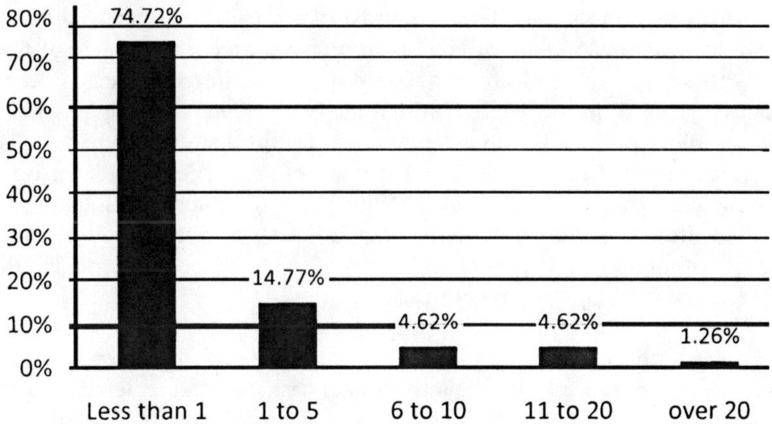

Source: Global Terrorism Database

More generally, there is an extensive psychological literature supporting the conclusion that under the right circumstances, punishment may elicit increases in proscribed behavior. Thus, in their formulation of reactance theory, Brehm and Brehm (1981: 4) argue that when an individual or group is threatened with some new form of social control they are immediately motivated to act to eliminate this control and restore their original freedom. Relatedly, much psychological literature (Duckitt and Fisher, 2003; LeVine and Campbell, 1972) suggests that threats from out-groups generally increase the cohesion of in-groups and also the pressure on in-group deviants to conform and to support in-group leaders.

Criminology literature also provides some support for backlash models. Thus, early labeling theorists (Becker, 1963; Tannenbaum, 1938) pointed out that punishment leads to identity changes in individuals as well as social changes in society that result in criminal offenders increasing their deviant behavior following their official labeling; a concept Lemert (1951: 77) famously referred to as "secondary deviance." Sherman (1993) has argued that whether punishment results in deterrence will depend on whether offenders experience sanctioning as legitimate, the social bonds between the sanctioning agent and the individuals or groups being sanctioned, and the extent to which offenders can deny their shame by seeking support from others in the community. Support for the conclusion that punishment is more likely to be seen as legitimate by the punished when the punishment is perceived to be procedurally fair is supplied in several survey-based studies by Tyler (2000; for a review, see Tyler, 2006).

My colleagues and I recently used GTD data (LaFree, Dugan and Korte, 2009) to contrast deterrence and backlash perspectives based on the efforts of the British to stop terrorist violence in Northern Ireland committed by the Irish Republican Army and their allies. Based on a region about the size of Connecticut, with a population of about 650,000, the republicans launched nearly continuous strikes from the 1960s through the early 1990s that made Northern Ireland the most politically violent region in the European Community (later the Union) during this period. We identified six high profile counter terrorist interventions used by the British from 1969 to 1992 to reduce republican violence in Northern Ireland and then we used statistical tests to determine whether the future risk of attacks during this period increased, decreased or remained the same after each of the major interventions.

Figure 5.7 shows that the results of these British interventions were more consistent with backlash than deterrence explanations. Three of the six British interventions produced significantly higher risks of future terrorist strikes by republicans and two interventions had no significant effects. The five interventions that were either followed by no change in terrorist strikes or significantly more terrorist strikes included two targeted assassinations of terrorist leaders (Loughall and Gibralter incidents), attempts to treat terrorists more like common criminals than politically-motivated activists (criminalization), a military curfew (Falls), and a partial suspension of due process rights for those suspected of terrorism (internment). The only clear cut support for deterrence among these six interventions was the use of a major military surge called Operation Motorman which significantly reduced the risk of new attacks.

And this is not the only study of terrorism to identify backlash effects. The basic finding that the imposition of harsh criminal justice and military interventions to reduce terrorism may well be counterproductive has been found in a wide variety of countries and under varying political circumstances (Collins, 2004; Geraghty, 2000; Kenney, 2003; Lichbach, 1987; Malvesti, 2002; Nevin, 2003; Soule, 1989; Turk, 2002). Given the evidence that deterrence-based thinking with regard to terrorism is often demonstrably unsuccessful, we must ask ourselves why it remains the most common reaction of governments to terrorist threats. One obvious answer is that governments that experience terrorist strikes

Figure 5.7. Violent Attacks in Northern Ireland, 1969-1992

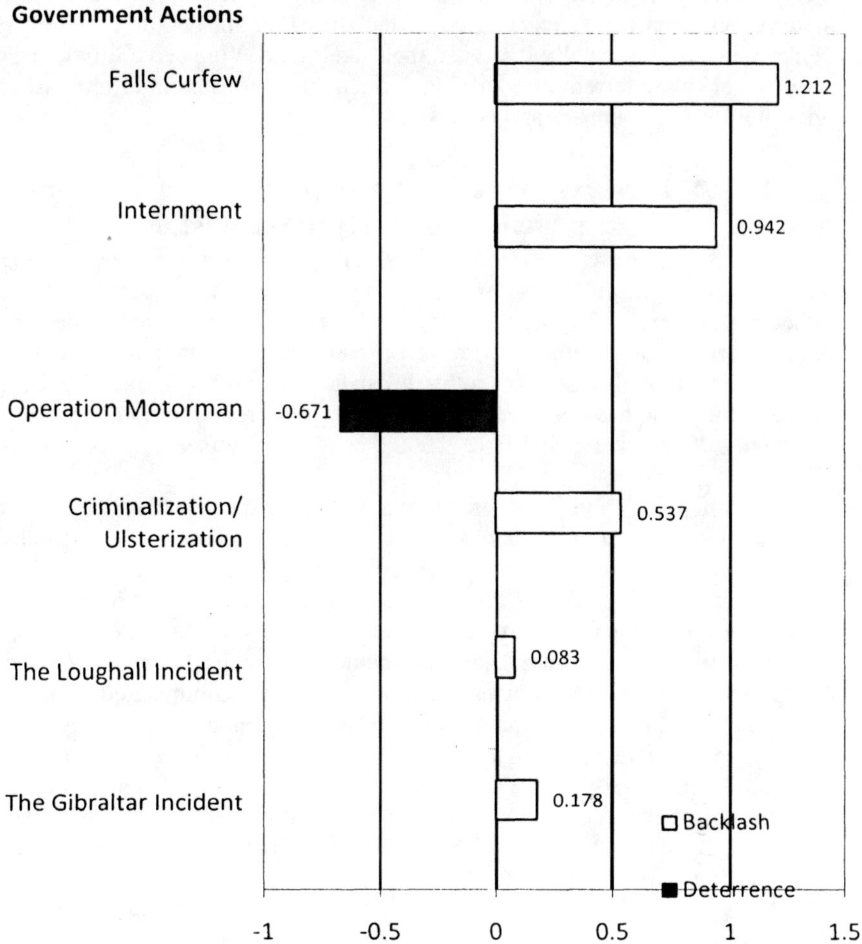

Source: LaFree, Dugan, and Korte (2009)

face tremendous pressure to take some action and often times there appear to be few obvious alternatives to harsh military or criminal justice interventions. The British began experimenting with a variety of counter-terrorist strategies after their forces moved into Northern Ireland in 1969. Only one of the interventions we examined showed signs of significantly reducing risks of more republican violence.

I should hasten to add that this is a case study. We do not know whether government counter terrorist strategies have had similar effects in other regions of the world, on different groups or individuals, or indeed, even in this region of the world during different time periods. Nevertheless, our results strongly suggest that in terms of the operation of the IRA in Northern Ireland at least, many deterrence-based measures adopted by the British either had no effect on future terrorist strikes or actually increased their likelihood. We need a lot more careful analysis of the deterrent and backlash effects of various counter terrorist strategies in different countries and contexts.

Myth 10: Terrorist groups are impervious to governmental counter terrorist policies and rarely make mistakes.

Just as some researchers and policy makers are overly optimistic about the abilities of governments to use deterrence measures to stop terrorist groups, other researchers and policy makers are overly pessimistic about the chances that terrorist organizations will make mistakes and miscalculations that can be exploited. Although research on the desistance of terrorist groups has been neglected, the topic has been receiving increased research attention in recent years (Cronin, 2008; Jones and Libicki, 2008; for a review see LaFree and Miller, 2009).

My colleagues and I (Dugan, Huang, LaFree and McCauley, 2009) recently used the GTD to examine the targeting strategies of two terrorist groups that were based in Turkey and were especially active during the 1970s and 1980s: the Armenian Secret Army for the Liberation of Armenia (ASALA) and the Justice Commandos of the Armenian Genocide (JCAG). At the end of the First World War, the Armenian Diaspora included roughly 1.4 million people in thirty-four countries. Armenians worldwide had been traumatized by the brutal attacks that killed approximately one million Armenians in Turkey in 1915. Fifty years after these mass attacks, many Armenians felt considerable impatience with their traditional leadership groups who had been unable to advance recognition of the attacks, let alone advance national liberation for Armenians remaining in Turkey and the USSR. This discontent laid the foundation for ASALA and JCAG.

In figure 5.8, I show total terrorist attacks committed by ASALA and JCAG from 1975 to 1988 from the GTD. Figure 5.8 shows a dramatic increase in attacks by both groups, peaking in 1980 for JCAG and 1981 for ASALA. Following these peaks, attack levels fall off dramatically, especially for ASALA. While ASALA staged forty six attacks in 1981, by 1984 the annual total had dropped to only five attacks and four years later ASALA had stopped attacking altogether. While JCAG never had as many attacks as ASALA, the number of attacks launched by JCAG also fell dramatically after 1982. Our goal in this research project was to figure out what explained the sudden desistance in violent attacks of ASALA and JCAG after the early 1980s.

After modeling many possible explanations for this sudden desistance, our conclusion was that the most convincing explanation was a strategic shift by ASALA in its targeting strategy. Before the early 1980s, ASALA was careful to target Turks and avoided non-Turkish and especially Armenian, casualties.

Figure 5.8. Attacks by ASALA and JCAG, 1975 to 1988

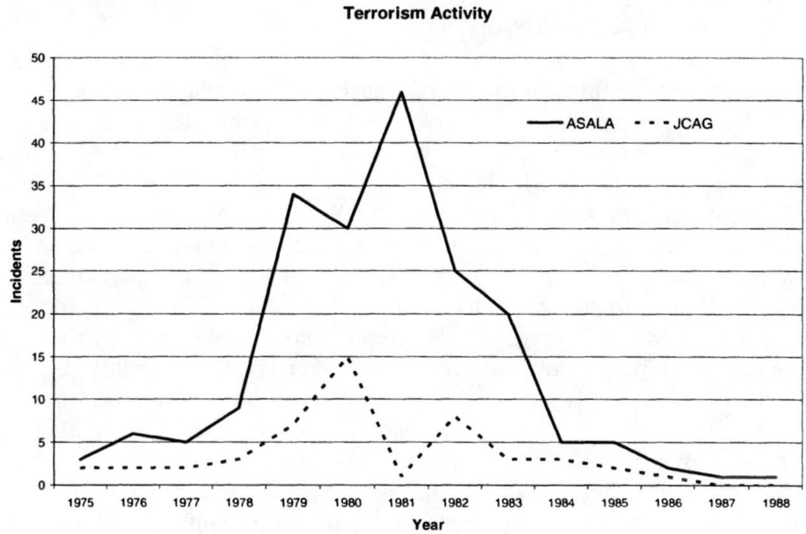

Source: Dugan, Huang, LaFree and McCauley (2009)

But starting in the early 1980s, they became far less discriminate in their targeting methods. The pivotal historical event in our analysis was an especially brutal attack on Paris's Orly Airport in 1983. An explosive device detonated prematurely in the terminal area by the Turkish Airlines counter, killing eight people (four French, two Turkish, one American, one Swedish) and wounding over fifty more. The expansion of increasingly inept attacks such as the one at Orly created a polarized and hostile climate within ASALA and in Armenian perceptions of ASALA. We concluded that this change in targeting strategy seriously undermined the legitimacy of ASALA among its supporters in the Armenian Diaspora and in the West. Interestingly, although JCAG was not involved in the Orly bombing and in general had a much more disciplined approach to the use of terrorist violence, JCAG attacks also declined rapidly following Orly. These results suggest that when a terrorist organization that depends heavily on a Diaspora over-reaches in terrorist targeting, it may offer a strong opening for discrediting terrorism as a tactic, even discrediting terrorist groups that have not over-reached.

Perhaps the most general lesson from ASALA's rise and fall is a perspective on terrorist motivation. Most terrorists want to mobilize and lead others to support their cause. Terrorists who claim to represent an ethnic or communal group want to mobilize and lead their own people in preserving communal culture and values. Therefore, the most important audience of terrorist activity may often not be the enemy target of attacks, but rather the terrorists' own sympathizers and supporters. Any terrorist group that loses sight of its major audience is vulnerable.

Discussion and Conclusion

Historically, terrorism and its consequences have not been major specialization areas for researchers in the social and behavioral sciences. This could be regarded as a dangerous situation given that as a method terrorism tries to exploit lack of knowledge to provoke emotional overreaction. There are indications in recent years of much greater engagement by social researchers. Terrorism research solicitations by the National Science Foundation, the National Institute of Justice and the Bureau of Justice Administration, and the creation of the Department of Homeland Security's Centers of Excellence program have all strengthened support for social scientific studies of terrorism and responses to terrorism. The Minerva program (*Washington Post*, 2008), funded by the Department of Defense, promises to increase further levels of support. Moreover, spurred by brutal attacks such as the Madrid and London bombings, funding of social science research on terrorism and responses to terrorism has also expanded greatly in Europe (Eder and Senn, 2008).

Several of the myths discussed in this paper could be more easily summarized as "the myth of the super terrorist." This would apply to the assumption that terrorist attacks are ubiquitous (Myth 3), use sophisticated weaponry (Myth 6), and are incredibly lethal (Myth 7) and that terrorist groups are always long lasting (Myth 8) and never make strategic errors (Myth 10). As we have seen, terrorist attacks are highly concentrated in geographical space, rely to a large extent on readily available, unsophisticated weaponry, and frequently involve few or no fatalities. The typical terrorist group disappears in less than a year and there is ample evidence that terrorists frequently make strategic errors. What makes terrorism so incredibly challenging is precisely the asymmetric weakness of its perpetrators. A half century ago, William Wolf (1957) drew this comparison memorably in an essay about the possible impact of a wasp on a speeding automobile with four passengers. If a wasp that flies into the window of a moving car causes a driver to lose control and crash, an insect weighing less than half an ounce, armed with a tiny syringe containing a drop of irritant, can take the lives of four men and convert a large, powerful car into a heap of scrap. Thus, "action and reaction can be ridiculously out of proportion (33)."

The exceptional originality of the 9/11 attacks are directly connected to several of the other myths discussed here, including the perception that attacks were rapidly increasing just before 9/11 (Myth 1), the perception that the United States is the most likely country to be targeted by terrorists (Myth 2), and the assumption that most terrorist attacks involve disgruntled groups from one country attacking civilians in another country (Myth 5). The 9/11 attacks likely do represent a watershed of sorts—the end of the wave of primarily Marxist-

Leninist inspired terrorism that dominated the world until a few years after the collapse of the Soviet Union and the rise of transnational jihadi-style terrorism that began in the 1990s and rose dramatically following the 9/11 attacks. As we have seen, there are many strategic reasons why the U.S. makes a good target for terrorist attacks. Nevertheless, it is important to keep in mind that at least up until this point in history, the vast majority of terrorism has been carried out by domestic groups on local targets.

This leaves Myth 9, the assumption that deterrence measures are universally the best response to terrorism. At present there is very little extant literature on categorizing and measuring counterterrorism policies and efforts. But from the research that does exist, there is ample evidence to suggest that striking back forcefully does not always achieve the hoped for policy objectives and may trigger backlash effects that make things considerably worse. Sorely needed are more sophisticated analyses of countermeasures according to a taxonomy that spans the lifecycle of terrorist groups and events, from addressing grievances and countering ideological radicalization, to deterring attacks and punishing perpetrators.

Objective research on terrorism is especially critical because policy in this area is likely to be driven—even more than with common acts of violence—by exceptional cases. We need to guard against what Thomas Schelling (1962) described many years ago as "a routine obsession with a few dangers that may be familiar rather than likely." Social science research can help.

Notes

1. We should hasten to add that most of the 1993 data in the GTD were lost by the original data collectors and we have never been able to recover them fully (LaFree and Dugan, 2007). Unfortunately, 1993 was a very active year for worldwide terrorist attacks. For figure 5.1 and the other trend analysis we estimate 1993 rates by taking the average value for 1992 and 1994.

2. The 1993 World Trade Center Bombing was not included in the analysis because the perpetrators of the event were not affiliated with any of the 53 terrorist groups identified by this study at the time when the attack occurred.

3. The GTD excludes attacks related to open combat between opposing armed forces, both regular and irregular. However, the GTD includes attacks against the military if the military is there as an internationally recognized peacekeeping force, if the attack is against military forces on leave away from their area of operation (as in the attack on the *USS Cole*), or if the attacks are against military personnel who are in their place of residence (LaFree and Dugan, 2007).

References

Asal, Victor, and R. Karl Rethemeyer. "Targeting and Attacking America: Ideology and Capability." Unpublished Manuscript, University of New York at Albany, 2007.

Atran, Scott. "Genesis of Suicide Terrorism." *Science* 7 (March 2003): 1534-39.

Becker, Howard S. *Outsiders: Studies in the Sociology of Deviance*. Glencoe, IL: Free Press, 1963.

Behlendorf, Brandon. "Spatial Choices and Terrorist Incidents." Paper presented at the annual meeting of the American Society of Criminology, St. Louis, MO, November, 2008.

Benjamin, David, and Steven Simon. *The Next Attack: The Failure of the War on Terror and a Strategy for Getting it Right.* New York: Time Books, 2005.

Braithwaite, John. "Pre-empting Terrorism." *Current Issues in Criminal Justice* 17 (2005): 96-114.

Brehm, Sharon Stevens, and Jack Brehm. *Psychological Reactance: A Theory of Freedom and Control.* New York: Academic Press, 1981.

Clarke, Ronald V. and Graeme R. Newman. *Outsmarting the Terrorists.* Westport, CN: Praeger, 2006.

Collins, Stephen D. "Dissuading State Support of Terrorism: Strikes or Sanctions?" *Studies in Conflict and Terrorism* 27 (2004): 1-18.

Crenshaw, Martha. "Why America? The Globalization of Civil War," *Current History* 100 (2001): 425-32.

———. "The Causes of Terrorism." Pp. 99-118 in *Violence: A Reader*, edited by Catherine Besteman. New York: New York University Press, 2002.

———. "Why the United States is targeted by terrorism," Presentation at the annual meeting of the International Studies Association, San Diego, CA, 2006.

Cronin, Audrey Kurth. *Ending Terrorism: Lessons for Defeating al-Qaeda.* Abingdon, Oxon: Routledge for the International Institute for Strategic Studies, 2008.

Cutter, Susan. "Geo-coded Terrorism Attacks in India." Unpublished Manuscript, University of South Carolina, 2005.

Duckitt, John, and Kirstin Fisher. "The Impact of Social Threat on Worldview and Ideological Attitudes." *Political Psychology* 24 (2003): 199-222.

Dugan, Laura, Julie Huang, Gary LaFree, and Clark McCauley. "The Armenian Secret Army for the Liberation of Armenia and the Justice Commandos of the Armenian Genocide." *Asymmetric Conflict* (forthcoming).

Dugan, Laura, Gary LaFree, and Alex R. Piquero. "Testing a Rational Choice Model of Airline Hijackings." *Criminology* 43 (2005):1031-66.

Eder, Franz, and Martin Senn, eds. *Europe and Transnational Terrorism: Assessing Threats and Countermeasures.* Baden, Germany: Nomos, 2008.

European Commission. "Defining Terrorism." *Transnational Terrorism, Security and the Rule of Law.* www.transnationalterrorism.eu. (accessed October 10, 2008).

Enders, Walter, and Todd Sandler. "Distribution of Transnational Terrorism among Countries by Income Class and Geography after 9/11."*International Studies Quarterly* 50 (2006): 367-93.

Falkenrath, Richard. "Analytic Models and Policy Prescription: Understanding Recent Innovation in U.S. Counterterrorism." *Journal of Conflict and Terrorism* 24 (2001): 159-81.

Frey, Bruno S., and Simon Luechinger. "Terrorism: Deterrence May Backfire." *European Journal of Political Economy* 20 (2002): 1-23.

Geraghty, Tony. *The Irish War.* Baltimore, MD: The Johns Hopkins University Press, 2000.

Greener-Barcham, Beth K. "Before September: A History of Counter-Terrorism in New Zealand." *Australian Journal of Political Science* 37 (2002): 509-24.

Higson-Smith, Craig. "A Community Psychology Perspective on Terrorism: Lessons from South Africa." Pp. 3-22 in *The Psychology of Terrorism*, edited by Chris Stout. Westport, CT: Praeger, 2002.

Hoffman, Bruce. *Recent Trends and Future Prospects of Terrorism in the United States.* Santa Monica, CA: Rand, 1998.

Jacobs, Bruce. "Crack Dealers and Restrictive Deterrence: Identifying NARCS." *Criminology* 34 (1996): 409-31.

Jenkins, Brian M. "International Terrorism: A New Model of Conflict." in *International Terrorism and World Security*, edited by David Carlton and Carla Schaerf. London: Croom Helm, 1975.

———. *The New Age of Terrorism.* RAND: National Security Research Division. 2007. www.rand.org/pubs/reprints/2006/RAND_RP1215.pdf (accessed December 16, 2009).

Jones, Seth G. and Martin C. Libicki. *How Terrorist Groups End: Lessons for Countering al Qaeda.* Santa Monica, CA: Rand Corporation, 2008.

Kenney, Michael. "From Pablo to Osama: Counter-terrorism Lessons from the War on Drugs." *Survival* 45 (2003): 187-206.

Klepper, Steve, and Daniel S. Nagin. "Tax Compliance and Perceptions of the Risk of Detection and Criminal Prosecution." *Law and Society Review* 23 (1989): 209-40.

LaFree, Gary. "Countering Myths about Terrorism." 38th Annual Theodore Standing Lecture. State University of New York, Albany. April, 2008.

LaFree, Gary, and Laura Dugan. "How Does Studying Terrorism Compare to Studying Crime?" Pp. 53-74 in *Criminology and Terrorism,* edited by Mathieu DeFlem. New York: Elsevier, 2004.

LaFree, Gary, and Laura Dugan. "Introducing the Global Terrorism Database," *Political Violence and Terrorism* 19 (2007): 181-204.

LaFree, Gary, and Laura Dugan. "Tracking global terrorism, 1970-2004." *To Protect and to Serve: Dilemmas in Policing Terrorism and Serving the Public.* (forthcoming.)

LaFree, Gary, Laura Dugan and Raven Korte. "The Impact of British Counter Terrorist Strategies on Political Violence in Northern Ireland: Comparing Deterrence and Backlash Models." *Criminology.* (forthcoming)

LaFree, Gary, and Erin Miller. 2008. "Desistance from terrorism: What can we learn from criminology?" *Asymmetric Conflict* (forthcoming).

LaFree, Gary, Sue-Ming Yang and Martha Crenshaw. Forthcoming 2009. "Trajectories of Terrorism: Attack Patterns of Foreign Groups that have Targeted the United States, 1970 to 2004," *Criminology and Public Policy.*

Leiken, R. S., and S. Brooke, S. "The Quantitative Analysis of Terrorism and Immigration: An Initial Exploration." *Terrorism and Political Violence* 18 (2006): 503- 521.

Lemert. Edwin M. *Social Pathology.* New York: McGraw-Hill, 1951.

LeVine, Robert A., and Donald T. Campbell. *Ethnocentrism.* New York: Wiley, 1972.

Lichbach, Mark Irving. "Deterrence or Escalation? The Puzzle of Aggregate Studies of Repression and Dissent." *Journal of Conflict Resolution* 31 (1987): 266-297.

Lum, Cynthia, Lesley Kennedy, and A. Sherley. "Are Counter-Terrorism Strategies Effective?: The Results of the Campbell Systematic Review on Counter-Terrorism Evaluation Research." *Journal of Experimental Criminology* 2 (2006): 489-516.

Malvesti, Michele L. "Bombing Bin Laden: Assessing the Effectiveness of Air Strikes as a Counter-Terrorism Strategy." *The Fletcher Forum of World Affairs* 26 (2002): 17-29.

McCauley, Clark. "Jujitsu Politics: Terrorism and Responses to Terrorism." Pp. 45-66 in *Collateral Damage: The Psychological Consequences of America's War on Terrorism*, edited by P. Kimmel and C. Stout. Santa Barbara, CA: Greenwood Publishing, 2006.

Merari, Aerial. "Academic Research and Government Policy on Terrorism." *Terrorism and Political Violence* 3 (1991): 88-102.

Nagin, Daniel S., and Raymond Paternoster. "Enduring Individual Differences and Rational Choice Theories of Crime." *Law and Society Review* 27 (1993): 467–496.

Neumayer, Eric, and Thomas Plumper. "Foreign terror on Americans," Unpublished manuscript, London School of Economics. 2008.

Nevin, John A. "Retaliating Against Terrorists" *Behavior and Social Issues* 12 (2003): 109-128.

Paternoster, Raymond. "The Deterrent Effect of the Perceived Certainty and Severity of Punishment: A Review of the Evidence and Issues" *Justice Quarterly* 4 (1987): 173–217.

Paternoster, Raymond, and Sally S. Simpson. "Sanction Threats and Appeals to Morality: Testing a Rational Choice Model of Corporate Crime." *Law and Society Review* 30 (1996): 549-583.

Piquero, Alex R., and Stephen G. Tibbetts. "Specifying the Direct and Indirect Effects of Low Self-Control and Situational Factors in Offenders' Decision Making: Toward a More Complete Model of Rational Offending." *Justice Quarterly* 13 (1996): 481-510.

Pridemore, William Alex, and Joshua D. Freilich. "The Impact of State Laws Protecting Abortion Clinics and Reproductive Rights on Crimes against Abortion Providers: Deterrence, Backlash or Neither?" *Law and Human Behavior* 31 (2007): 611-627.

Ross, Laurence, and Gary LaFree. "Deterrence in Criminology and Social Policy." in *Behavioral and Social Science: Fifty Years of Discovery,* edited by N. J. Smelser and D. R. Gerstein. Washington, DC: National Academies Press, 1986.

Schelling, Thomas. "Forward to Roberta Wohlstetter." *Pearl Harbor: Warning and Decision*. Stanford, CA: Stanford University Press, 1962.

Schmid, Alex. "Statistics on Terrorism: The Challenge of Measuring Trends in Global Terrorism," *Forum on Crime and Society* 4 (2004): 49-69.

Schmid, Alex, and A. J. Jongman. *Political Terrorism: A New Guide to Actors, Authors, Concepts, Databases, Theories and Literature*. Amsterdam: North-Holland, 1988.

Sharp, Gene. *The Politics of Nonviolent Action*. Boston: Porter Sargent, 1973.

Sherman, Lawrence W. "Defiance, Deterrence, and Irrelevance: A Theory of the Criminal Sanction." *Journal of Research in Crime and Delinquency* 30 (1993): 445-473.

Silke, Andrew. "Becoming a Terrorist."Pp. 29-54 in *Terrorists, Victims and Society: Psychological Perspectives on Terrorism and its Consequences,* edited by A. Silke. West Sussex, England: Wiley, 2003.

Simpson, Sally S., Nicole L. Piquero, and Raymond Paternoster. "Exploring the Micro-Macro Link in Corporate Crime Research." in *Research in the Sociology of Organizations,* edited by P. Bamberger and W.J. Sonnenstuhl. Greenwich, CT: JAI Press, 1998.

Smelser, Neil. *The Faces of Terrorism: Social and Psychological Dimensions*. Princeton, NJ: Princeton University Press, 2007.

Smith, Brent L., and Kelly R. Damphousse. "The Life Course of American Eco-Terrorists: Informal and Formal Organizations." *Criminology and Public Policy* (forthcoming).

Smith, Brent L., Kelly R. Damphouse, Freedom Jackson, and Amy Sellers. "The Prosecution and Punishment of International Terrorists in Federal Courts: 1980-1998."*Criminology and Public Policy* 1 (2002): 311-338.

Soule, John W. "Problems in Applying Counter terrorism to Prevent Terrorism: Two Decades of Violence in Northern Ireland Reconsidered." *Terrorism* 12 (1989): 31-46.

Tannenbaum, Frank. *Crime and the Community*. New York: Ginn, 1938.

Turk, Austin. "Confronting Enemies Foreign and Domestic: An American Dilemma?" *Criminology and Public Policy* 1 (2002): 345-350.

Tyler, Tom R. *Why People Obey the Law: Procedural Justice, Legitimacy, and Compliance*. New Haven: Yale University Press, 1990.

———. "Multiculturalism and the Willingness of Citizens to Defer to Law and Legal Authorities" *Law and Social Inquiry* 25 (2000): 983-1019.

———. "Psychological Perspectives on Legitimacy and Legitimation" *Annual Review of Psychology* 57 (2006.): 375-400.

U.S. Department of State. *Country Reports on Terrorism, 2007*. Washington, DC: Office of the Coordinator for Counterterrorism, April 2008.

Van Brakle, Mischelle, and Gary LaFree G. "Rational Choice and Terrorist Target Selection: Lessons from the South African Experience." Paper presented at the annual meetings of the American Society of Criminology, Atlanta, Georgia, 2007.

Washington Post. 2005. "Chinese Detainees are Men without a Country: 15 Muslims, Cleared of Terrorism Charges, Remain at Guantanamo with Nowhere to go." August 24.

Washington Post. 2008. Military's Social Science Grants. Maria Glod. Sunday, August 3, A05.

Wolf, William. 2000 (originally published in 1957). In Eric Frank Russell, *Wasp*. London, Victor Gollancz.

Wright, Richard T., and Scott H. Decker. *Burglars on the Job: Streetlife and Residential Breakins*. Boston, MA: Northeastern University Press, 1994.

———. *Armed Robbers in Action: Stickups and Street Culture*. Boston, MA: Northeastern University Press, 1997.

Terrorism Panel Summary

Kelley Moult*

Presenter: *Gary LaFree*, Director of the National Consortium for the Study of Terrorism and Responses to Terrorism, University of Maryland

Discussants:+ *Joseph Kielman*, Science Advisor to the Science and Technology Directorate, Department of Homeland Security

John Wigle, Chief: Worldwide Incidents Tracking System, National Counterterrorism Center

Moderator: *Brian Forst*, Professor of Justice, Law and Society, School of Public Affairs, American University

This panel discussed evidence from the Global Terrorism Database (GTD), and what these results suggest for national and international terrorism policy. Discussion topics centered on the importance of data to creating good policy responses, government's use of data, and the difficulties of collecting and analyzing terrorism data.

The Global Terrorism Database (GTD) is an open-source database that collects information on global terrorist events and includes some 80,000 U.S.-based, international and transnational terrorist incidents. Currently the database spans the period 1970-2007, and contains information on the date and location

* Ph.D. Student, School of Public Affairs, American University.

+ The views expressed by the participants are their own and in no way reflect the views of either the Department of Homeland Security or the National Counterterrorism Center.

of events, weapons used, target characteristics, and the group or individual responsible (when available). The GTD is considered the most comprehensive unclassified data base on terrorist events in the world, and is based on information from 3,500,000 news articles and 25,000 news sources.

Gary LaFree's paper evaluates ten popular "myths" about terrorism that center on the characteristics of terrorism, terrorist groups, their attacks, and what the appropriate counterterrorism strategies should be. Many of these myths paint a picture of organized, strategic "super-terrorists" whose attacks are ubiquitous, sophisticated and incredibly lethal. In contrast, the data from the GTD show that terrorist attacks tend to be geographically concentrated, reliant on unsophisticated weaponry, and involve few fatalities. The events of September 11, 2001 helped create the perception that terrorist attacks were increasing in frequency, were mostly attacks from 'outsiders' on another country, and that the United States was the most likely target. Data from the GTD counter those perceptions, showing instead that domestic terrorists have perpetrated the vast majority of terrorist attacks against local targets.

For those interested in policy, perhaps the most striking finding from the GTD data relates to the value of deterrence-based responses to terrorism. This data suggests that instead of decreasing terrorist incidents, striking back with force may well result in backlash events that significantly worsen long-term outcomes. Although LaFree cautions that more analysis is necessary, preliminary findings indicate that U.S. counter-terrorism policy may benefit from social science research to ensure that policy is not created based on unlikely scenarios.

In response, Joseph Kielman highlighted how important properly understanding security threats are to policymaking in this arena. Understanding existing threats is not only central to grasping what terrorism represents in terms of U.S. national security, but is also a critical to any discussion about how distribute government resources in order to counter such threats. The U.S. Department of Homeland Security (DHS) relies on data like those found in the GTD to make these kinds of evidence-based policy decisions.

In addition to the personal and economic devastation it wrought, September 11th, 2001 was a watershed moment for the organization of America's national security infrastructure. The creation of DHS brought together over twenty pre-existing federal departments to address homeland security and lead the federal government's counter-terrorism policy initiatives. DHS was tasked with coming up with a reasoned response to terrorism, and necessarily needed to understand the risks that were involved, while simultaneously mounting an effective and economic policy response. Data-driven analysis remains an important tool in this endeavor, and the GTD continues to play a valuable role in promoting a *reasoned response,* rather than simply a *large-scale reaction* to risk, events, or threats. While DHS was largely reactive early on, it has attempted to move more toward this "reasoned response" approach over the last six years.

While the temptation is to focus on future risk, early terrorist incidents that occurred in the U.S.— examples include the 1993 World Trade Center bombing, the 1995 Oklahoma City Bombing, and the Unabomber's campaign in the mid-1990s—are equally important in crafting a policy response. The FBI dealt with these early incidents as criminal issues, although they were by and large terrorist issues. The current policy question for government is how to conceive of and address such terrorist incidents? How can quantitative databases like the GTD aid in preparing for these kinds of occurrences by being prospective, if not predictive, in understanding the threats that exist.

Terrorism data like those found GTD raise a number of important questions. The first of these deals with the nature of world itself. In many ways, society has changed a great deal since the late 1990s and early 2000s; increased globalization and the development of new technologies has created a society more interconnected and interdependent than ever before. One wonders whether these changes have also ushered in a different era of terrorism, and allowed some key features of the threat to be ignored, or to seem less relevant as they might have been. If the world has indeed become less local, we should consider what effect has this had on how terrorist groups form and are motivated. While some of these answers are not captured in instruments like the GTD (and perhaps shouldn't be), there is a need to question whether we should be seeking out ways of gathering this kind of information as we move forward.

A second key question is whether there are new and unique forms of terrorism that demand both a reorientation and an expansion of the definitions used to drive efforts like the GTD. As a direct result of available data, LaFree's research, like most of the field, focuses on terrorist attacks that have violent consequences and cause deaths. As we move into the future, other forms of terrorism, which pose equally significant if not entirely different threats, will be increasingly salient. Data collection efforts must evolve to meet the shifting landscape. Consider cyberterrorism as an example: it can cause large amounts of potential damage and is an outgrowth of the way in which the world has changed. The advent of the twenty first century has brought with it changes that have impacted the way that terrorism operates and functions.

Kielman closed his remarks by arguing for increased efforts at understanding how similar changes in factors such as financial concerns, resources, food, and the environment may be indirect causes of terrorist action, both locally and globally. These different causes of terrorism may influence the information that the GTD collects, the methods that it uses to do so, and how the technologies and techniques at our disposal can be used to understand the risks of the future.

In his response to LaFree's essay, John Wigle welcomed the focus on data, and highlighted the importance of different data sets that may track different information, since these varied data increase not only our ability to understand and illuminate the constituent parts of the terrorism issue, but help to develop a targeted policy response. The myths highlighted in the paper drill down on important issues, and suggest the need for additional research to understand the terrorism policy questions facing the U.S. government. Wigle argued that the GTD is an essential tool that can help government personnel and private citizens understand terrorism and evaluate policy.

For example, LaFree's "Myth 10" holds that terrorist groups are "impervious to governmental counter terrorism policies and rarely make mistakes." Wigle sees the GTD data revealing that strategic shifts may cause terrorists to "over-reach" and provide a strong opening for discrediting both terrorism as a method, and the terrorist organizations themselves. From a policymaker's perspective it would be interesting to understand some of the factors behind this "over-reaching." It may be useful to know whether there are things that can be done to induce terrorist organizations to over-reach sooner, and whether competition for attention by terrorists leads to an escalation that may culminate in over-reaching. Similarly, we may speculate as to the value of so-called "big stick" counterterrorism policies such as "Operation Motorman," the aggressive British Army campaign waged in 1972 against the Provisional Irish Republican Army in Northern Ireland. Further, after the success of the Iraqi surge, some may argue that these policies work, but there may be other factors that have bearing on these successes, such as the hearts and minds of civilians. From a policymaking perspective it would be interesting to be able to evaluate empirically the importance and effect of such factors.

Although it is easy to view terrorism in present-day and emotional terms, Wigle sees great value in using empirical analyses to consider whether our emotional reactions are in fact based in some kind of truth, or whether we are making poorly informed decisions that exacerbate the problem. These kinds of mistakes may blunt the immediate counter-terrorism effects of the policy and, in the worst cases, lead to secondary effects capable of causing additional harm. To illustrate his point, Wigle linked misconceptions about weapons of mass destruction to the invasion of Iraq, and misinformation about the value of torture and the abomination of Abu Ghraib.

The forum discussed at some length the nature of terrorism data and its importance to policy-making. The existence of data sets like the GTD can provide an opportunity to counter the perception that treatment of terrorism has been politicized and to include outsiders like academics in the policy-making process. Further, such data helps to inform the academic community about policy decisions. Collaboration between government and outside stakeholders lends further credence to the reliability of government's own data collection efforts and the trends highlighted by those data. Panelists agreed that terrorism statistics should take a higher national priority, like labor statistics for example, where the data are rigorously scrutinized for accuracy and methodological rigor. These kinds of data are very important, since they arm stakeholders with the tools to understand how terrorist groups form and what they do. They also provide a unique opportunity to evaluate empirically how policy has positively or negatively affected the issue globally, and what policy directions should be pursued in the future. Databases such as these provide the opportunity to examine terrorism based on evidence, when arguably too much of what we read and observe is based on conjecture, rather than empirical information.

In his remarks, Brian Forst applauded the fact that the GTD overcomes many of the biases that afflict other research, such as focusing on transnational events and ignoring events that are home-grown. He highlighted that this data has contributed to policymaking by showing that strong sanctions against terrorism are more likely to produce backlash effects, which confirms much anecdotal evidence and conjecture on the point. According to Forst, it has also shown that transnational terrorism is much more difficult to deal with than national attacks, and that successful interventions take time due to the need to learn language and cultures in order to be able to insinuate oneself into the society. This has highlighted one of the great ironies of modern-day terrorism, namely that there is an element of symmetry to asymmetric warfare: ignorance of local culture is a barrier to both terrorists and counter-terrorist activities alike.

Forst questioned how GTD's open source data, which is culled from print reports from a set of news sources and electronic databases, affects the quality of information it houses. At the very least, because each source has its own criteria about which stories to report, which may or may not vary with the news cycle of the day, the data's standards are at best uneven. This raises a question as to whether the GTD serves as a representative sample of terrorist events, which seems unlikely given what we know about the news reporting of other more traditional crimes. For example, only about 50 percent of all felony victimizations are reported to the police, and a small fraction of those are reported in open source media. These sources may also introduce a geographical bias, since few crimes in New York are reported in the print media unless they are homicides or billion-dollar swindles, while small town papers report the theft of a bicycle. While it is possible to rely on official sources of crime statistics like the Uniform Crime Report to be able to contextualize crime reports, there is no similar source for terrorism incidents.

LaFree responded with a suggestion that terrorism data is perhaps uniquely suited to open-source methods since, unlike any other crime, its success is gauged by whether incidents receive media attention. Legitimate questions arise as to the role of media control and saturation on the reporting of terrorist incidents. Does a country like Burma, which has only twelve incidents in the GTD, not experience terrorism, or does it control the media coverage of those events to the extent that we don't know about it. This is a key question for the GTD project going forward: whether per capita exposure to the media predicts terrorism in the database, and the extent to which increases in terrorist incidents in the database is a function of media saturation. The data is currently being compared to other sources, such as FBI data on indictments in terrorism cases, which may provide a means to check its validity.

LaFree went on to argue that terrorism data has numerous limitations beyond its open sourcing. First, there are no universal definitions of terrorism, which means that incidents have to be classified on a case-by-case basis. Second, distinguishing local events from transnational attacks is not as simple as it may seem. Three important factors impact the distinction between national and transnational terrorism: (1) the place where the attacks occur; (2) the ethnicity of the victims; and (3) the ethnicity of the offenders. So, for example, is it an international terrorist incident if a Pakistani group attacks the Pakistani embassy in Germany? How do you classify terrorist events perpetrated by an organization comprised of international actors and organized in accordance with a global ideology, but whose mission, operational focus, and specific orientation are concentrated in one country, like Al Qaeda in Iraq?

Third, distinctions between counter-terrorism and counterinsurgency have become blurred, but may be important in terms of policy, since possible connections exist between counterinsurgency efforts in one country and eventual terrorist attacks in another country. Definition and application of terms like "combatant" are therefore critical. For example, in a lot of the violence in Iraq there is difficulty in distinguishing between combatants and non-combatants, between the military and the police. There are police that work with military at checkpoints, and military that work with the police, there are civilian special agents who are in vehicles with soldiers when they are attacked. Sometimes those in the anti-terrorism community apply somewhat arbitrary rules when classifying these incidents, and in essence end up cramming human beings into 1s and 0s. Wigle suggested that while organizations like the National Counterterrorism Center (NCC) use the statutory definition of terrorism, this may mean that where a designated terrorist organization conducts an attack against combatants, part of the picture may go missing. In these cases, while the tactics, procedures, and methods are the same, the target is different, which may cause the incident to fall outside of the purview of NCC's database, the Worldwide Incident Tracking System.

Fourth, classifying groups as terrorist is not straightforward, since there are groups like Hamas and Hezbollah who use both legitimate political means and terrorist strategies. Other groups start out as terrorists and then use legitimate political discourse when the approach official seats of power. Fifth, terrorism data is plagued by the wide reluctance of governments to share information about foiled terrorist plots or alleged incidents. However, this problem is not unique to terrorism studies, and researchers and policy-makers can look to other fields for methodological cues. The case/control method that is used in medicine could be a solution to this problem. For example, we could compare improvised explosive device (IED) attacks with targets that could have been attacked and were not. We could also collect data on groups that have grievances, some of which use terrorism and some of which do not, and add this to existing data to create variation. These questions are academic, but also have important policy consequences.

The panel's discussion also covered the 'next steps' in data on terrorism. Dr. LaFree underlined that the GTD represent the first but certainly not the last step in trying to understand many of the questions facing the anti-terrorism community. While trends can be culled from the GTD data, we need to think much more strategically and narrowly around key kinds of policy questions like IEDs, suicide terrorism, and the use of liquid explosives. There is great promise in building and combining the various datasets into a body of data that can help fill in parts of the terrorism puzzle. Similarly, other projects are planned to link the GTD data with FBI indictment information and crime data on extremist organizations, whether terrorist or non-terrorist, to see if there are any precursor events that would provide clues to future events. The GTD is an event database, but the panelists agreed that a database on terrorist groups would also be useful, since the GTD only contains information on perpetrator groups when there is a claim of responsibility following an event.

What is more, it is important to pursue questions about why terrorist groups end: researchers tend to put more emphasis on "beginnings" rather than "ends," both for crime and for terrorism. Focusing on the termination of terrorist organizations may lead to further understanding about the strategic missteps of terrorists. We should start thinking strategically about these questions to avoid democracy's tendency to think selectively about the things right in front of us. It is time to engender a focus on new forms of terrorism (such as cyberterrorism, which the GTD does not examine) as we move into what may well be a new era in terrorism.

Chapter 6

What Do We Expect from Our Government Representatives On Immigration?

Guillermina Jasso[*+]

Promote, then, as an object of primary importance, institutions for the general diffusion of knowledge.

George Washington, 1796

Can it be, that Providence has not connected the permanent felicity of a nation with its Virtue?

George Washington, 1796

Justice is the first virtue of social institutions, as truth is of systems of thought. . . . Being first virtues of human activities, truth and justice are uncompromising.

John Rawls, 1971

---

* Silver Professor and Professor of Sociology at New York University.

+ I thank Jennifer Hunt, Eric Larson, and Robert Warren for valuable comments. I also gratefully acknowledge New York University for its intellectual and financial support.

Introduction

I am a scientist, not a policymaker. My job is to understand the way the world works. Others can take the understandings that my fellow scientists and I progressively construct, refine, and sharpen, and use them to advance the human project—to make more intelligent public policy in the United States and around the world. I have studied international migration and immigration to the United States for over thirty years now, and these pages collect questions, comments, and insights whose discussion may be helpful to a new and bold Administration.

At the outset it is useful to sketch a model of the way that science and policy processes work in what Rawls (1971:4-5, 453-462) would call "a well-ordered society." First, the public and private sectors provide freely available information—raw data, if you will; for example, both the government (i.e., the people's representatives) and private surveys provide information about immigrants. Second, scientists use the basic information to test and estimate their accounts of immigrant flow, composition, behavior. Third, policymakers use both the basic information and the scientific accounts to construct policy options. Fourth, the people use both the basic information, the scientific accounts, and the policy options to reach conclusions about the best course to follow. Finally, governmental entities enact laws and implement them, mindful of the people's ideas and in a spirit of acting both justly and as representatives of "we the people."

Thus, at the outset, I reformulate the Conference question—What do we expect from our government?—to the more apt question in a country whose government is "of the people, by the people, and for the people": What do we expect from our government representatives?

Obviously, neither good science nor good policy is possible without good information. And neither the people nor their governmental representatives can attain excellence in understanding the issues and choosing a course of action without integrity in the handling of information. Finally, inventiveness brings to the table new scientific ideas and new policy options.

Accordingly, this paper answers the question—What do we expect from our government representatives?—with three words: *Information, Integrity,* and *Inventiveness.* I briefly note and in some cases describe a selection of areas in the science and policy of immigration where more and better governmental information and a rededication to integrity are urgently needed and where inventiveness would save or soothe. The particular examples are a highly limited selection. There are many more.

Moreover, I do not discuss the important matter of how the government deals with its customers—for example, how immigration agencies deal with applicants for a variety of immigration services, such as access to visas, employment authorization documents, and naturalization. On that topic, see the Annual Reports of the U.S. Citizenship and Immigration Services (USCIS) Ombudsman. The office of the Ombudsman was established by the Homeland Security Act of 2002, which also mandated annual reports to Congress. Of course, in some cases, a single governmental action would extraordinarily improve both service to customers and the quality of information available to scientists and policymakers; a prime example is case management at USCIS.

I also note at the outset that the government agencies from which I draw examples—notably the Department of State, the Department of Homeland Security, and the U.S. Census Bureau (an agency of the Department of Commerce)—do some relevant things superbly well, even heroically. Nevertheless, we expect them to reach for perfection—in the same way that we expect ourselves to reach for perfection. After all, they represent us.

The paper is organized as follows. Section 2, "Preliminaries," provides a brief overview of the science of international migration and of the contemporary U.S. immigration context. Section 3 outlines what we expect from our government representatives—more and better information and a vigorous new integrity, seasoned with a little inventiveness.

Preliminaries

The Science of International Migration

As in all scientific fields, the first challenge is to pose the core questions, writing and re-writing them as knowledge about immigration advances and first principles in general sociobehavioral science dig deeper and deeper. A tentative list of candidates for central questions might include:

1. What are the migrant's characteristics and behavior at entry?
2. How do the migrant's characteristics and behavior change with time in the destination country?
3. What are the characteristics and behavior of the children of immigrants?
4. What are the impacts on the origin and destination countries?

It is obvious from the questions that there are three basic actors in the migration process: the migrant him- or herself, others in the origin country, and others in the destination country. Reasoning about the questions quickly leads to foundational ideas about immigrant self-selection, pertinent law in both origin and destination countries (including immigrant selection systems embodied in immigration law), processes of assimilation and integration, and a variety of impacts on both individual and society in both origin and destination countries.

Not surprisingly, topics central to basic sociobehavioral science surface in the migration arena. Thus, migration research, besides gaining important knowledge about migration also sheds light on fundamental processes.[1]

Some Basics of Contemporary U.S. Immigration

As shown in table 6.1, under current U.S. immigration law, foreign-born persons in the United States include legal permanent residents (LPR), LPRs who have become naturalized citizens of the United States, persons in a variety of legal temporary statuses, and persons in an illegal status.

Table 6.1. Types of Foreign-Born Persons in the United States

1. Legal permanent residents (LPR)
2. LPRs who have naturalized
3. Legal temporary residents (nonimmigrants)
3.1. On LPR track
3.2. Aspiring to LPR
3.3. Not aspiring to LPR
4. Unauthorized

The United States admits about a million persons a year to LPR (table 6.2).[2,3] The system of visa allocation provides numerically unlimited visas to the spouses, minor children, and parents of adult U.S. citizens (a set collectively called "immediate relatives of U.S. citizens"). Numerically limited visas are granted to three main categories of immigrants: (1) family immigrants, comprised of the adult children and siblings of U.S. citizens (a set collectively called "close relatives of U.S. citizens" to distinguish them from "immediate relatives of U.S. citizens") and the spouses and children of LPRs; (2) employment immigrants, comprised of five subcategories; and (3) diversity immigrants (winners of the lottery visas designated for persons from countries underrepresented in recent immigration). Two additional categories of LPR visas have subsets of both numerically limited and numerically unlimited type. These are: (4) humanitarian immigrants (including refugees, asylees, and parolees); and (5) legalization immigrants, that is, illegal immigrants who are becoming legal, including registry-provision immigrants (who qualify in virtue of length of illegal residence) and cancellation-of-removal immigrants, plus immigrants targeted by special legalization legislation (such as the Nicaraguan Adjustment and Central American Relief Act of 1997, or NACARA).

Table 6.2. Recent and Current Annual Flows of New Legal Permanent Residents

Fiscal Year(s)	Number
A. Average annual flow	
1991-1995	781,848
1996-2000	771,307
2001-2005	980,344
B. Annual flow	
2006	1,266,047
2007	1,052,322
2008	1,107,010

Note: Flows of new legal permanent residents (LPR) represent all persons granted legal permanent residence during the period. In most years, over half of all new LPRs are already living in the United States. Figures refer to the total, non-IRCA-legalization number of new LPRs. This number was reported as "total non-legalization" in Table 4 of the INS and DHS *Yearbooks* through the 2004 *Yearbook*. The *Yearbooks* for 2005-2008 do not report the non-IRCA-legalization total, but it is possible to obtain it by subtracting the IRCA legalization total from the grand total in Table 7. During the period 1991-2008 IRCA legalizations declined from a high of over a million in 1991 to less than a thousand in every year since 1998, with a low of 8 in 1999 and totals of 188, 217, 93, and 116 in Fiscal Years 2005, 2006, 2007, and 2008, respectively (DHS *Yearbooks*, table 4 through 2004, table 7 thereafter).

Many people around the world are ineligible to receive a visa to visit the United States because they are poor; they fall under the public charge ground of ineligibility. The process of applying for an immigrant visa is arduous and time-consuming. Persons waiting for numerically limited visas may have to wait many years. The current upper extreme is almost twenty three years for persons from the Philippines approved for visas as the siblings of U.S. citizens; at the other extreme, visas in some of the employment-based categories (such as that for priority workers, including world-renowned scientists, artists, and executives) are available immediately. Besides the wait for numerically limited visas, all visa applications take processing time. In general, the visa process lasts from the date when the first application is filed (known in numerically-limited visa cases as the "priority date") to the date that legal permanent residence is granted.

What Do We Expect from Our Government Representatives?

Fundamentally, there are three things we expect from our government representatives: information, integrity, and inventiveness.

Information

The information required for immigration science and policy focuses on two overlapping sets of persons: (1) foreign-born persons in the United States; and (2) applicants for immigration services. Foreign-born persons in the United States may be among the applicants for a variety of immigration services, such as adjustment to LPR, employment authorization, or naturalization; and the applicants include not only foreign-born both in the United States and abroad but also native-born, such as some of the U.S. employers seeking to sponsor prospective employees and some of the U.S. citizens seeking to sponsor the immigration of spouses and relatives. In general, all U.S. agencies which play a part in the immigration process or collect data on foreign-born persons are involved in providing the information critical for science and policy.

With respect to foreign-born in the United States, both science and policy need information about two things: (1) the size of important subsets of the foreign-born; and (2) their characteristics and behavior.

U.S. law engenders several subsets of foreign-born persons in the United States, and these differ importantly in their rights and constraints. They include, starting with the subset with the most rights and fewest restrictions and progressing to the subset with the fewest rights and restrictions:

1. naturalized citizens;
2. legal permanent residents (LPR) who have lived in the United States for five years (and all of whom are thus eligible for naturalization);
3. legal permanent residents who have lived in the United States for less than five years;[4]
4. legal temporary residents holding priority dates for admission to LPR and who have blanket permission to work;
5. legal temporary residents holding priority dates for admission to LPR but who do not yet qualify for blanket permission to work and have restricted permission to work;
6. legal temporary residents holding priority dates for admission to LPR but who do not yet qualify for blanket permission to work and do not have permission to work at all;
7. legal temporary residents who are not in the LPR queue but have blanket permission to work;
8. legal temporary residents who are not in the LPR queue but have restricted permission to work;
9. legal temporary residents who are not in the LPR queue and do not

have permission to work at all;

10. holders of legal temporary visas which have expired and holders of valid visas (from subsets 5, 6, 8, and 9) who accept unauthorized employment; and
11. persons without any kind of visa or permission to enter.

The first of these eleven subsets can be identified and studied via data collected by the U.S. Census Bureau in the decennial censuses and in demographic surveys such as the Current Population Survey and the American Community Survey. There is varying interest in assessing the size and composition of the other ten subsets. For example, a mix of government and private researchers and policymakers has mounted efforts to estimate the size of some of the subsets. DHS researchers have estimated the second subset—legal permanent residents eligible to naturalize—and the second and third subsets combined—all LPRs (Rytina 2004, 2005, 2006, 2008, 2009); and the fourth through ninth subsets—all legal temporary residents (Grieco 2006). Lowell (2000) estimated the size of the H-1B component of the fourth through ninth subsets (all legal temporary residents). Wadhwa et al. (2007) estimated the employment-based component of the fourth, fifth, and sixth subsets combined (legal temporary residents who are in the LPR queue in the United States). Moreover, researchers and policymakers go to heroic lengths to estimate the size of the tenth and eleventh subsets combined—illegal aliens (Hoefer, Rytina, and Baker 2008, 2009; Hoefer, Rytina, and Campbell 2006, 2007; Passel and Cohn 2008; Warren 2003).[5]

It is axiomatic in social science that human behavior cannot be understood without understanding the environment faced by the protagonist. In the case of foreign-born persons, the environment includes the set of opportunities and restrictions based on visa status. That is, the environment is different for each of the eleven subsets identified above. It is impossible to understand schooling choices, labor supply decisions, wage rates, wage trajectories, home ownership, travel patterns, or knowledge of English, for example, without understanding the environment faced by foreign-born persons. And understanding the environment they face is impossible without information about their visa status.

Similarly, it is impossible to assess or design immigration policy without information on visa status, as noted in the 1994 report of the U.S. Commission on Immigration Reform (CIR 1994:xxxi, 184-185). In the same vein, the U.S. General Accounting Office (1998) assessed existing data, concluding that information on the foreign-born population, by visa status, is critically needed for informed policymaking.

Information: Improving Information on the Foreign-Born Collected by the U.S. Census Bureau

The main sources of information on the foreign-born population are the decennial Censuses, the Current Population Survey, and the American

Community Survey conducted by the U.S. Census Bureau. These data sources provide not only tabulations but also public-use microdata which scientists intensively use. However, there is a grave mismatch between U.S. law and the questionnaire items used in these censuses and surveys (hereafter termed Census data). This mismatch is particularly evident in the lack of information on visa status and the lack of sensitivity to visa status in other questionnaire items (such as the year-of-entry item).

While asking direct questions on visa status is fraught with peril, creative approaches may well be found for eliminating or mitigating the current data limitations. It is important to prevent Census data from becoming anachronistic —pertaining to a world in which all foreign-born are alike in the eyes of the law and face the same opportunities and constraints.

Above we noted that it is impossible to understand the characteristics and behavior of the foreign-born without understanding the environment they face. Accordingly, it is impossible to understand response patterns to Census questions without understanding the visa-dependent environment faced by foreign-born persons. Persons in the ten subsets listed above which cannot currently be identified in Census data face very different environments, and thus any questionnaire items that would identify one or more of the subsets would increase knowledge about immigrant behavior and improve data quality.

Illustration: Visa-Dependent Environment and Labor Force Participation

Many foreign-born persons in the United States are prohibited from working. These include, besides the obvious case of illegal entrants, the spouses of a large number of legal temporary visa holders—such as spouses of academic students (F2 spouse of F1), spouses of vocational students (M2 spouse of M1), spouses of temporary workers (H4 spouse of H worker), spouses of extraordinary-ability temporary workers (O3 spouse of O1 worker), and spouses of athlete and entertainer temporary workers (P4 spouse of P worker). However, other spouses are not prohibited from working (though they may face significant restrictions and require special work authorization), for example, spouses of exchange visitors (J2 spouse of J1) or intracompany transferees (L2 spouse of L1). Thus, Census data on labor force participation of non-naturalized foreign-born persons (especially women) married to non-naturalized foreign-born persons cannot be correctly interpreted. Is there differential work ethic? Is there differential compliance with the law?

Illustration: Visa-Dependent Environment and Naturalization Rates

Only LPRs can naturalize (ignoring the golden few who, as with battlefield grants of citizenship or the new Military Accessions Vital to National Interest (MAVNI) pilot program, are made citizens without the usually requisite period of lawful permanent residence or, as in the case of adopted children, at least passing through the LPR stage). The data collected by the Census Bureau certainly provide information on the number of persons who are naturalized. But no inference can be drawn about naturalization rates by origin country, given that the number eligible to naturalize—that is, the proportion LPR, or, more precisely, LPR with the requisite duration of residence—may vary widely across origin country.

Illustration: Visa-Dependent Environment and the Census Year-of-Entry Question

Consider the effect of immigration law and the visa-dependent environment on the Census year-of-entry question. The year-of-entry question leaves open to broad interpretation the phrase "come to live" and thus gives rise to ambiguities. Moreover, a deep flaw is the mismatch between the question and U.S. immigration law. Whether the item is worded, "When did this person come to the United States to stay?" (1980 and 1990 Censuses) or "When did this person come to live in the United States?" (2000 Census), it is still the case that for a nontrivial fraction of the foreign-born it is against the law to ever have "come to stay" or "come to live." Such persons will have a difficult time responding to the question. Further, even persons who at the time of the census or survey have permission to live permanently in the United States (LPRs) will be constrained in responding because they may fear that admitting that they "came to live" or "came to stay" at a time when it was against the law for them to do so could lead to penalties.

This mismatch between U.S. immigration law and the year-of-entry question arises from a fundamental element in U.S. law, known as the Presumption of Immigrant Intent (Section 214(b) of the Immigration and Nationality Act). This cornerstone of U.S. immigration law holds that an applicant for a temporary visa is presumed to be an immigrant—presumed to intend to live permanently in the United States—unless he or she can prove otherwise to the consular officials abroad and the immigration agents at ports of entry. Refugees are exempt from this disabling presumption, as are applicants for certain kinds of nonimmigrant visas—notably those applying for H1 temporary worker and L1 intracompany transferee visas. For example, if an applicant for a tourist visa (B-2) or an academic student visa (F-1) tells the consular official that he or she would like to live in the United States, the visa will probably not be issued. The burden of proof is on the visa applicant.

Not surprisingly, the presumption of immigrant intent is widely known and arouses strong reactions around the world. A quick internet search will uncover much evidence of this. To illustrate, consider this excerpt from a briefing by State Department Deputy Spokesman Philip T. Reeker on July 10, 2002: "If the applicant cannot prove to the satisfaction of consular officers that he or she, the applicant, does not intend to immigrate, the visa application is refused. And indeed, if you go abroad, you will discover that many, many people around the world understand the difficulty, often, in overcoming that assumption and actually qualifying for a visa to the United States."

Thus, the current year-of-entry questionnaire item, besides containing ambiguities that damage data quality, also has the potential to arouse fear among the foreign-born of being placed in legal jeopardy. It might be prudent for the Census Bureau to consider removing the question or undertaking a major revision.

Modifying the Questionnaire Items

Both behavioral questions and aggregate-size questions critical for science and policy require information on visa status. None of these questions can be answered with currently available Census data. New or revised questionnaire items would significantly improve Census data.

A portion of the aggregate-size question—i.e., estimating the size of the combined tenth and eleventh subsets and some combination of subsets from among the remaining eight unidentified subsets—could be accomplished by using the "grouped answers" approach (also termed the two-card follow-up method) designed by staff at the General Accountability Office (U.S. GAO 2006; Larson 2007). This method asks each respondent to place himself or herself into a group of multiple visa types; the various "grouped answers" are then used to estimate specific visa types. As Passel (2007:22) notes, "In spite of some promising tests, the method has not been applied on a large scale." (The Census Bureau's report of one such test is included as Appendix IV in U.S. GAO 2006; another is reported in chapter 3 and appendix II in U.S. GAO 1999.)

With respect to the behavioral questions, inroads could be made by eliminating the year-of-entry item and replacing it with a questionnaire item (or set of items in a split-ballot design) concerning the timing of important visa-status events. Some possible questionnaire items that could be asked of foreign-born, non-naturalized respondents are: (1) If you are a legal permanent resident (LPR), in what year did you become an LPR? (2) If you are eligible to become a naturalized citizen of the United States, in what year did you become eligible? (3) If you ever came to the United States with a temporary visa, in what year did you enter with a temporary visa for the first time? (4) In what year did you first enter the United States for a stay of at least 60 days? (5) In what year did you first enter the United States? Similarly, other questionnaire items could tap duration, for example: (6) Since the first time you entered the United States, how much time in total have you spent in the United States?[6]

Other questionnaire items could also be improved. For example, the questionnaire item on language, "Does this person speak a language other than English at home?" could be changed (possibly in a split-ballot design) to "If this person speaks a language other than English at home, what proportion of the time does he or she speak a non-English language?"

A questionnaire item on parental birthplace would be most useful. Again, it might be possible to judiciously craft a split-ballot design, to incorporate such questions as "Where do your parents live?" and "If your parents have ever been in the United States, how much time has each spent in the United States?" Note that a set of well-crafted parental birthplace items (fielded in a split-ballot design) would be useful in helping to identify the subset of the native-born mentioned in footnote 5—native-born persons who were raised abroad by foreign-born parents and who moved to the United States as adults.

Because visa status is endemic and has a long reach, it should receive particular attention. Two points are especially important: (1) questionnaire items should not place respondents in jeopardy, real or imagined; and (2) questionnaire items should provide information necessary for the main estimation and testing tasks. Note that attentiveness to visa status should permeate not only the design of visa-status questions but the design of all questions asked of foreign-born persons (and, indeed, questions asked of native-born persons as well, because of the existence of that newcomer subset of the native-born discussed in footnote 4 and immediately above).

Information: Improving Information on the Foreign-Born Collected by the U.S. Department of State

The State Department processes all foreign persons applying abroad for temporary or permanent visas to the United States. As described earlier, some of the permanent visas are numerically limited and typically there are waiting lists for most numerically limited visa types. Between 1980 and 1995, and again in 1997, the State Department published the waiting lists for each of the numerically-limited family and employment visas as of the first of January of each year—including both principals and accompanying family members—and providing figures for the top fifteen or so origin countries. This information is extremely valuable to both researchers and policymakers. Yet after 1997 this information was never again provided.

Recently there was a good omen. The Visa Bulletin for March 2009 (U.S. Department of State, 2009) included the worldwide totals for waiting lists in the five family preference categories as of January 2009. It is earnestly to be hoped that this is a sign of better things to come and that the State Department will resume the practice of providing annual counts.

The worldwide family waiting list in 1997 was 3,538,430 (U.S. Department of State 1997). The worldwide figure for 2009 is lower—2,723,352. The 2009 report, while not providing country totals by visa type, does provide overall figures for the top ten countries—in order, Mexico, Philippines, Dominican Republic, China, India, Vietnam, Bangladesh, Haiti, El Salvador, Pakistan. The Mexico waiting list totaled 1,046,809 in 1997; twelve years later, the total is 961,744 registrants.

This information is critical to any assessment of immigration law and policy, as has been understood since the days of the U.S. Select Commission on Immigration and Refugee Policy (1981:352-456, esp. 377); see also the first Triennial Comprehensive Report on Immigration (1999), mandated by the Immigration Reform and Control Act of 1986. It is also critical for understanding the behavioral correlates of the visa process. A growing number of commentators are linking departure of highly skilled prospective immigrants who studied and/or trained in the United States to the long visa waits (Wadhwa et al. 2007). Further, many immigration researchers believe that persons on the waiting list comprise at least a fraction of the illegal population. Finally, the State Department visa waiting list is one of the six subsets of the population identified by Wadhwa et al. (2007) who are in the queue for numerically-limited employment-based visas (where the queue extends from the filing of the first petition—which in the case of numerically limited visas yields the priority date—to granting of LPR).

We highlight two sets of information, the first on applicants for LPR, the second on the LPR population.

Information: USDHS Applicants

USCIS receives more than six million applications a year for a variety of services. According to figures compiled in the CIS Performance Analysis System (PAS), receipts exceeded six million in 1997 and again in every year from 2000 to 2006, with a high of 7,949,554 in 2001 (CIS Ombudsman, 2007:113-114). Adjudications reached a high of 7,479,575 in 2005 (CIS Ombudsman, 2007:113-114; see also CIS Ombudsman, 2008:29 and GAO, 2007:6).[7] Information on some of these applications is critical for science and policy.

As noted above, the State Department visa waiting lists cover an important subset of the pre-LPR queue. Two other important subsets come within the purview of USCIS:

- Prospective immigrants for whom the I-130 ("Petition for Alien Relative") or I-140 ("Immigrant Petition for Alien Worker") has been filed but not yet adjudicated.
- Prospective immigrants whose I-485 ("Application to Register Permanent Residence or Adjust Status") has been filed but not yet adjudicated. These include both applicants for numerically-limited visas for whom a visa number has become available and also applicants for numerically-unlimited visas.

The size of the pre-LPR queue for employment visas is a pressing question and one for which there is no official answer. As the CIS Ombudsman observed in the 2007 annual report to Congress (2007: 13):

> Failing to correct the system annually results in hundreds, if not thousands, of wasted hours by all levels of USCIS leadership in trying to account for an often asked question by Congress, the Ombudsman, stakeholders, and others: "Exactly how many employment-based green card applications does the agency have pending?" USCIS still cannot answer that question today with certainty.

This information, however, hinges on a comprehensive case management system, something which, as noted in the CIS Ombudsman's 2008 *Report* (2008:9, 21, 24) still eludes CIS, constituting a "pervasive and serious problem" at CIS and becoming the subject of the Ombudsman's first recommendation (see also the recommendations in earlier reports of the CIS Ombudsman (e.g., 2007:35)). Estimates of these pending adjudications, along with receipts, denials, and approvals, are compiled in the Performance Analysis System. Researchers and policymakers caught a glimpse of PAS estimates, because some of the estimates were serendipitously published in the 2007 CIS Ombudsman's *Report* (2007:113-114). The PAS estimates were used in Wadhwa et al. (2007) and also above.

Information: USDHS LPRs

USCIS also maintains a large variety of information on legal permanent residents. This information ranges from basic data on annual cohorts of new immigrants—which are used to prepare the published tabulations in the U.S. DHS annual *Yearbook of Immigration Statistics*—to address changes, green card renewal, and naturalization. Some of these data systems are particularly important for science and policy. Here are three illustrations:

1. Public-use microdata on annual cohorts of new legal permanent residents. Published tabulations are certainly useful. There is no substitute, however, for public-use microdata, which enable a sharper look at new LPRs and even estimation of basic behavioral models. For example, while the published tabulations provide the total number of new immigrants who achieve LPR as the spouses of U.S. citizens—the visa type accounting for the largest fraction of new immigrants each year, approximately a third of all adult immigrants—only the microdata make it possible to track the sex ratio by origin country among these immigrants. The U.S. Immigration and Naturalization Service (INS) provided these microdata from the years 1972 to 2000 (see, for example, INS 1996:201), and they are still sold by the National Technical Information Service (NTIS). It would be extremely useful if DHS were to reinstitute this practice, and make available the microdata for the cohorts from 2001 to the present and then continuing on into the future.

2. LPRs whose green cards have reached the ten year expiry date and have not renewed them (or naturalized). At the present time, the population at risk consists of all immigrants who obtained LPR in the period 1989-1999. This information would be useful for estimating the number of LPRs who have left the country (albeit with some error, given that some immigrants, such as the elderly, may think there is no situation for which they would need a valid green card).

3. LPRs who have naturalized. At one time, INS had a project linking naturalization data to immigrant data for three immigrant cohorts—1977, 1982, and 1994 (INS 1997:138-141). These linked microdata sets were also sold by NTIS. Again, it would be most valuable for USCIS to both reinvigorate the project and to make the linked microdata available for public use for as many years as possible. Note that these immigration-naturalization matched data permit estimation of naturalization rates for adult immigrants (Baker 2007; INS 1997:138-141; Jasso and Rosenzweig 1982:281, 286; Jasso and Rosenzweig 1995).

Information: USDHS Combined File of LPRs and Applicants

A good case management system would readily provide much of the information discussed above: the size of the population in each of the eleven subsets identified above; and the number of applicants in the pre-LPR queue, by visa type and by stage in the queue, including the subset in the State Department waiting lists. As well, it would make it possible to obtain estimates of emigration and of sponsorship behavior.[8]

Integrity

We expect from our government representatives a complete and wholehearted devotion to truth and to principle. Of course, our government representatives, like all of us humans, are sometimes severely tested. In a spirit of mutual encouragement, deeply mindful of our own failings, we might discuss a few areas where we may be in need of rededication.

Integrity: Immigration Law, Legalization

Immigration at times becomes a contentious issue, and thus perhaps it is not surprising that government officials, including our elected representatives in Congress, sometimes say things that contradict the very law they are sworn to uphold. A case in point involves the question of what action to take with respect to the several million illegal aliens in the country. A nontrivial number of government officials, joined by aspiring government officials, have painted a picture of U.S. immigration as having two streams, a legal one and an illegal one, declared themselves foes of the illegal stream, and denounced any effort to legalize illegals. Yet it is no secret that enshrined in U.S. immigration law are several legalization programs—not merely one but several—and that the idea of legalizing illegals has an honorable history dating to 1929 and passage of the Registry Act of March 2, 1929, which permitted persons who had been illegally in the United States since before July 1, 1924, to adjust to legal permanent residence. As stated in the official DHS-USCIS Field Adjudicator's Manual, Section 23.7, "Registry is a provision of immigration law that enables certain unauthorized aliens in the U.S. to acquire lawful permanent resident status" (available at the USCIS website—see also the application procedures at the USCIS website). The entry date required for eligibility currently stands at January 1,1972.

Besides the registry provisions, U.S. law also includes cancellation-of-removal provisions. Moreover, the United States instituted in 1997 a legalization program for persons from Cuba, El Salvador, Guatemala, Nicaragua, and countries of the former Soviet Union (NACARA—the Nicaraguan Adjustment and Central American Relief Act of November 19, 1997) and in 1998 for persons from Haiti (HRIFA—the Haitian Refugee Immigration Fairness Act of October 12, 1998). While the number of legalizations do not reach the millions, they are not trivial. According to the 2008 DHS *Yearbook* (table 6), in the ten-year period from FY 1999 through FY 2008, a total of 301,652 persons were granted LPR through cancellation-of-removal, NACARA, and HRIFA. The number of registry legalizations is understandably much smaller— for example, a little over 216 persons in FY 2007 and 179 in FY 2008 (table 7).

These provisions of U.S. immigration law, together with the number of legalizations they enable, make plain two facts. First, it is inaccurate to speak of two streams of persons—children of the light and children of the dark—for instead there is a sequence of steps and the same persons go from one step to the next, from illegal to legal. Second, it is inaccurate to speak of legalization of illegals as a new idea that must not be allowed to intrude into the American body of law—for it is already there, indeed, has been there since 1929.[9]

The elected official of integrity who opposes legalization of illegals would work tirelessly to repeal the registry provisions, the cancellation-of-removal provisions, NACARA and HRIFA, and any other section of current law which makes it possible for illegals to legalize.

Integrity: Immigration Law, Punishment for Illegals

It is a basic principle of retributive justice and of criminal law that the punishment should be proportional to the offense—or, as Gilbert and Sullivan's *Mikado* sings, "to let the punishment fit the crime." It is thus odd and strangely fascinating to find in immigration law a nonmonotonic relation between punishment and duration of unlawful presence. According to current law, the punishment for unlawful presence of between 180 days and one year is inadmissibility for three years; and the punishment for unlawful presence of more than one year is inadmissibility for ten years.(INA 212(A)(9)(B)(i)) One would thus expect that the longer the duration of unlawful presence, the longer the term of inadmissibility. Yet, as seen in the previous section, if duration of unlawful presence exceeds thirty seven years (currently), there is no punishment but instead a reward: LPR.

Integrity: Interpreting Census Information, Language

Everyone who works with data—scholars, policymakers, legislators and their staffers, Census Bureau personnel—faces the often daunting task of choosing words to label and describe characteristics, processes, and other phenomena. It is not easy for any of us. Sometimes, in the interest of brevity, we attach imperfect labels, adding a footnote such as, "we will use 'just reward' as shorthand for the more precise but longer 'observer-specific/rewardee-specific just reward.'" Occasions arise, however, when shorthand expressions seriously compromise truth. When the topic is a contentious issue like immigration, shorthand expressions may endanger serious and dispassionate discussion.

The place of English in the life of an individual or household presents an interesting example. Several Census questionnaires include the following question: "Does this person speak a language other than English at home?" If the answer is "yes," two further questions are asked: "What is this language?" and "How well does this person speak English?" (the latter with four response categories—very well, well, not well, not at all).

As anyone who has worked with data will attest, it is natural, when faced with the actual language reportedly spoken at home to want to refer to the person as a speaker—say, a Swedish speaker or a Basque speaker. Of course, we know the label may not be strictly correct, may in fact be misleading. We know that the person may mostly speak English, may only on the phone (at home) with relatives in another country speak Swedish or Basque. In most research it would not matter much; the final sentences we write lose much of their color, and lose the rest of it in revision. And saying "Swedish speaker" and "Basque speaker" does not arouse much passion—except in connection with certain films or certain separatists. But say "Spanish speaker" and all around heart rates shoot up.

The language item starts out on the straight and narrow. The Census 2000 document, "Origins and Languages," states that the item "identifies people who use another language in addition to or in place of English" and the ACS 2009 "Guide" instructs the respondent to answer "yes" "if the person sometimes or always speaks a language other than English at home" and to answer "no" "if the person speaks only English, or if a non-English language is spoken only at school or is limited to a few expressions or slang."

But by the time the item reaches public release, it has shed the "in addition to" or "sometimes" qualifier. For example, the Census Bureau issued a "Facts for Features" bulletin on the occasion of Hispanic Heritage Month 2005 in which it states that "Spanish speakers constitute a ratio of more than 1-in-10 U.S. household residents."

Two years later, on September 12, 2007, the Census Bureau issued a public release based on the ACS 2006 survey titled, "New Census Bureau Data Reveal More Older Workers, Homeowners, Non-English Speakers." That is, speaking a language other than English at home, instead of or in addition to English, morphed into "non-English speaker." The actual text reads: "In 2006, about eight million more people spoke a foreign language at home than in 2000. Nationally, one in five (19.7 percent) over age five spoke a language other than English at home, compared to 17.9 percent in 2000."

Fortunately, integrity is a continuous variable, and it often grows. Two years later (on February 19, 2009), the Census Bureau issued a press release titled, "Census Bureau Data Show Characteristics of the U.S. Foreign-Born Population." This time the title of the release does not include any reference to language and the caption in the text reads "English Language Ability" instead of "Non-English Speakers."

However, the narrative continues, the "speaks a language other than English at home" formulation without the qualifiers "sometimes" or "in addition to." It states: "About 97 percent of the foreign-born population from Mexico and the Dominican Republic age five and over speak a language other than English at home."

The language problems do not end there. The Census Bureau defines a household (and its members) as "linguistically isolated" if all persons age fourteen and older both (1) speak another language at home, and (2) report that they speak English at a level below "very well." Imagine a household comprised of two parents, two children under 14, and a grandparent. Imagine further that the parents and children always speak to each other in English, and the grandparent speaks only the non-English language. If the parents speak in accented English, they may report that they do not speak English "very well"—even if they are world-renowned U.S. university professors. And thus the household (and all its members) are classified as "linguistically isolated."

Integrity: Interpreting General Information, Workers

The term "work" plays many parts in immigration law—and in immigration discussions. And thus we find at least two situations in which "people" morph into "workers," and even "children" morph into "workers."

1. *Recipients of employment-based visas.* It is well-known that employment-based visas are awarded not only to the principal who qualifies for the visa but also to the principal's spouse and minor children. Yet government officials and staffers sometimes unwittingly provide erroneous descriptions and characterizations. It is not unusual to hear references to "workers" to whom we give LPR visas and use the number for all the employment visas—about half of which do not go to "workers" but to their spouses and children. Thus, it is sometimes said, we provide 140,000 visas annually to workers, when in fact the actual number of workers is about half that. It may be tedious to always and scrupulously add the phrase "and their spouses and children" but for the public servant who holds steadfastly to truth it soon becomes second nature.

2. *Undocumented.* Analysts both inside and outside the government provide estimates of the number of undocumented (or, equivalently, unauthorized or illegal) aliens in the country. As if by magic, these are

> transformed into "workers." Twelve million undocumented workers. Yet the scholars and analysts who provide the estimates take great pains to make clear that their estimates include everyone, regardless of age and regardless of labor force participation (Hoefer, Rytina, and Baker 2008, 2009; Hoefer, Rytina, and Campbell 2006, 2007; Passel and Cohn 2008; Warren 2003).

Integrity: Immigration Policy

The United States was founded on the premise that all humans have an inalienable right to life, liberty, and the pursuit of happiness. Most Americans are proud to be in the vanguard of the human project. They join with George Washington (1796) in seeking to be an example to the world. Yet there are sections of U.S. immigration law that give pause, notwithstanding their legitimate genesis. Integrity dictates a new look. Here are some examples.

Integrity: Poverty and Travel

When we were children, we learned that all humans are heirs to the planet and all its good things and all its civilizing treasure. From St. Augustine we learned, "The world is a book, and those who do not travel read only a page." From every great book we learned that we can fall on hard times, that we can go off to seek our fortune, that sometimes a change of air, or a new tongue, can restore the spirit. And from our parents we learned courtesy; we learned a natural reciprocity that impels us to say to the fruitseller in a far-off land, oh, you would enjoy my country, you should visit it someday.

But in fact our immigration law abjures poverty.[10] Poor people are inadmissible, a provision of law dating back to the Immigration Act of 1882, for we fear that they may become a public charge. I once heard Patricia Roberts Harris, Secretary of Health and Human Services (and a principal in the U.S. Select Commission on Immigration and Refugee Policy) say how much she believed that poor people had built this country, and that we should again let poor people come to the United States.

Integrity: Poverty and Family

To prevent the immigration of persons who may become a public charge, current law requires an affidavit of support for most family-based immigrants. The affidavit of support is tied to the poverty line, which hinges on family composition.

Meanwhile, it is well known that some new LPRs do not bring all their children with them to the United States. Commentators speculate that some LPRs may prefer to have the children raised in the origin country by grandparents.

But what is little known is that immigration officials, finding that the affidavit of support cannot cover all the children listed on an immigration application, tell the principal applicant that only two or three can be approved and, therefore, the applicant must choose which children to bring to the United States and which to leave in the origin country.

I have seen consular officers, long after leaving the visa section duties of their early career, recall with infinite sadness the part they played in separating children from parents, not unlike Chinese authorities asking parents to choose which children would be sent to the fields during the re-education era.

Integrity: Work and Marriage

Some Americans find marriage a high and joyous good. And some consider the camaraderie that arises from equality an essential ingredient of that high joy. And some among us have even joined our pen to Aristotle's "love is possible only to equals" and Ovid's gentle story of Baucis and Philemon (who were the same age and did the same work and wanted to die together). Yet our country routinely and casually imposes inequality on hundreds of thousands of marriages. It does so by granting nonimmigrant spouse visas which prohibit work (as noted above).

Of course, this distorts the visa process. There is abundant anecdotal evidence that some H-1B workers seek LPR exclusively so that their spouses may gain work authorization, with no intention of remaining permanently in the United States. Data from the New Immigrant Survey are consistent with that notion, indicating that, while 78 percent of the 2003 cohort intend to stay in the United States, less than 60 percent of the highly-skilled principals of EB-1 and EB-2 have a similar inclination (and 71 percent of the principals in the college-graduate and skilled-worker subsets of EB-3), as reported in Jasso (2009).[11] Moreover, some researchers also suggest that work restrictions on spouses generate other distortions, such as reducing the quality of spouses and, if there is assortative mating, of the skilled workers themselves (Hunt 2009).

The damage to integrity is of course deeper than distortion of the visa process.

Integrity: American Indians

Fundamental to integrity is a sense of evenhandedness, a sense of justice. It was indeed evenhandedness which led to progressive refinement of immigration law, as it has progressively shed bars based on race and gender. Meanwhile, American appreciation of the achievements of the natives of the pre-Columbian Western Hemisphere grows, and with it an impulse to connect to all those spiritual, if not always physical, ancestors.

The United States has enacted many laws and entered into many treaties involving American Indians. One of these treaties was the John Jay Treaty (1794-95), which, among other provisions, guaranteed safe passage to American Indians across the new border with Canada. Of course, free passage was a moot point in the Pre-Restriction Era. When the United States closed its borders to the world beyond the Western Hemisphere and instituted the national origins quota system, there was sufficient concern for American Indians born in Canada, that

Congress passed the Act of April 2, 1928, which states: "Be it enacted by the Senate and House of Representatives of the United States of America in Congress assembled, That the Immigration Act of 1924 shall not be construed to apply to the right of American Indians born in Canada to pass the borders of the United States: Provided; That this right shall not extend to persons whose membership in Indian tribes or families is created by adoption." [S. 716.] 45 Stat., 401. The Immigration and Nationality Act of 1952 modified the law to require at least 50 percent of American Indian blood. As part of guaranteeing free passage, American Indians born in Canada may become LPRs (8 CFR 289.2).

However, other American Indians—American Indians born in countries other than Canada—are not similarly granted access to legal permanent residence in the United States. To be sure, there are historical reasons for favoring the Canada-born. Still, the modern sensibility wonders about the lack of evenhandedness.

Inventiveness

The United States is itself a marvelous invention. Every one of its institutions and procedures was invented. The same spirit of inventiveness informs immigration law and policy and can help us navigate our way to a better future. This section begins with two inventive immigration programs—one already well-established, the other being piloted—and continues with a starter list of ideas that could become pilots or experiments.

Inventiveness: Diversity Visa Program

When the U.S. Select Commission on Immigration Policy was considering policy alternatives, one of the guiding ideas involved portfolio diversification. The national interest called for immigrants from many backgrounds, with a range of experiences. The heavily family-oriented nature of immigrant visa allocation tended to "bring more of the same." Moreover, there was a noticeable lack of immigration from Africa, and many Commission voices sought to strengthen the flow from Africa. Further, progressive waves of blood kin would have less of the energy and courage of pioneer immigrants.

Eventually, the Commission hit upon a lottery system to simultaneously diversify the immigrant flow, provide visas to persons from Africa, and enrich the pool with new pioneers. After some experimentation, the Immigration Act of 1990 established the Diversity Visa Program, which provides 55,000 visas annually (reduced since 1999 to 50,000 in order to provide 5,000 visas to the NACARA program), allocated by lottery, to applicants from countries underrepresented in recent immigration flows and their spouses and minor children; "underrepresented" is defined as having fewer than 50,000 LPRs in the last five years.

Today the Diversity Visa Program is flourishing. Since the fall of 2003, application has been electronic, on the internet. Since 2003 the number of applications hovered around 6 million annually, but in the fall of 2007 it jumped to 9.1 million and in the fall of 2008 to an unprecedented 13.6 million, presumably as internet use has increased around the world. As expected, the Diversity Visa Program has substantially increased the flow of immigrants from Africa. In the period 2001-2008, the proportion of Africa-born of all diversity-visa admissions to legal permanent residence ranged from 35.2 percent in 2005 to 45.8 percent in 2007 (U.S. INS and U.S. DHS, *Yearbook of Immigration Statistics*, 2001-2008).

Inventiveness: MAVNI Program

Private firms are not the only ones seeking personnel from abroad. After months of deliberation, the Department of Defense announced a pilot program intended to recruit soldiers with three main types of needed skills—medical, language, and cultural. The Military Accessions Vital to National Interest (MAVNI) pilot program begins with a small experiment, recruiting about 300 medical professionals and 550 speakers of 35 languages (including Arabic, Chinese, Hindi, Kurdish, Pashto), for a total of 1,000 recruits. Depending on the experience with the pilot, the program may be substantially increased.

Inventiveness: Starting a List of Ideas

1. *Future immigrants, learning English, and becoming Americans*—future LPRs in the visa waiting list abroad. As noted above, there are long waiting lists for numerically-limited visas—almost three million persons worldwide in the family preferences alone (Visa Bulletin, March 2009). Some of these future LPRs are probably already in the United States, either on valid nonimmigrant visas or illegally. But some unknown, possibly large, proportion is abroad. With every year that passes, it becomes more and more difficult for these future LPRs to acquire the English language skills that will be their lifeblood once they arrive in the United States. And, though there is some argument on this point, it is widely believed that children learn a second language best if they learn it before age twelve or so.

It would therefore be useful to consider ways of beginning the Americanization of future LPRs even before they arrive in the United States or acquire legal permanent residence. One approach is to utilize the vast American network around the world to provide advance training in English as well as some modicum of socialization into American life.[12]

The American network around the world has many components, emanating from both the public and private sector, that could be enlisted in this effort. Here we mention four.

The first component of the U.S. global network that could be used in this effort consists of the schools operated by the Department of Defense, via the Department of Defense Education Activity (DoDEA) for the children of military personnel stationed at military installations abroad. Currently, there are DoDEA schools in twelve foreign countries—Bahrain, Belgium, England, Germany,

Guam, Italy, Japan, Korea, the Netherlands, Portugal, Spain, and Turkey. Unfortunately, the twelve countries do not include even one of the top ten countries in the family visa waiting list. Nonetheless, these DoDEA schools can play a useful part by accepting children who are on the visa waiting list and live nearby.

The second component of the international U.S. network consists of the American-sponsored overseas schools assisted by the Department of State via the Office of Overseas Schools, a unit of the Bureau for Administration, which reports to the Under Secretary for Management. This network covers schools in 134 countries, including all the top ten countries in the visa waiting list except El Salvador. These are private schools. One can imagine scholarships, lotteries, pilot programs to facilitate admission to these schools for children on the visa waiting list.

The third component of the American global network includes all the programs of the Bureau of Educational and Cultural Affairs, which reports to the Under Secretary of State for Public Diplomacy and Public Affairs. The Bureau's many units include the Office of English Language Programs, which develops English language teaching and teacher training programs for U.S. embassies and consulates and for host country organizations. Office staff include over twenty Foreign Service Regional English Language Officers (RELO) with expertise in teaching and learning English. The Office has worldwide coverage; RELOs are posted in three of the major countries represented in the family visa waiting list—Mexico, India, and China.

Finally, it would be impossible to overlook the growing network of American universities with branches abroad. These branches all have courses on the host country language(s) for the visiting American undergraduates. It might be a logical extension of their mission to also conduct courses on English for host country students.

Small, experimental, pilot programs could assess the possibilities for enlisting the substantial American presence abroad in the service of providing English language training and early Americanization for future LPRs around the world. Future LPRs could be invited to participate in these programs at an early point in the visa process, for example, when the I-130 (Petition for Alien Relative) or I-140 (Immigrant Petition for Alien Worker) are approved (and applicants for numerically-limited non-current visas go on the visa waiting list) or when they submit Form DS-230 (Application for Immigrant Visa and Alien Registration).

The motto might be: "Get them in early and often."

2. *Future immigrants, learning English, and becoming Americans—future LPRs in the United States*. It goes without saying that it would be useful to invite future LPRs in the United States to English classes and a broad range of Americanization experiences.

3. *Permanent and temporary migration.* A fundamental distinction in U.S. immigration law pertains to temporary visas and permanent visas. Applicants (with some exceptions) apply for one or the other; and numerical caps on permanent visas are set by Congress partly in response to discussions about how many immigrants the country can absorb. Of course, as everyone knows, temps become perms, and perms become temps. Nonimmigrants discover they would love to stay in the United States, and immigrants discover they really are not suited to the American way. And some immigrants, as was noted earlier, already know at the time of application that they will not live permanently in the United States, their reason for wanting LPR linked to prohibitions on spouses working in many of the temporary visa categories.

Consider an experiment in which otherwise qualified applicants for certain visas—for example, professional athletes applying for P-1 visas or new PhDs applying for H-1B visas—were randomly selected to receive an immigrant visa instead of the temporary visa. It would be possible to assess the saving in workload hours for U.S. government officials, and it would be possible to contrast the outcomes of the treatment and control groups—in visa stress, in productivity, in Americanization.

Notes

1. Examples of basic topics illuminated by migration research include identity formation, group formation, language acquisition, development of civic virtue, and discourse with and about the gods.

2. The acronym LPR is used for both lawful permanent resident and lawful permanent residence. The context should make clear whether reference is to a person or to a status.

3. Immigration figures in table 6.2 refer to the total, non-IRCA-legalization number of new LPRs. This number was reported as "total non-legalization" in table 4 of the INS and DHS *Yearbooks* through the 2004 *Yearbook*. The *Yearbooks* for 2005-2008 do not report the non-IRCA-legalization total, but it is possible to obtain it by subtracting the IRCA legalization total from the grand total in table 7. During the period 1991-2008 IRCA legalizations declined from a high of over a million in 1991 to less than a thousand in every year since 1998, with a low of 8 in 1999 and totals of 188, 217, 93, and 116 in Fiscal Years 2005, 2006, 2007, and 2008, respectively (DHS *Yearbooks*, table 4 through 2004, table 7 thereafter).

4. Some LPRs with less than five years of U.S. residence are eligible to naturalize.

5. This list ignores a subset of the native-born which is also migration-relevant. This consists of persons who (1) were born in the United States, (2) were raised since early childhood abroad by foreign-born parents, and (3) as adults migrated to the United States. This subset is an ideal "control group" in studies of immigrant behavior, because they share many, perhaps most, background characteristics with immigrants, including the migration stress associated with adjusting to a new country, but not the arduous experience of applying for a visa and hence none of the constraints or visa stress associated with the visa process or with illegality.

6. Robert Warren (personal communication) proposes a simple procedure in which the respondent looks at a handheld computer screen and enters the number of months in the United States and visa type corresponding to each year. Such a procedure could be fielded in a split-ballot design.

7. At the end of FY 2006, the number of pending applications stood at 3,415,409 (CIS Ombudsman 2007:113-114).

8. Such a case system could readily be designed by some of the employers petitioning for H-1B visas.

9. For further discussion and recent estimates, see Jasso, Massey, Rosenzweig, and Smith (2008).

10. The poverty of members of religious orders who have taken a vow of poverty is politely ignored, and the "poor Clare" morphs into a "religious worker."

11. The New Immigrant Survey (NIS) is the first national longitudinal survey of new legal immigrants to the United States. For a brief overview of the NIS project, see Jasso (2008), and for comprehensive information as well as to download data or documentation, see the project website (http://nis.princeton.edu).

12. This approach is by no means without its challenges. For example, it is widely believed that Americans posted abroad endure substantial culture shock when they return home. Thus, the American experience offered by Americans abroad may differ from that offered by Americans in the United States.

References

Baker, Bryan C. "Trends in Naturalization Rates." Office of Immigration Statistics, Department of Homeland Security, 2007.

Bean, Frank D., Rodolfo Corona, Rodolfo Tuiran, Karen A. Woodrow-Lafield, and Jennifer van Hook. "Circular, Invisible, and Ambiguous Migrants: Components of Difference in Estimates of the Number of Unauthorized Mexican Migrants in the United States." *Demography* 38 (2001): 411-422.

Costanzo, Joseph M., Cynthia Davis, Caribert Irazi, Daniel Goodkind, and Roberto Ramirez. "Evaluating Components of International Migration: The Residual Foreign Born." Working Paper #61. Washington, DC: U.S. Bureau of the Census. Population Division, 2002.

Grieco, Elizabeth M. "Estimates of the Nonimmigrant Population of the United States: 2004." Office of Immigration Statistics, Department of Homeland Security, 2006.

Hill, Kenneth. "Illegal Aliens: An Assessment." Pp. 225-245 in *Immigration Statistics: A Story of Neglect,* edited by Levine, Hill, and Warren. Washington DC: National Academy Press, 1985.

Hoefer, Michael, Nancy Rytina, and Bryan C. Baker. "Estimates of the Unauthorized Immigrant Population Residing in the United States: January 2007." U.S. Department of Homeland Security, Office of Immigration Statistics, 2008.

———. "Estimates of the Unauthorized Immigrant Population Residing in the United States: January 2008." U.S. Department of Homeland Security, Office of Immigration Statistics, 2009.

Hoefer, Michael, Nancy Rytina, and Christopher Campbell. "Estimates of the Unauthorized Immigrant Population Residing in the United States: January 2005." U.S. Department of Homeland Security, Office of Immigration Statistics, 2006.

———. "Estimates of the Unauthorized Immigrant Population Residing in the United States: January 2006." U.S. Department of Homeland Security, Office of Immigration Statistics, 2007.

Hunt, Jennifer. "Which Immigrants Are Most Innovative and Entrepreneurial? Distinctions by Entry Visa." (working paper 14920, NBER, 2009).

Jasso, Guillermina. "New Immigrant Survey." Pp. 499-500 in *International Encyclopedia of the Social Sciences.* 2nd ed. Vol. 5, edited by William A. Darity Jr. Detroit: Macmillan Reference USA, 2008.

Jasso, Guillermina. "Ethnicity and the Immigration of Highly Skilled Workers to the United States." *International Journal of Manpower* 30 (2009): 26-42.

Jasso, Guillermina, Douglas S. Massey, Mark R. Rosenzweig, and James P. Smith. "From Illegal to Legal: Estimating Previous Illegal Experience among New Legal Immigrants to the United States." *International Migration Review* 42 (2008): 803-843.

Jasso, Guillermina, and Mark R. Rosenzweig. "Estimating the Emigration Rates of Legal Immigrants Using Administrative and Survey Data: The 1971 Cohort of Immigrants to the United States." *Demography* 19 (1982): 279-290.

———. "Do Immigrants Screened for Skills Do Better Than Family-Reunification Immigrants?" *International Migration Review* 29 (1995): 85-111.Reprinted in *The Economics of Migration, Volume III*, edited by Klaus F. Zimmerman and Thomas K. Bauer. Elgar Publishing, 2002.

Larson, Eric. "Estimating Irregular Migration in a Survey: The 'Two-Card Follow-Up' Method." (UN/POP/MIG-6CM/2007/01). Paper presented at Sixth Coordination Meeting on International Migration. 2007. Available at www.un.org/esa/population/meetings/sixthcoord2007/P01_GAO.pdf.

Lowell, B. Lindsay. "H-1B Temporary Workers: Estimating the Population." Working paper. Institute for the Study of International Migration, Georgetown University, 2000.

Passel, Jeffrey S. "Unauthorized Migrants in the United States: Estimates, Methods, and Characteristics." OECD Social, Employment and Migration Working Paper No. 57. Directorate for Employment, Labour and Social Affairs, Employment, Labour and Social Affairs Committee, Organization for Economic Co-operation and Development, 2007. Available at www.oecd.org/dataoecd/41/25/39264671.pdf

Passel, Jeffrey S., and D'Vera Cohn. "Trends in Unauthorized Immigration: Undocumented Inflow Now Trails Legal Inflow." Washington, DC: Pew Hispanic Center, 2008.

Rawls, John. *A Theory of Justice*. Cambridge, Massachusetts: Harvard University Press, 1971.

Rytina, Nancy F. "Estimates of the Legal Permanent Resident Population and Population Eligible to Naturalize in 2002." U.S. Department of Homeland Security, Office of Immigration Statistics, 2004.

———. "Estimates of the Legal Permanent Resident Population and Population Eligible to Naturalize in 2003." U.S. Department of Homeland Security, Office of Immigration Statistics, 2005.

———. "Estimates of the Legal Permanent Resident Population and Population Eligible to Naturalize in 2004." U.S. Department of Homeland Security, Office of Immigration Statistics, 2006.

———. "Estimates of the Legal Permanent Resident Population in 2006." U.S. Department of Homeland Security, Office of Immigration Statistics, 2008.

———. "Estimates of the Legal Permanent Resident Population in 2007." U.S. Department of Homeland Security, Office of Immigration Statistics, 2009.

The Triennial Comprehensive Report on Immigration. Washington, DC: Government Printing Office, 1999.

U.S. Bureau of the Census. "F. Origins and Languages." *Uses for Questions on the Census 2000 Forms: Federal Legislative and Program Uses*. 1998.

U.S. Bureau of the Census. *Facts for Features. Hispanic Heritage Month 2005: September 15-October 15*. (CB05-FF, 14-3 (Rev.)) 2005.

U.S. Bureau of the Census. *New Census Bureau Data Reveal More Older Workers, Homeowners, Non-English Speakers*. (CB07-CN.10.) 2007.

U.S. Bureau of the Census. *Your Guide to the American Community Survey*. (ACS-30(2009), (8-2008)). 2008.

U.S. Bureau of the Census. *Census Bureau Data Show Characteristics of the U.S. Foreign-Born Population*. (CB09-CN.01.) 2009.

U.S. Commission on Immigration Reform. *U.S. Immigration Policy: Restoring Credibility*. Washington, DC, 1994.

U.S. Department of Homeland Security, Citizenship and Immigration Services Ombudsman. 2004-2008. *Annual Report*. Washington, DC: Government Printing Office.

U.S. Department of Homeland Security, Office of Immigration Statistics. 2002-2008. *Yearbook of Immigration Statistics*. Washington, DC: Government Printing Office.

U.S. Department of State. *Report of the Visa Office*. Washington, DC: Government Printing Office, Various years.

U.S. Department of State. 1997. "Visa Bulletin for April 1997." Vol. 7, No. 73. Posted online.

U.S. Department of State. 2009. "Visa Bulletin for March 2009." Vol. 8, No. 6. (Incorrectly labeled; this should be Vol. 9, No. 6.) Posted online.

U.S. Government Accountability Office. *Estimating the Undocumented Population: A "Grouped Answers" Approach to Surveying Foreign-Born Respondents.* GAO-06-775. Washington, DC: Government Printing Office, 2006.

U.S. General Accountability Office. *Immigration Benefits: Additional Efforts Needed to Help Ensure Alien Files Are Located when Needed.* GAO-07-85. Washington, DC: Government Printing Office, 2006.

U.S. General Accounting Office. *Immigration Statistics: Information Gaps, Quality Issues Limit Utility of Federal Data to Policymakers.* GAO/GCD-98-164. Washington, DC: Government Printing Office, 1998.

U.S. General Accounting Office. *Survey Methodology: An Innovative Technique for Estimating Sensitive Survey Items.* GAO/GGD-00-30. Washington, DC: Government Printing Office, 1999.

U.S. Immigration and Naturalization Service. *Statistical Yearbook of the Immigration and Naturalization Service*. Washington, DC: Government Printing Office, 1979-2001.

U.S. Select Commission on Immigration and Refugee Policy. *U.S. Immigration and the National Interest: Staff Report of the Select Commission on Immigration and Refugee Policy.* Washington, DC: Government Printing Office, 1981.

Wadhwa, Vivek, Guillermina Jasso, Ben Rissing, Gary Gereffi, and Richard B. Freeman. *Intellectual Property, the Immigration Backlog, and a Reverse Brain-Drain: America's New Immigrant Entrepreneurs, Part III.* Kansas City, KS; Kaufmann Foundation, 2007. Available at http://ssrn.com/abstract=1008366.

Warren, Robert. *Estimates of the Unauthorized Immigrant Population Residing in the United States: 1990 to 2000.* Department of Homeland Security, 2003.

Washington, George. "Farewell Address." Originally published in *American Daily Advertiser*, a Philadelphia newspaper, September 19, 1796. It appears in numerous collections of Washington's writings and of American state papers.

Immigration Panel Summary

Alison Brooks*

Presenter: *Guillermina Jasso*, Silver Professor and Professor of Sociology, New York University

Discussants: *Susan Martin*, Donald G. Herzberg Associate Professor of International Migration, Executive Director of the Institute for the Study of International Migration in the Edmund A. Walsh School of Foreign Service, Georgetown University

Moderator: *Rita Simon*, University Professor, School of Public Affairs, American University

Introduction

Immigration is one of the most complex policy issues facing the American government. The issue has clear implications for the well-being of our nation's economy and the legitimacy of existing legal regimes, to say nothing of the effects it has on the lives of millions of immigrants. The panel addressed each of these broad themes in a wide-ranging discussion that touched on the role of government, the value of transparency and evidence-based policy, and the relative merits of a majoritarian, opinion-driven policy process.

Guillermina Jasso

In presenting her essay, "Q. What Do We Expect From Our Government Representatives on Immigration? A. Three Things: Information, Integrity, Inventiveness," Jasso's focused on three things she believes the American people should expect from their government's immigration policy: information, integrity, and inventiveness. She began the discussion by distinguishing three types of foreign-born people in the U.S.: (1) legal permanent residents (LPRs); (2) LPRs who became naturalized, legal temporary residents; and (3) illegal residents.

Regarding the expectation of information from our government

* Ph.D. Student, School of Public Affairs, American University.

representatives, Jasso explained that information on foreign-born residents in the U.S. and applicants for immigration services must be made public in order to craft intelligent immigration policy. The government sources for immigration information include the Census Bureau, the Department of Homeland Security (DHS), and the Department of State. Although the Census Bureau does provide some basic information on immigration patterns, the Bureau does not contextualize any of the data they publish. Therefore, only limited information can be extrapolated (e.g., we cannot ascertain why the Census Bureau classifies an immigrant a certain way).

Conversely, agencies like the State Department have been more willing to provide detailed immigration data. To illustrate her point, Jasso, explained that, "in the years 1980 to 1995 and then again in 1997, the State Department published . . . the waiting lists for numerically limited visas. This was an extremely valuable piece of information—this is what kept researchers and policymakers in touch with the backlogs." Jasso recommended the State Department publish these lists again, and urged DHS to update its case management system to meet information needs and to keep track of backlogs. Jasso argued that an enlightened discussion on immigration policy is only possible if the U.S. government is willing and able to pursue an evidence-based approach to the issue. Of course, this is much more difficult for a government that does not consistently collect and disseminate statistics on the issue. That this absence of data may complicate actual policy-making is of particular concern in light of the issue's political intensity, and the wide-ranging effects it has for the millions of people who aspire to become American citizens.

In addition to a more transparent, rational policy-making process, Jasso argued that the existing system would benefit from a rededication to integrity, truth, and principle. To illustrate the problems with the current approach, she asserted that the punishment for illegal migrants is neither consistent nor proportionate to the 'crime' committed. For example, "if you are unlawfully present in the U.S. between 180 and 365 days, the punishment is that you become inadmissible for one year. If you are unlawfully present for over a year, you become inadmissible by [*sic*] ten years. . . . If you've been unlawfully present for 37 years, you get a reward: legal permanent residence." Further, Jasso explained that if a less-wealth family is trying to immigrate to the United States, oftentimes the system's financial requirements demand that the family split up, leaving some people at home in the native country. Additionally, Jasso argued that the factors by which a person is denied entry are questionable (e.g., a person may not be admitted if they are poor).

Jasso urged both the Congress and the Obama Administration to pursue an inventive approach to reform, predicated on thinking creatively to craft immigration policy that makes sense for all involved. For example, Jasso suggested offering seminars on American culture and English language classes for people abroad who are on the waiting list to receive legal permanent resident status. These workshops would facilitate assimilation and would enhance the reputation of the United States overseas.

Ultimately, Jasso's remarks centered on her belief that the U.S. government should adopt a pro-immigration stance, and focus on reforming a policy that in current form creates strange incentives, punitive economic requirements, and irrational public discourse. As a starting point, Jasso suggested that rather than making the transition process long and arduous, reforms that emphasize information, integrity, and inventiveness would promote the success of new immigrants to our country.

Susan Martin

In her presentation, "Credibility and U.S. Immigration Policy," Susan Martin approached the issue from an evaluative, research driven perspective. Specifically, she presented a set of benchmarks recommended for use when evaluating the U.S. immigration system. Before accepting a position at Georgetown University, Martin served as the director of the U.S. Commission on Immigration Reform, which was mandated by Congress in the 1990s to advise both the President and Congress on U.S. immigration policy. The benchmarks presented were originally established by the Commission in 1994 as a means to measuring the credibility of U.S. immigration policy. Martin argued that the benchmarks are still useful as a way of thinking about what we should expect from our government in managing migration.

These three benchmarks include: (1) the immigration system should effectively and efficiently admit those whose admissions are in the interest of the U.S.; (2) those who do not fit the characteristics established by our immigration system should be kept out; and (3) those who have no legal right to stay should be removed, and if removal is either impossible or inadvisable, their status should be regularized. To preface her comments, Martin noted that there are only 200 million international migrants in the world, representing about 3 percent of the world's population. She pointed out that "migration is the exception, not the rule, for the vast majority of people. The majority of people never leave their country of origin or if they leave their country, they do it for short periods of time and return. It's only a very few people in the world who migrate for longer periods and even fewer who migrate permanently."

Regarding the first benchmark, Martin explained that although the U.S. admits more people to become legal, permanent residents than any other country in the world, and has a large program for temporary stays (e.g., workers and students), its immigration system is faced with extensive backlogs and long waits. To illustrate the extent of this backlog, Martin noted that "if you are the spouse or minor child of a permanent resident wanting to come to the United States . . . the wait may now be five or six years just to be able to reunite with your immediate family. . . . That becomes one of the driving forces for illegal migration because a lot of families decide to come anyway rather than wait and be separated for such an extended period of time." Additionally, the system used by the United States to select immigrants is not based on publicly determined criteria and frequently excludes people who would generally be seen as desirable candidates for migration. This includes, for example, highly-skilled workers whose abilities are in demand, who in most cases are still subject to long waiting periods. As is clear, Martin believes that the current system is neither as effective nor efficient as it could or should be, a reality that has negative consequences for both the United States and the country's prospective migrants.

Martin continued by discussing her second benchmark—keeping undesirable people out of the country. She began by noting that approximately 12 million people are in the U.S. without authorization, a failure she believes stems from an emphasis on border enforcement rather than on other more productive law enforcement options. Dr. Martin proposed that enforcement should be focused at the worksite and should involve helping employers determine who has authorization to work. To Martin, this may be a more appropriate strategy since a large percentage of illegal migration is driven by the desire for employment. Martin also recommended a system that provides alternative ways for employers to address their labor needs, including policies that facilitate offshoring, which would reduce the need for businesses to rely on illegal immigrant labor. Martin pointed out that "in interviews with immigrants who have come here illegally, the large draw for them is the job market. And the reason employers hire them is that they are looking for workers who will work at the wages and under the working conditions that are being offered, and very often there aren't American workers who are willing to do that."

Finally, Martin addressed the subject of her third benchmark: the process of removing immigrants who are in the U.S. illegally. She lamented the fact that current policy—and many of the proposed reform efforts—focus on reducing the due process rights of those illegal immigrants involved in the removal process. She asserted that this is the wrong approach and we should not take away a person's rights in such a pivotal, life-changing situation. To Martin, the removal process could be greatly improved by removing such administrative barriers, and creating a more user-friendly, transparent system. Doing so, for example, would require developing a way to monitor the whereabouts of people with deportation notices that have not left the country. Such a move could strengthen the national security interests of the country, and would go a long way toward legitimizing the overall removal process. Such a system would require a significant amount of trust and cooperation from immigrant communities, however, which is hard to imagine under the current approach. What is more, Martin stated that in order to improve the removal process, policy-makers must have a serious, dispassionate discussion about who should be regularized, how, and with what rights.

Martin concluded that, based on these benchmarks, the U.S. immigration system requires a great deal of improvement. She asserted that our government representatives have the obligation to create a system that makes sense for all stakeholders and serves the public's interest in the rule of law, national security, and a vibrant immigrant culture. We should expect our government to have a sensible, unemotional debate of the merits of various immigration policies and look beyond partisan politics to find solutions that are both creative and fair. However, Martin believes that immigration reform should not be made a policy priority until the economy improves. The issue's importance demands a serious public discussion and a careful legislative process, which in Martin's view are less likely in a political climate affected by high unemployment and growing budget deficits.

Rita Simon

Rita Simon examined the relationship between U.S. immigration policy and public opinion in her presentation, "Immigration and Public Opinion." She began by reminding the audience that although the U.S. is a country of immigrants, the public often has a negative opinion of the immigrant population. This is ironic because "the Declaration of Independence charged the King with attempting to keep the colonies depopulated, refusing to recognize naturalization acts passed by the colonial assemblies, and restricting westward settlement." Simon attributed this paradox to the practice of viewing immigrants with "rose-colored glasses turned backwards," meaning that "those immigrants who came earlier—whenever earlier happens to be—are viewed as having made important and positive contributions to our society, economy, and culture. But those who seek entry now—whenever now happens to be—are viewed at best with ambivalence and more likely with distrust and hostility." For example, after World War II, the public was most suspicious about those seeking entry from Japan and Germany—countries who had been our adversaries during the war. Simon explained that "the reversal from a positive to a negative contribution occurs when respondents are asked about immigrants who are currently entering the United States in large numbers. These groups are perceived as more of a bad than a good thing for the United States." Currently, Mexicans are looked down upon as having contributed little to the U.S. through their immigration.

Since 1946, and most recently in 2008, pollsters have asked Americans, "Should U.S. immigration be kept at its present level, increased, or decreased?" At no time did more than 18 percent of the American public favor increasing the number of immigrants admitted. Simon noted that this poor public opinion of immigrants is pervasive—even recent immigrants are suspicious of large numbers of people entering the country. She explained that although public opinion toward immigration has generally been negative, more recent polls indicate slightly more positive attitudes toward immigrants than earlier ones. Recent polls indicate that increasing numbers of Americans believe that immigrants are good for the country, do not increase crime, and make the country more open to new ideas and cultures.

Public opinion polls show that if immigration policy was formed based solely on the public's attitude, our country would likely be even more restrictive in terms of how many immigrants are admitted each year. Though Simon did note that opinion toward immigrant groups are somewhat fluid, and do tend to change with the political climate. Dr. Simon's presentation implicated a central question of governance in a constitutional democracy: To what extent should policy be driven by the will of the majority, or should elected leaders serve as trustees, developing policy based on their view of the greater common good, regardless of their constituents' opinion on the matter?

Questions and Answers

The first audience question asked the panel how realistic it would be to hold employers accountable for hiring illegal migrants given that private businesses are driven by profit and built around low labor costs. Further, the audience member speculated that such a practice would lead to a police state. In her response, Martin of Georgetown University, asserted that verification of work authorization is not going beyond existing employment norms for both workers and businesses. She expressed support for updating and improving the electronic verification system, and argued that the government has never seriously addressed employment verification because a large number of American businesses benefit from having access to illegal labor sources. In her view, this tacit acceptance of illegal behavior on the part of employers is neither "what we should expect from our government [n]or what we should tolerate." Martin concluded by arguing that if as a society we think employers should have access to such low-cost labor sources, then we should provide the legal means by which they can access it.

Another audience member asked the panelists if they believed that the new Obama administration would improve access to immigration data, thereby enhancing the scholarly community's ability to evaluate the effectiveness of current policy. Jasso explained that President Obama signed an executive order on his policy for increased information dissemination and Attorney General Holder has put it into effect. She is hopeful that data on the numbers of immigrants that had not been reported over the last several years will again become available to the public.

The final question raised the issue of reducing illegal immigration. Martin reiterated that the best way to address the problem is by targeting employers and strictly enforcing labor standards. Jasso added that it is important to know who comprises the illegal migrant population and explained that many researchers believe that a sizeable fraction of people who are on the waiting list for legal permanent resident status are already illegally in the country. Jasso also emphasized the importance of information. In her mind, good policy derives from well-informed legislators.

Part Three:

Focusing on Processes

Chapter 7

Transition Time at the National Level: The Government, Congress, and Party Leaders

Walter J. Oleszek*

Change and transition are constants in political affairs, and that is what this paper is about. It focuses on a limited number of issues that highlight the change dynamic: the size and reach of the national government, the key role of legislative oversight in holding governmental agencies and officials accountable, and the reorientation of roles that confronts congressional party leaders in the 111th Congress (2009-2011). At the outset, it is worth providing a brief review of what the 2008 elections wrought and the challenges that face the new President and new Congress.

The Contemporary Context

The November 2008 elections made history in a number of respects. The first African American, Barack Obama, was elected president of the United States. As President Obama said, "I don't look like all those other presidents" on our currency (Dionne, 2008). His election is truly a momentous event given our

* Senior specialist in American national government at the Congressional Research Service; Adjunct professor, School of Public Affairs, American University. The views expressed here are solely those of the author. They do not represent the views of the Library of Congress, the Congressional Research Service, or The American University.

nation's history of slavery, the Civil War, Reconstruction, *Brown v. Board of Education* (1954), the civil rights marches, and so many other struggles that paved the way to this change. His election sent a message to everyone, here and abroad, that the highest office in America will no longer always be occupied by someone with a white face. Obama's personal background also reflects a fundamental change in American society: its growing diversity and demographic complexity.[1]

The 2008 elections were noteworthy in other ways as well, such as the return of unified government (one party in charge of the legislative and executive branches); the first back-to-back, double-digit election victories for the House majority party since the 1950-1952 electoral cycle; the election of the first Vietnamese American, Joseph Cao, R-La., to the House of Representatives; and, on the opening day of the new Senate, potential Senators from Illinois and Minnesota could not be sworn into office because of continuing political controversies in those states.

Significantly, President Obama and members of the 111th Congress take office in the midst of the most serious economic crisis since the Great Depression. The country is in a deep economic recession, which officially started in December 2007. The economic downturn is predicted to be the longest and most severe since World War II. Every day the press and media highlight the plethora of bad news: the growing joblessness; plant closings; home foreclosures; the erratic swings of the stock market; banking failures; the collapse of giant financial institutions (Lehman Bros., Wachovia Corp., and Bear Stearns, for example); the decrease in the value of peoples' retirement plans; frozen credit markets; the decline in industrial production; the bankrupting of many businesses; and the global spread of the economic meltdown. On top of these interrelated and multiple economic crises, the legislative and executive branches will have to grapple with other major challenges in health, energy, the environment, education, and the conflicts in Iraq and Afghanistan.[2] "I cannot remember a time when Congress had an agenda of this size, scope, and difficulty," remarked former Representative Lee Hamilton, D-Ind., who spent thirty-four years in the House (Hook, 2009).

The top priority facing Congress and the President is to restore the economic health of the nation and prevent the recession from spiraling downward into another depression. To achieve these objectives, many policymakers and economists agreed that Congress needed to rapidly pass a fiscal stimulus package, costing upwards of $1 trillion.[3] "The state of our economy calls for action: bold and swift," exclaimed President Obama. With consumer confidence and spending in decline, business investment on a downward path, and a slump in global trade, huge spending by the federal government, along with tax cuts (to promote consumer spending), appear to many as the best option for restarting the economy. "We are all Keynesians now" is the prescription that dominates policymaking today.[4]

Congressional enactment in mid-February 2009 of a nearly $800 billion fiscal stimulus package (the American Recovery and Reinvestment Act) is the largest in history. It is roughly equal to the total annual discretionary budget of the United States and represents the most massive governmental intervention in the economy since the Depression. Among other initiatives, the Federal Reserve and the Treasury Department pledged $7.6 trillion "to contain the ever-widening collapse of the economy" (Parker, 2009: 38).[5] Noteworthy, too, is that the 110th Congress passed a $700 billion financial bailout package which granted wide-ranging discretion to the Treasury Secretary "to buy up trouble mortgage-related securities in a desperate attempt to unclog credit markets and clean up the balance sheets of banks and other financial institutions teetering on collapse" (Ives and Ota, 2008; see also, Stokes and Hegland, 2008). In short, the national government is responding in big and numerous ways to try and revive the economy and to better regulate and supervise unfettered laissez-faire economics.

The economic crisis has sparked a new debate about an issue that is as old as the Republic: the size and role of the national government. The libertarian Cato Institute, a Washington-based think tank, even ran a full-page ad in several newspapers juxtaposing a statement by President Obama—"There is no disagreement that we need action by our government, a recovery plan that will help to jumpstart the economy"—with their own rejoinder: "With all due respect Mr. President, that is not true." Instead, the group of economists who endorse Cato's view contend that lower "tax rates and a reduction in the burden of government are the best ways of using fiscal policy [the government's tax and spending program] to boost growth" (*Washington Post*, 2009). Some analysts suggest nationalization or partial nationalization as options to deal with the banking crisis (Stokes, 2009; Sanger, 2009; Appelbaum and Cho, 2009).

With renewed debate about the scope and power of government, the primary objectives of this paper are three-fold. It will provide a brief overview of the perennial debate about the role, reach, and size of the national government. The paper will then focus broadly on Congress's oversight role, and its importance in holding the national government accountable for its actions and decisions. As part of this analysis the paper will suggest several ways to strengthen a fundamental responsibility of Congress—legislative oversight—that is often last in members' hierarchy of priorities after representation and lawmaking. (The term *lawmaker* or *representative*—rather than *overseer*—suggests where many House and Senate members prefer to focus their time, energy, and resources.) Third, congressional party leaders are in a period of transition with a new president in the White House. It is worth reviewing several of these developments. Lastly, the paper will close with summary observations.

The Role of Government: Clashing Views

"The role of government in a free society must be a matter of continuous negotiation among members of its public," wrote Princeton Professor Michael Walzer (1984). This fundamental idea is the essence of self-government by the people through their elected representatives. From the beginning, our Founding

Fathers argued about the role of the national government and their basic argument continues to this day. Two schools of thought emerged during the early period, one articulated by Thomas Jefferson and the other by Alexander Hamilton.

Jeffersonian v. Hamiltonian Views

Jefferson was an advocate of limited government: "That government governs best that governs least." Government closest to the people—state and local units—is to be preferred, according to Jefferson, to a robust and remote national government. As Jefferson said in his March 4, 1801, inaugural address:

> Still one thing more, fellow-citizens—a wise and frugal Government, which shall restrain men from injuring one another, shall leave them otherwise free to regulate their own pursuits of industry and improvement, and shall not take from the mouth of labor the bread it has earned. This is the sum of good government, and this is necessary to close the circle of our felicities (Richardson, 1897: 311).

Jefferson even recommended that each generation should have its own "rebellion" to accommodate changing views and circumstances. (As president, Jefferson was not reluctant, however, to use government to double the size of the country with the Louisiana Purchase.)

Jefferson's rival, Alexander Hamilton, preferred a strong, energetic, and activist national government if the new nation was to survive and prosper. A proponent of the implied powers of the national government, Hamilton wrote in *Federalist* No. 31 that: "A government ought to contain in itself every power requisite to the full accomplishment of the objects committed to its care, and to the complete execution of the trusts for which it is responsible, free from every other control but a regard to the public good and to the sense of the people." Hamilton especially favored a strong executive as essential to good government. In brief, Hamilton's philosophy was that the national government could be a positive instrument for addressing common problems that no individual or locality could resolve by itself, such as maintaining a strong defense against foreign adversaries, promoting the general welfare, or creating a national currency. Or as Abraham Lincoln put it, "Government is people coming together collectively to do that which they could not do as well, or at all, individually" (Hallard, 1996: 9).

Fast forward to the contemporary era and it seems evident that the Hamiltonian view has largely prevailed over the Jeffersonian perspective. To be sure, Jefferson's ideas of small government and states' rights resonate powerfully with millions of Americans including many lawmakers, analysts, scholars, media commentators, and association leaders. Grover Norquist, the head of Americans for Tax Reform, is an ardent advocate of smaller government. As he stated, "I don't want to abolish government. I simply want to reduce it to the size where I can drag it into the bathroom and drown it in the bathtub" (Edwards, 2001).

Presidents, too, have championed limited government and urged support for reversing its growth. "Government is not the solution to our problem," said President Ronald Reagan in his 1981 inaugural address. "Government is the problem." Fifteen years later in his State of the Union message, President William Jefferson Clinton stated, "The era of big government is over." Clinton did try a "third way" to promote activism, reconciling peoples' skeptical views of big government with a progressive agenda. The third way approach to governing was neither liberal nor conservative. It claimed to join free-market strategies with governmental policies that "provide workers with job training, health care, and some pension security" (Edsall, 1998).

The fundamental reality, however, is that the era of big government is not over: it is back (or really never went away) as today's federal actions to address the economic crisis underscore. "Not since Lyndon B. Johnson and Franklin D. Roosevelt," wrote a congressional journalist, has a President like Obama "moved to expand the role of government so much on so many fronts—and with such a demanding sense of urgency" (Hook, 2009).[6] Of course, the national government has taken on numerous functions and responsibilities throughout American history, even during the 19th century when there was small government compared to the contemporary period. Consider the subsidies for the transcontinental railroad or the creation of our land-grant college system. The 20th century—from the Progressive era to World War I, from the New Deal to the Great Society—witnessed a huge expansion in the size and power of government. Expansion was driven by a number of overlapping factors.

Why Governmental Growth?

Domestic and international crises tend to expand the reach of the federal government. Wars, for instance, are significant in fueling the growth of federal responsibilities. War threatens the nation itself, and the government—the president as Commander-in-Chief and other federal entities—often accrue new and expanded prerogatives to protect the country. The intelligence community, for instance, grew rapidly during the Cold War as the U.S. faced a major threat from a nuclear-armed super power: the Soviet Union. After 9/11, Congress and the president established a new Department of Homeland Security to meet the challenge of nihilistic terrorists who will employ any means to kill Americans and wreck havoc on the country.

Complexity is another factor triggering governmental growth. New problems and issues constantly arise that call for governmental action. For example, to address the Great Depression—with the banking system in collapse and unemployment approaching 25 percent—President Franklin D. Roosevelt's New Deal created many new federal programs and agencies that did not disappear after the economic emergency ended, such as Social Security and the Tennessee Valley Authority. Today, as the world's sole superpower, the federal government must deal with an array of issues with global dimensions, from trade to currency exchange rates to global warming. To be sure, a population of over 300 million people creates its own unique set of governmental issues (health care, transportation, law enforcement, energy, and so on).

Scientific and technological developments also fueled the growth of the national government. When the Soviet Union launched Sputnik in 1957, the government responded by creating the National Aeronautics and Space Administration (NASA) and investing tax dollars in schools and universities across the country to promote scientific and engineering programs. Scholars and analysts from Upton Sinclair's *The Jungle* (1906) to Rachel Carson's *The Silent Spring* (1962) to Ralph Nader's *Unsafe at Any Speed* (1965) spotlighted issues—the dreadful conditions in meat-packing plants, environmental damage, and unsafe automobiles, respectively—that spawned federal initiatives and programs. Moreover, as the government expanded its responsibilities and capacities, it was only natural that individuals and groups would look to their national officeholders for the resolution of various issues and problems.

The Size of Government

In short, a host of military, economic, and social challenges, along with many other factors (industrialization, immigration, public demand, and so on), led to a large expansion in the size and reach of the national government. Of course, it is not self-evident what "too big" for the federal government really means. One measure of size is federal expenditures as a share of gross domestic product (about 3 percent of GDP in 1929 compared to 20.2 percent in 2008). Another is the federal budget, which is over $3.5 trillion today and will continue to grow in the future because of mandatory retirement and health costs associated with our aging population. A third way to measure the size of government is the number of employees (today, around 2.7 million federal employees), which has remained relatively constant in size for years.

How can the government continue to perform its many new and old functions while generally keeping its size down? One answer is that federal work is being outsourced (privatized) to contract firms. The Pentagon, for example, reached a milestone of sorts at the start of this century when the number of its private sector employees (734,000) exceeded its civilian workforce (700,000). These contract employees "perform service jobs from mowing lawns to testing weapons systems" (Nakashima, 2001). One scholar has put the true personnel size of the government at about 15 million employees: the 4.1 million civilian, military, and postal workers plus the 10.5 million "shadow" employees who work "under federal contracts and grants or mandates imposed on state and local governments" (Light, 1999).[7] The number of private contractors seems likely to soar as "more and more companies" enter the government contracting world following enactment of President Obama's stimulus package (Allen and Prarie, 2009). (Federal spending on contracts increased from $12.8 billion in 1978 to $531.8 billion in 2008 [Davidson, 2009].)

Contracting out federal functions to the private sector has its advantages (cost, flexibility, or speed, for example), but it can complicate Congress's job of overseeing the performance of these "third party" entities. Public-private partnerships are sometimes difficult for federal administrators and congressional committees to monitor and hold accountable. There is often an absence of coordination among the multiplicity of legislative panels and federal executives responsible for the work done by private contractors. The experience in Iraq with Blackwater Worldwide (now called Xe), a private security firm, underscores the difficulty.

Congress and the president must determine whether the public or private sector is best suited to implement various programs or policies and, concomitantly, how to bolster accountability and transparency among the entities that actually perform the job. As the Inspector General of the Department of Energy said about the $40 billion allocated in the economic stimulus package for energy loans and grants: "Absorbing the money, making sure it gets into the hands of the right recipients . . . are going to be significant challenges" (Power and King, Jr., 2009). The stimulus package is "the ultimate test of government's ability to deliver, from a vast array of federal agencies and departments down to state and local offices across the country" (MacGillis, 2009). The surge of stimulus money granted to many federal agencies will produce challenges for various entities responsible for monitoring the expenditure of funds: in-house "watchdogs," the Government Accountability Office (GAO), and congressional committees.[8] President Obama has appointed Vice President Joe Biden to be the chief executive branch supervisor of the economic stimulus law, ensuring that it is economically and efficiently carried out.

There are other ways to measure the growth in the size of government, such as the number of *Federal Register* pages (for example, 3,450 in 1937 compared to 80,700 in 2008), pages in the tax code, or the increase in tax collection. Do any one of these measures, singly or in combination, indicate what is the right size for government? Is the central government too big, too small, or just right? Peoples' views are likely to be shaped by the context of the times or the values they hold. If the economy is strong, the country is at peace, and most individuals are doing well, then individuals lean toward limited government. If conditions are the reverse, then many people will support the view of William Cohen, a former GOP lawmaker from Maine and Secretary of Defense, "The government is the enemy until you need a friend" (Dionne, 1996). A similar sentiment was expressed by a former U.S. ambassador to France: "In a war, people need more government than in peace; in a recession they need more government than in prosperity" (Rohatyn, 2001).

As for values, this nation from its frontier beginning has emphasized liberty, freedom, and an individualistic tradition. Immigrants flooded the nation as a land of opportunity where everyone had a chance to start anew and make something of themselves, even going from "rags to riches." Governmental interference in peoples' personal and private affairs or business enterprises was typically unwelcomed. Yet as various analysts have long noted, Americans tend to be ideologically conservative but operationally liberal. On the one hand, many individuals may emotionally view government as a necessary evil, but rationally they support federal programs that benefit them. As Representative Barney Frank, D-Mass., explained, if you ask people whether they favor "government spending or a tax cut—the tax cut will win. But if you substitute . . . almost any specific form of government spending [it] will beat a tax cut" (Hook, 1999).

The public has long complained about an overcommitted and underachieving federal establishment. Citizens focus more on the failures of government (Hurricane Katrina is a recent example) rather than its many achievements. A study by The Brookings Institution identified 544 of the greatest accomplishments of the federal government, as determined by 450 scholars, over a 55-year period (1944-1999). They listed laws such as promoting equal access to public accommodations, rebuilding Europe after World War II, reducing disease (polio, for instance), and strengthening the nation's highway system (see Gribben, 2000 and Light, 2001). Yet people today remain skeptical, even cynical, about an activist government. Various explanations account for this perception, such as bureaucratic inefficiencies and unresponsiveness, government-bashing by various pundits, officeholders, and media commentators, or the constant assumption of new functions and issues (spreading democracy worldwide, global climate change, etc.) that challenge government competence (Galston, 2009).

Summing Up

The national government's role and scope suggests several explicit or implicit points or principles that merit review. They include:

- The public appears to be of two minds about whether there is too much government. Citizens may pay lip service to Thomas Jefferson's admonition that the best government is one that governs least, but their actions frequently belie their words. Farmers, for example, might say they dislike too much government, but they strongly support farm subsidies. The political and personal rhetoric is often Jeffersonian but public actions are generally Hamiltonian.

- Since at least the 20th century, the national government has gained enormous influence. Wars, economic calamities, attitudinal changes (citizens' increased expectations of federal government assistance), and the nationalization of scores of issues (such as air and water pollution) are among the factors that stimulated an expansion of government, a phenomenon experienced by many other nations.

- Government is not the only instrument for resolving problems, but it is a major actor in solving many. An important responsibility of the national government is to address issues that individuals or communities cannot handle themselves, such as protecting the nation's environment or undertaking huge infrastructure projects. Even so, issues traditionally under the purview of the states and localities—for instance, schools, roads, or fire and police protection—does not mean, as Representative David Obey, D-Wis., noted, "that they're *exclusively* state and local responsibilities" (U.S. News and World Report, 1981).

- Today's broad consensus that the government must spend more to restart the economy does not minimize the importance of the marketplace and the crucial role of risk-taking entrepreneurs and small businesses in restoring economic prosperity. As history demonstrates, the initiatives and innovations of large and small businesses operating in a free-market system can expand the economic pie, producing large benefits for society-at-large.[9]

- There are limits on a government that spends beyond its means. With the debt ceiling raised to $12.1 trillion by the stimulus package and fiscal deficits as far as the eye can see, there is large concern among decision-makers, economists, and others about how the nation will stem the rising tide of red ink (tax hikes, spending cuts, or both, for example); whether other nations will continue to purchase U.S. debt; and when policymakers will address the long-term, unfunded commitments (Social Security, Medicare, and other entitlements) that by some estimates exceed $56 trillion.[10]

Congress Oversees the Executive Establishment

Despite periodic efforts by lawmakers and presidents to shrink the size of government, it is probably not reasonable to expect any significant rollback to the eras of Teddy Roosevelt or Woodrow Wilson. Analysts and pundits recognize this reality by suggesting that "big government" is not the right issue; rather, policymakers need to focus on "smart," "effective," "competent," "responsive," "better," or "re-invented" government. However the federal establishment is characterized, it is essential that Congress exercise its constitutional authority to check the discretionary power that it delegates to federal executives and departments.

Oversight is an implicit constitutional obligation of the Congress. According to historian Arthur Schlesinger, Jr., the framers believed it was not necessary to make specific reference to "oversight" in the Constitution. "[I]t was not considered necessary to make an explicit grant of such authority," wrote

Schlesinger. "The power to make laws implied the power to see whether they were faithfully executed" (Schlesinger and Burns, 1975). Over the years Congress has bolstered its ability to carry out its obligation to oversee the bureaucracy through various laws, amendments to House and Senate rules, and periodic increases in staff and budgetary resources.

Congress has a multiplicity of tools and techniques to monitor and hold federal officials accountable. They include committee hearings; the creation of select committees; the authorization and appropriations processes; casework; informal legislative and executive staff consultations; audits and investigations by the Government Accountability Office (GAO) and Inspectors General (IGs); and the Senate's confirmation prerogative. Congress requires so many different devices because each has its strengths and weaknesses, and it is often necessary to employ several in combination if the House and Senate are to assess adequately executive branch performance and program effectiveness. Importantly, oversight enables Congress to challenge unwarranted assertions of executive branch power.

The Checking Power of Oversight

One of the most dramatic developments in the modern era is a huge expansion of executive influence. If the Founding Fathers returned to observe their handiwork, they might be shocked by the role and reach of today's President and the creation of a "presidential branch" of government. This expansion, as noted above, has been decades in the making. Moreover, the Bush-Cheney administration accelerated this trend after 9/11, especially in national security matters.

Assertions of executive authority after 9/11 by President George W. Bush are well known, and include such things as domestic wiretapping; blocking White House aides from testifying before congressional committees; the creation of secret prisons abroad; and interpreting, or not enforcing, certain provisions of laws as he saw fit. As justification for these actions, Vice President Dick Cheney declared that "it would have been unethical or immoral for us not to do everything we could to protect the nation" (Ward and Solomon, 2008). There was some push-back by Congress against executive claims of authority, such as revising the Foreign Intelligence Surveillance Act (FISA) to provide additional guidelines regarding warrantless surveillance (see Starks, 2008: 1900-02; and Harris, 2008: 66-70), as well as decisions by federal courts (see, for example, the Supreme Court's June 2004 decisions in *Hamdi v. Rumsfeld* and *Rasul v. Bush*) that constrained executive power even in wartime.

Overall, Republicans largely supported President Bush's decisions and generally avoided hard-hitting investigations of the administration. However, there were notable exceptions. Consider, for example, the oversight activities of GOP Senators Charles Grassley, John McCain, and Tom Coburn or, in the House, the review work of GOP Representatives Tom Davis, who castigated the administration's performance in the aftermath of Hurricane Katrina as chair of the Government Reform Committee, and Judiciary Chairman James

Sensenbrenner's fifty-six reviews of the USA-Patriot Act.[11] Then Majority Leader John Boehner's office even issued a sixty-three page report highlighting the oversight activities of fourteen House committees. No doubt Leader Boehner issued the report to counter criticisms directed at congressional Republicans for doing insufficient oversight work and their willingness to back the Bush administration's expansive view of presidential power.

The prevalent view was that during the period when Republicans controlled Congress and the White House (2001-2007),[12] the legislative branch was reluctant to conduct hearings and investigations that might embarrass the administration. As GOP Representative Ray LaHood (now Secretary of Transportation in the Obama administration) explained: "Our party controls the levers of government. We're not about to go out and look beneath a bunch of rocks and try and cause heartburn. Unless [executive officials] really screw up, we're not going to go after them" (Nather, 2004: 1190). Another GOP lawmaker, Representative Chris Shays, who lost his Connecticut seat in the November 2008 elections, said: "We ended up functioning like a parliament, not a Congress. We confused wanting a joint agenda with not doing oversight" (Brownstein, 2006). Added journalist Ronald Brownstein, the Republican Congress "viewed itself less as an independent branch of government than as a junior partner to the White House in the American equivalent of a parliamentary system" (Brownstein, 2007). Why did Congress perform as if it were an adjunct of the White House? In the judgment of Representative Frank (2006):

> I believe we have seen an overreaching by the President. I believe we have seen a seizing of power that should not have been seized by the executive branch. But executive overreaching could not have succeeded as much as it has without congressional dereliction of duty.

When Democrats won control of the 110th Congress (2007-2009), House Majority Leader Steny Hoyer declared: "We are going to provide the time for committees to do oversight of the executive department and of the way the people's money is being spent and the effectiveness of the policy implementation of the president" (Chaddock, 2006). There is no doubt that oversight and investigations were a top priority for Democrats. Given divided government, Democratic-led committees had policy and political incentives to investigate the Bush administration. As one scholar concluded:

> [P]olicy divergence is most likely to occur under divided government, so the majority party in Congress will want to constrain the agencies under the president's control. In addition, members of the majority party may believe that they can benefit from using oversight to emphasize policy differences between their party and the president's party, and if in the case of such hearings and investigations they embarrass a president and his agency, this is not an insignificant [political] side benefit (Shipan, 2005).

Henry Waxman, D-Calif., the former chair of the House Oversight and Government Reform Committee, conducted scores of investigations of the Bush II administration and was known as "Mr. Oversight" on Capitol Hill. Some people could say, without too much exaggeration, that his review work produced a significant increase of oversight activity in the 110th Congress. A study by The Brookings Institution concluded: "What [was] most striking about activity throughout the 110th Congress, especially in the House, was the dramatic increase in the amount and scope of oversight of the executive following years of relative inattention and deference under the Republican majority." Moreover, a "good deal of the oversight during the 110th Congress was devoted to Iraq, the dominant public concern, which had been largely neglected in the previous Congress. But oversight ranged across diverse subjects, was mostly serious in its approach, and often had real consequences for policy and administration" (Binder et al., 2009).

In the 2008 elections, Democrats won control of the House, Senate, and White House for the first time since 1992. If divided government provides incentives for more oversight, unified government is often a disincentive for aggressive investigative activity by congressional committees. At issue is whether the Democratic 111th Congress will conduct vigorous and rigorous oversight if and when there are allegations of incompetence, failures of performance, or wrongdoing against their own President or high officials in the Obama administration. History demonstrates, as the Carter administration can attest, that unified government is no bar to tough investigative oversight. Senate Majority Leader Harry Reid of Nevada has already proclaimed, "I don't work for Obama" (Cusack et al., 2009). And Speaker Pelosi is certainly a strong leader who will defend the House's prerogatives (Thrush, 2009). Moreover, she sent a mid-February 2009 letter to House committee chairs stressing the importance of "rigorous oversight of all aspects of federal spending and government operations to help achieve deficit reduction and fiscal responsibility." She also directed the chairs to submit to her by mid-March a timetable of their planned oversight hearings (Wolfensberger, 2009).

There are inherent constitutional and political tensions between Congress and the President even during periods of unified government. For example, will President Obama relinquish powers that the White House accumulated during the Bush II presidency or support congressional initiatives to do so. Only time will tell. In various interviews and statements, President Obama has indicated that he would not use signing statements to undermine the intent of laws or deploy military troops abroad contrary to legislation enacted by Congress and signed into law. On the other hand, there is the view that presidents do not give up powers they have acquired. "It's one thing to campaign against excessive executive power and it's another to give it away once you have it," remarked a Princeton professor (Chaddock, 2009; see also Mahler, 2008).

Other Key Oversight Purposes

Congress's "watchdog" role is important for other overlapping reasons besides checking executive power. First, oversight shines the spotlight of public attention on many significant issues, allowing the American people to make informed judgments about executive activities and actions. "The informing function of Congress," wrote Woodrow Wilson in 1885, "should be preferred even to its legislative function." He went on to say:

> Unless Congress have and use every means of acquainting itself with the acts and dispositions of the administrative agents of government, the country must be helpless to learn how it is being served; and unless Congress both scrutinize these things and sift them by every form of discussion, the country must remain in embarrassing, crippling ignorance of the very affairs which it is most important it should understand and direct.

Another fundamental purpose of oversight is to protect Congress's policymaking role and its place in our constitutional separation of powers system as the "first branch" of government. The huge growth of the executive branch has produced a policymaking rival to the Congress. Administrators do more than simply "faithfully execute" the laws according to congressional intent (which may be vague). Federal agencies are filled with knowledgeable career and noncareer experts who, among other things, write rules and regulations that have the force of law; formulate policy initiatives for Congress and the White House; interpret statutes in ways that may expand their discretionary authority or, in addition, undermine legislative intent; and shape policy development by "selling" their ideas to lawmakers and committees via the hearings process, the issuance of agency reports, and in other ways. The large policy role of the executive branch underscores the critical role of oversight in emphasizing Congress's authority over executive entities.

Oversight is also crucial to the lawmaking process. Only by investigating how a law is being administered can Congress discover deficiencies in the original statute and make necessary adjustments and refinements. There are, of course, a number of political purposes associated with oversight, such as generating favorable publicity for programs; urging the elimination or major reduction of agencies; responding to requests from special interests to influence agency decisions; or winning electoral support from constituents or various groups. Oversight thus occurs in a political context where the relationship between Congress and administrative agencies can range from cooperation to conflict.

Some New Arrangements

Oversight has long been a topic of concern on Capitol Hill. A comment made by former Speaker Thomas "Tip" O'Neill—Members "like to create and legislate, but we have shied from both the word and deed of oversight."—no doubt still resonates with many of today's lawmakers (O'Neill, 1979). Since

Speaker O'Neill made that comment, the House and Senate have adopted numerous House and Senate rules changes, and have passed various laws (for example, the Government Performance and Results Act) to encourage and promote more and better oversight. More recently, the House on January 14, 2009, adopted a resolution (H. Res. 40) by a vote of 423 to 0 requiring committees (subcommittees thereof) to conduct at least three hearings a year—at least one every 120 days—on the topic of waste, fraud, and mismanagement in the agencies under the committee's jurisdiction, and additional hearings if auditors cannot verify an agency's financial report, or if the GAO designates as "high risk" a program under a panel's jurisdiction.

If many House members view oversight as tedious, thankless, and time-consuming, something that has to be shoehorned into their other priorities (lawmaking, representation, campaigning, fund-raising), then the result might be perfunctory rather than diligent and thorough reviews of agency activities and program performance.[13] There is no question that House and Senate leaders recognize the importance of oversight, and various lawmakers excel at it and have deservedly earned high praise for their investigative work. And there is no doubt more oversight activity occurs on Capitol Hill than many people realize. How much monitoring of agency activities is done by Congress is not easy to measure quantitatively, because it is subsumed in many hearings, meetings, or informal settings whose purposes may be secondary to reviewing program and policy administration.[14]

Moreover, there is no precise scholarly consensus on the definition of oversight and without that it is hard to measure the extent of review activity on Capitol Hill. Some say oversight is "after the fact" review of statutory implementation; others suggest that anything Congress does, formally or informally, to affect the executive branch is oversight. Suffice it to say that undercounting surely characterizes the amount of oversight carried out by House and Senate committees because it occurs in so many ways and is a byproduct of so many legislative activities.

Because it is difficult to get an accurate count of how much oversight activity actually occurs in the House and Senate, every legislative reform effort—from the Legislative Reorganization Act (LRA) of 1946 to adoption of H. Res. 40 in 2009—highlights a common theme: Congress needs to do "more and better" oversight. Although people may disagree on what constitutes "quality" oversight, there are several essential components that seem to foster effective oversight. They include: (1) a committee chair committed to doing oversight on a sustained basis; (2) the involvement of committee members; (3) an experienced and professional staff; (4) bipartisanship; (5) preparation and documentation in advance of any public hearing; (6) coordination and cooperation with other relevant committees; and (7) follow-through to ensure that recommendations of the committee(s) are acted upon. Helpful, too, is a cooperative administration. Absent cooperation, committees may need to use compulsory processes (subpoena and contempt) to obtain the information they need and the testimony of pertinent witnesses.

It is the qualitative dimension of oversight that likely gives pause to many lawmakers because of their many other commitments and responsibilities. Are there things that might permit the House and Senate to more effectively oversee an executive branch that is so massive in size and reach? With respect to the TARP and the economic stimulus bill, Congress created special oversight panels to monitor the spending of federal funds so as to prevent waste, fraud, and abuse. Among several other ideas that might strengthen oversight are:

(1) *Outside Oversight Advisory Group.* Encourage committees to establish, on a selective basis, an outside advisory group to assist them in their most important investigative reviews. The Washington area is filled with experts on various topics (academics, former Members, think tank analysts, former journalists, etc.) who would be willing to assist committees without any remuneration. These ad hoc panels could be created, as needed, by the committee chair in consultation with the ranking member. The ad hoc panels could automatically dissolve when their work is over or whenever the chair deems it appropriate.

(2) *Workload Management.* Time is probably lawmakers' most precious commodity. There is simply not enough of it, and oversight often suffers as a result. Is there a way to reduce some of the institution's workload? Not since the 1946 LRA, so far as is known, has Congress analyzed its responsibilities with an eye toward identifying certain workload areas that might be dropped. Are there responsibilities that Congress can shed or delegate to another entity? Are there processes or procedures that can be modified to allow more opportunities for oversight? With new issues understandably being added to Congress's agenda and many old ones still of high priority, perhaps it is time for a systematic review of how Congress handles its workload to determine if changes can be made that might attract broad support. Institutionally, can Congress subtract anything from its agenda portfolio? Are there scheduling or other changes that could ease the time demands on individual lawmakers as they confront an ever-expanding workload?

(3) *Oversight and Investigative Staff.* For decades, the House Appropriations Committee has had a "Survey and Investigations" staff. Most of the staff aides are former GAO, FBI, or other individuals skilled in investigative work. The staff does review work at the behest of the chair and ranking member. Perhaps other committees should be authorized to have a separate, long-tenured, full-time professional staff exclusively devoted to the conduct of oversight and investigations.

(4) *Casework.* Every lawmaker's office receives scores of constituent communications. Many of them deal with the problems constituents are having with various administrative agencies. Is there a way to encourage all or most Member offices to identify and categorize their casework inquiries—mindful of privacy and other requirements—and transmit them to a central congressional database to determine if citizens are having problems with certain agencies or programs? Such information could lead to focused investigations to remedy these problems.

(5) *The Public as Watchdog.* "Transparency" is a key word affecting government. The more people who have access to what the government is doing, the more chances there are for private citizens to do oversight. Critics of Congress's oversight say it needs to follow a "police patrol" model: the 1946 LRA's standard of "continuous watchfulness" of the programs and agencies under each panel's jurisdiction. Instead, Congress often observes the "fire alarm" approach: it waits until a crisis hits the front pages before the relevant committees review agencies' responses to the "fire." In today's Internet age, there may be value to a "public engagement" model. The Federal Funding Accountability and Transparency Act of 2006, informally called the "Google your government" law, enables citizens to search and track online billions of dollars in federal grants and contracts.[15]

The potential inherent in technology is that it enables interested persons or watchdog groups to monitor federal spending and make its evaluations known to Capitol Hill lawmakers. A new government Web site—www.recovery.gov, launched February 17—allows citizens to track the projects that receive money from the stimulus package.[16] With heightened transparency, the blogosphere may spur congressional oversight of government spending and activities. Online watchdogs, with their grass-roots networking capacity, seem well-positioned to help Congress promote better administrative performance by encouraging informed dialogue between lawmakers and constituents about how money is spent to implement national policies and programs. As Thomas Jefferson said, "Information is the currency of democracy" (Bang-Jensen, 2009).

Challenges for Congressional Party Leaders

Unified government is no guarantee of a smooth relationship between the legislative and executive branches. After all, the House, Senate, and White House are filled with strong-willed individuals who have their own policy goals, political objectives, and ideological preferences. Forging winning coalitions on priority issues is no easy task either for congressional leaders or presidents. The most recent example of unified government for Democrats occurred during the first two years of the Clinton administration (1993-1994). Democrats controlled each chamber then with numbers almost equivalent to the 111th Congress: 258 to 176 in the House and 57 to 43 in the Senate. Professor Ross Baker (2008) summarized President Clinton's rocky start with the Congress:

> Clinton's problems started with his proposal to enable gays to serve openly in the armed forces. His principal antagonist in this fight was not a Republican, but the Democratic chairman of the Senate Armed Services Committee, Sam Nunn of Georgia. After backing down on that issue, Clinton proposed an emergency stimulus package that quickly passed the House but was scuttled by the outnumbered Republicans in the Senate through a filibuster—Democrats didn't have the 60 votes to end it. Clinton's early missteps, combined with collapse of the national health insurance initiative, captained by Hillary

> Clinton, contributed to the Republican capture of both houses of Congress in the 1994 elections.[17]

Democrats have studied Clinton's first year in office, and they understand the need for Congress and the president to get off to a fast and successful start. And to date they have achieved those objectives, given rapid congressional action in passing an economic stimulus measure that is historic in cost, scope, and ambition. "[G]etting a package of this size done that quickly, I think most knowledgeable Washington insiders would have said 'impossible,'" noted Peter Orszag, Obama's director of the Office of Management and Budget (OMB) (Victor and Friel, 2009: 35). (The nearly 1,100-page stimulus bill, H.R. 1, was introduced on January 26 and signed into law on February 17, 2009.)

At this juncture, both parties believe—or hope—that they are on the winning end of the vote to pass the stimulus measure. (Every House Republican voted against the bill. Only three Senate Republicans supported the measure; they provided the margin of support for passage of the legislation.) Majority party lawmakers realize that the 111th Congress cannot be "do nothing" or "do less than do nothing"—campaign themes often used by the minority party. The fundamental challenge for both congressional parties is to achieve legislative results that serve the public interest and that also promote their political advantage. Substantively, it is too early to assess whether the stimulus plan (and related actions) will revive the economy. Politically, however, it is evident that most congressional Republicans believe that opposing the recovery plan will result in electoral rewards for their party in the 2010 elections.[18]

Mid-term elections often produce electoral losses in the Congress for the president's party. In 1994, Democrats lost fifty-two seats in the House and eight seats in the Senate. Republicans captured control of the House for the first time in forty unbroken years. In President Bush's first mid-term election in 2002, Republicans picked up seats in both the House and Senate. This exceptional case is generally attributed to the tragic events of 9/11. Unless the 111th Congress produces legislative solutions to the key challenges facing the country—or are perceived by the public to be moving in the right direction—the Democratic majority might witness reductions in its numbers or the loss of control of one or both chambers in the 2010 elections. As Representative Chris Van Hollen, Md., the chair of the Democratic Congressional Campaign Committee, declared: "Our political fortunes are tied to Barack Obama's." The 2010 elections "will be a report card not only on Congress but the White House, too" (Thrush, 2009).

Unified government also means that Democrats must determine how to "strike a balance between separation of powers and intraparty cooperation, and between one-party hegemony and bipartisan cooperation" (Cohen and Friel, 2008). This balance may not be easy to achieve for at least three reasons. First, for the past eight years, whether in the majority or the minority, congressional Democratic leaders were often in the position of challenging and criticizing the Republican-led administration. Now, with Obama in the White House, they bear large responsibility for shepherding the administration's priorities to enactment.

Second, there is less need for congressional Democrats to develop an alternative agenda to the president's, although there is large pent-up demand for policy action on a number of important issues (energy, health, the environment, and so on). Democrats will not be reluctant to initiate legislation of their own on these and other matters. For example, two Senate chairmen (Max Baucus, Mont., and Edward Kennedy, Mass.) are working together to develop legislation that would revamp the health care system. "They are far ahead of the House, and Barack Obama's . . . administration appears content to let them lead on the issue—counting on Congress to use its own political capital to drive an overhaul as the Obama team focuses on other priorities" (Armstrong, 2008). When Thomas Daschle, the Senate's former Democratic leader, withdrew his nomination to be Secretary of the Health and Human Services Department because of tax problems, it further delayed administration action on overhauling the health system and underscored Congress's lead role in this field.

Third, to function effectively, unified government requires bicameral and inter-branch cooperation, coordination, and communication between and among the majority leaders of the House and Senate and the President. During the previous eight years, Democratic leaders were the face and voice of their party. Needless to say, they did not work closely with the Bush II administration. Now it is Obama's "bully pulpit" that will be used for communicating the party's agenda and message to the nation and the world, while congressional Democratic leaders amplify, explain, justify, or critique the president's—or their own—decisions. Just as the presidency is in transition during these early months of the new administration, so is the relationship between legislative leaders and the White House.

Another transition in the 111th Congress concerns congressional Republicans. Without their president in the White House, they will have a harder time delivering their message. Senate GOP leader Mitch McConnell, Ky, and House GOP leader John Boehner, Ohio, are among their party's principal national spokespersons, especially McConnell because the Senate's rules (the filibuster, for instance) grant the minority party the ability to have their views heard and to delay or block Democratic initiatives (Stanton, 2009). Congressional Republicans are expanding their message operations, hiring more communications directors, and "working feverishly," exclaimed Eric Cantor, Va., the House Republican whip, "to try and make sure we get our message out. . . . No one's irrelevant nowadays because you have a microphone." As a House GOP strategist stated, "there won't be many legislative victories [for Republicans] based on votes. Victories will come from how votes translate in the next morning's newspaper" (McPike, 2009).

The Republican's challenge, in brief, is at least three-fold: (1) deciding when to cooperate and when to oppose Democratic initiatives and President Obama's efforts; (2) determining when and how to use the lawmaking process to achieve their ultimate political aim—reclaiming majority status; and (3) defining their party's message. Should the party return to the doctrines articulated by President Ronald Reagan, such as limited government, lower taxes, deregulation, and a strong national defense? Or should the party move on and craft new policies that appeal to diverse and growing demographic groups (Hispanics, young people, Asians, independents, and so on)?

Concluding Observations

A major outcome of the 2008 elections was that it produced unified government. Elections in the main have two basic themes: "stay the course" or "it's time for a change." People certainly voted for change in 2008, and Barack Obama is the epitome of that change. Given the huge domestic and foreign challenges that face Congress and President Obama, elective officials now must deliver by using the authority and tools of the national government to enact changes that people want. As House Majority Leader Steny Hoyer put it, "Now our work is to turn from promise to performance, from speeches to statute" (Miller, 2009). In general, this means that government must continue to provide reasonable and credible "protection" of, by, and for the people. As former Senator Ernest Hollings, D-S.C. (1966-2005), once said:

> We have armies who protect us from enemies from without and the [Federal Bureau of Investigation] protects us from enemies within. We have Social Security to protect us from the ravages of old age. We have Medicare to protect us from ill health. We have clean air and clean water [laws] to protect our environment. We have [laws that mandate] safe working places and safe machinery. Our fundamental duties here are to protect (Hollings, 1997).

Several federal agencies explicitly mention or imply "protection" in their title, such as the Environmental Protection Agency, the Consumer Product Safety Commission, or the Occupational Safety and Health Administration. Needless to say, people want protection from the government itself as well as the economic marketplace.

Protection, however, is a costly enterprise. The huge sums authorized and appropriated to deal with the economic crisis is a perfect example. Not only is there understandable concern about the potential for the government's overreach in the nation's economy, there is also growing angst about the nation's escalating deficit and debt. Like any crisis, the soaring sums provide both opportunities and challenges. On the opportunity side, conditions seem right for a sustained effort by the legislative and executive branches to try to make government operate more efficiently, including the elimination of unnecessary federal programs and agencies. At bottom, there is no right size for government because political, economic, and social conditions are dynamic. Even still, a useful undertaking would be to reexamine what the government does with a view toward expanding or strengthening needed programs that work and ending those that have outlived their mission and value.

On the challenge side, public officials know that the government's huge expenses are in the entitlement area. Programs like Social Security and Medicare are wonderful programs that have helped the elderly to live longer, healthier, and more productive lives. On the other hand, to make major changes in either is difficult for at least two key reasons. First, real bipartisan support is necessary for any overhaul to minimize partisan attacks by one party or the other that would weaken the chances for success. Second, the elderly turn out to vote in large numbers. It might be necessary to develop a sustained public education initiative to persuade and convince senior citizens of the need for comprehensive change.

It is also worth noting that both parties like to spend money, albeit for different purposes and programs. As a general practice, Democrats like to spend more for social and safety-net programs and, in the current climate, increase the regulation of financial enterprises. Republicans, by contrast, prefer to increase spending for law enforcement and national security programs while limiting the government's role as a regulator of the environment or the free-market system. When George Schultz was OMB director under President Richard Nixon, he asked a question of the agency's most experienced budget expert and historian, "Tell me something just between you and me. Is there any difference between Republicans and Democrats when it comes to spending money?" The staff aide furrowed his brow and responded, "Mr. Schulz, there is only one difference: Democrats enjoy it more."[19]

Oversight is also more than a legislative function (Billings, 2009). The array of federal entities currently overseeing the stimulus package and the TARP—from the Federal Reserve to the Securities and Exchange Commission to the Treasury Department, not to mention congressional hearings and investigations by the GAO and Inspectors General—suggests a need for coordination of activities and findings among these entities.[20] Plus, who is the real coordinator: Congress, the President, the Treasury Secretary, or all of them? It is useful to have different institutions and individuals looking at things from their own unique perspective. However, the coordinative function probably rests fundamentally with the president, because of his unity of command. Congress, by contrast, is a decentralized institution that functions with hundreds of committees, subcommittees, task forces, and informal groups. It is a permeable institution open to access by citizens, whistle-blowers, and scores of groups and interests. Policy and oversight coordination and integration, except in times of crisis, is difficult to achieve for two separate legislative chambers with 535 independent-minded lawmakers.

Lastly, a challenge for President and the Congress is whether the often bitter partisan infighting can be set aside to produce policy achievements. Obama talked a great deal about a post-partisan presidency. An interesting question is what distinguishes "bipartisan" from "post-partisan"? Three GOP Senators were critical to the enactment of the stimulus package. To Senator John McCain, R-Ariz., this hardly constituted bipartisanship given the large numbers of House and Senate Republicans who voted against the stimulus package. Under Senator McCain's view, many more Republicans would have to be, as the saying goes, in on the takeoff as well as the landing before something might be called a bipartisan achievement. Perhaps a useful definition of bipartisan is bringing together Democrats and Republicans of different views, committee positions, and leadership posts to try and reach agreement on the major issues that divide the two parties. Two expectations implicit in this definition are that policy development would reflect genuine give-and-take between the two parties and that there is a real opportunity for policy input by the minority party.

Post-partisan is a vague term that is not easy to define. Some might suggest it reflects a new tone or method in dealing with members of the opposite party. President Obama, for example, has reached out to scores of Republicans on Capitol Hill, invited some to the White House for private sessions, or given rides to their constituencies to several on Air Force One. Post-partisan might mean establishing close, cordial working relationships with certain Republicans whom the president likes and trusts. It might mean a more respectful attitude in dealing with lawmakers who hold and articulate different views on legislation in the hopes of finding some common ground. It might reflect a more pragmatic approach to lawmaking: good ideas are to be evaluated on their merits regardless of someone's ideology or which party offers them. Or post-partisan might simply mean that President Obama is not a strong Democratic partisan in the mold of someone like Tom DeLay, R-Tex., when he served in the House as Majority Whip and then as Majority Leader. During the "fiscal responsibility summit" hosted by the President at the White House, Obama urged a bipartisan approach for both parties. "On the one hand, the majority has to be inclusive," he said. "On the other hand, the minority has to be constructive" (Wolf, 2009).

To conclude, the framers created a complex system of government with its array of checks and balances within a system of separated branches sharing and competing for power. Presidents, lawmakers, and the two political parties often disagree strongly about proposed solutions to national issues and problems. This is to be expected in a nation as large as ours with so many ethnic, religious, political, economic, or geographical differences. It is the function of representative government to deal with these differences, respect them and still reach a consensus on what a majority (sometimes a supermajority) believes to be in the national interest. As Madison wrote in *Federalist* No. 62: "A good government implies two things: first, fidelity to the object of government, which is the happiness of the people; secondly, a knowledge of the means by which the object can be best attained." The challenge for President Obama and the Congress is to attend to Madison's second criterion with renewed focus, energy, and cooperation so they can successfully accomplish Madison's first object.

Notes

1. President Obama, for example, was born to a white woman from Kansas and a black African from Kenya. His father left the family when he was two-years-old; he was raised in Hawaii and Indonesia; and he attended both Muslim and Catholic schools.

2. Dennis C. Blair, President Obama's director of national intelligence, underscored the global dimensions of the economic crisis and stated that it is the most serious threat

facing the United States, topping the issue of terrorism. The global economic crisis, he said, threatens "to topple governments, trigger waves of refugees and undermine the ability of America's allies to help in Afghanistan and elsewhere." Greg Miller, "Global Economic Crisis Called Biggest U.S. Security Threat," *Los Angeles Times*, February 13, 2009, (online edition).

3. There is controversy on a number of fronts, with respect to dealing with the economic crisis. Economists and policymakers disagree as to what constitutes the right mix of tax cuts and spending hikes. They also disagree on the specific items that should go in a stimulus package. Some argue that it is best to do nothing. Several GOP governors have indicated that they will not accept certain portions of the stimulus funding. Others worry about the huge price tag associated with the stimulus and the escalating deficit and debt that will be passed on to the next generation. Some dispute the notion that the government can spend its way out of a deep recession using money it does not have. See, for example, Martin Feldstein, "An $800 Billion Mistake," *The Washington Post*, January 29, 2009, A19; Joseph Stiglitz, "Do Not Squander America's Stimulus on Tax Cuts," *Financial Times*, January 16, 2009, 9; Eamon Javers and Jim VanDeHei, "The 'Do-Nothing Crowd' Says: Who Needs It?" *Politico*, January 28, 2009, 1; Donald Lambro, "Don't Kill Job Creation," *The Washington Times*, February 16, 2009, A21; Philip Rucker, "At Meeting, Governors Share Plans for Stimulus Funds," *The Washington Post*, February 22, 2009, A2.

4. In 1936, British economist John Maynard Keynes published his classic *The General Theory of Employment, Interest and Money*. One of its key observations was that in an economic downturn, the government should engage in deficit spending to restore the economy's well-being.

5. For a detailed look at federal efforts to aid the economy, see Clea Benson et al., "Sorting Out the Bailout," *CQ Weekly*, February 23, 2009, 394–409.

6. Some analysts suggest that President Reagan's conservative governance approach has not much relevancy to the current economic crisis. "A consequence of the economic events of the last two years has been to blow up [Reagan's governing] framework," explained William A. Galston, a domestic policy adviser to President Clinton. "President Obama now has his chance to make his case for a fundamentally different approach." Pete Wehner, a Bush administration official, said this about President Obama's expansion of the federal government's role: "He's really trying to reshape the landscape economically, [domestically], politically, and every other way." See Dan Balz, "Ambitious Blueprint a Big Risk the President Is Willing to Take," *The Washington Post*, February 27, 2009, A1 and A8.

7. See also, Paul C. Light, *The True Size of Government* (Washington, DC: Brookings Institution Press, 1990). Periodically, Professor Light updates the number of contract works. In his August 2006 revision, he compares the number of contract workers in 1999 (6,968,000) to 2005 (10,526,000), a 51.1 percent increase.

8. Transportation Secretary Ray LaHood has created a cross-agency "Transportation Investment-Generating Economic Recovery (TIGER) Team" to track how taxpayer dollars are spent so as to minimize waste, fraud, and mismanagement. See David R. Sands and Stephen Dinan, "Spending the Windfall Won't Be Easy," *The Washington Times*, February 18, 2009, A6.

9. In his budget message to Congress, President Obama stated: "It is true that we cannot depend on government alone to create jobs or to generate long-term growth. Ours is a market economy, and the Nation depends on the energy and initiative of private institutions and individuals. But at this particular moment, government must lead the way in providing the short-term boost necessary to lift us from a recession this severe and lay

the foundation for future prosperity." See *Congressional Record*, February 26, 2009, p. S2557. To be sure, there are many analysts, scholars, and others who worry about the government's heavy involvement in the economy and its assumption of responsibilities best left to the private sector and to state governments. As one scholar stated: "The greatest threat to our society now is not credit default swaps or mortgage-backed securities. It is the loss of our understanding of limited government, individual liberty, and the economic system that create a prosperous and free society." Gary Wolfram, "Obama, Central Planning, and the Constitution," *The Examiner*, February 27, 2009, 18.

10. For a different perspective of the unfunded liabilities issue, see Robert Kuttner, "The 'Deficit Hawks' Attack on Our Entitlements," *The Washington Post*, February 23, 2009, A19.

11. House Judiciary Chairman James Sensenbrenner identified 56 reviews of the USA-Patriot Act from 2001 to 2005 in the *Congressional Record*, February 1, 2006, H61-H62.

12. On May 24, 2001, Senator James Jeffords of Vermont announced that he was changing his party affiliation from Republican to Independent and caucusing with the Democrats. His switch shifted party control of the Senate from Republican to Democratic hands. The House remained in Republican control.

13. Members might also view oversight as electorally counterproductive: criticizing programs that many constituents like.

14. UCLA Professor Joel Aberbach found that oversight in the 1990s continues to be quite high and that the model developed. See Aberbach, *Keeping a Watchful Eye: The Politics of Congressional Oversight* (Washington, D.C.: The Brookings Institution, 1990). This model remains effective in explaining committee behavior. Also see Aberbach, "What's Happened to the Watchful Eye?" *Congress & the Presidency*, (Spring 2002): 3-23. Some people express concern that certain agencies and departments might suffer from too much oversight by too many congressional committees. See Stephen R. Heifetz, "The Risks of Too Much Oversight," *New York Times*, July 21, 2008, A21.

15. The federal government has an estimated 24,000 Internet sites. "Many departments and agencies host blogs, Facebook pages, YouTube channels, Twitter feeds and even ambitious virtual worlds on Second Life." See Mark Stencel, "Information Underload," *CQ Weekly*, February 16, 2009, 342.

16. This federal Web site is "supposed to post regular, detailed updates on stimulus contracts from Puerto Rico to Alaska and link to audits and reports from inspectors general and the Government Accountability Office. By law, *recovery.gov* must be user-friendly and allow for public feedback on the quality of projects." See Jeannette J. Lee, "Show Me the Money," *National Journal*, February 21, 2009, 52, and Ralph Lindeman, "OMB Issues Guidance to Agencies On Disclosures Under Stimulus Bill," *Daily Report for Executives*, February 19, 2009, online version. The stimulus package, as well as the earlier enacted Trouble Asset Relief Program (TARP), has a number of oversight provisions. For example, the American Recovery and Reinvestment Act (H.R. 1) created a Recovery Accountability and Transparency Board to monitor the investigative work of the inspector generals charged with tracking how all the stimulus money is spent. As for TARP, several oversight entities, including a Congressional Oversight Panel, have the responsibility "to assess the bailout fund's impact on financial markets, its transparency and whether it is helping to stem rising [home] foreclosures." Susan Schmidt, "Policing TARP Proves Tricky," *Wall Street Journal*, February 20, 2009, A4, and David M. Herszenhorn, "Stimulus Plan Ensures Boom Sector: Oversight," *New York Times*, February 20, 2009, A16.

17. Another factor that can be added to Baker's list is the House bank scandal. Scholars note that members of Congress with overdrawn bank accounts suffered high rates of defeat in 1994.

18. A Senate GOP spokesman highlighted one of their themes to keep Democrats on the defensive. "Democrats just spent $1 trillion we don't have. If they think that's a good long-term tactical move, they're mistaken." A House Democratic strategist replied: "House Republicans are sitting on their hands, measuring victory by the number of times they are on cable TV instead of the number of jobs they help to create." See Erin McPike, "Both Parties Seeing Advantage in Their Stimulus Positions," National Journal's *CongressDailyAM*, February 12, 2009, 11. Former Speaker Newt Gingrich "sees the stimulus bill as his party's ticket to a revival in 2010, as Republicans decry what they see as pork-barrel spending for projects like marsh-mouse protection." See Sheryl Gay Stolberg, "Cutting Slack Is So Old School," *New York Times*, February 22, 2009, E4.

19. From a May 28, 2008, speech—"Storms on the Horizon"—by Richard W. Fisher, president of the Federal Reserve Bank of Dallas, before The Commonwealth Club of California. See *Congressional Record*, January 6, 2009, E13.

20. It is interesting to note that the TARP legislation had four oversight bodies, the stimulus package only one.

References

Aberbach, Joel. *Keeping a Watchful Eye: The Politics of Congressional Oversight.* Washington, DC: The Brookings Institution, 1990.

———. "What's Happened to the Watchful Eye?" *Congress & the Presidency.* Spring 2002: 3–23.

Allen, Rand L., and John R. Prairie, "Now You Have to Tell the Government," *Legal Times*, January 9, 2009, 22.

Appelbaum, Binyamin, and David Cho, "U.S. Clears Path to Bank Takeovers," *The Washington Post*, February 24, 2009, 1(A).

Armstrong, Drew. "Senate Leaders Set to Take Lead With Health," *CQ Weekly*, November 24, 2008, 3142.

Balz, Dan. "Ambitious Blueprint a Big Risk the President Is Willing to Take," *The Washington Post*, February 27, 2009, 1(A) and 8(A).

Baker, Ross K. "Democrats, Not So Fast," *USA Today*, June 19, 2008, 11(A).

Bang-Jensen, Lise. "Spending Sites Make Politicos Take Transparency Seriously," *The Examiner*, February 25, 2009, 20.

Benson, Clea et al., "Sorting Out the Bailout," *CQ Weekly*, February 23, 2009, 394–409.

Billings, Deborah. "Lawmakers Put Steps in Stimulus Package to Ensure Oversight of Reinvestment Funds," *Daily Report for Executives*, February 14, 2009.

Binder, Sarah A., Thomas E. Mann, Norman J. Ornstein, and Molly Reynolds. "Mending the Broken Branch, Assessing the 110th Congress, Anticipating the 111th." The Brookings Institution. January 2009. http://www.brookings.edu/papers/2009/0108_broken_branch_binder_mann.aspx.

Brownstein, Ronald. "Who's Watching the President?" *Los Angeles Times*, March 21, 2007, online edition.

———. "Treating Oversight as an Afterthought has Its Costs," *Los Angeles Times*, November 19, 2006.

Cohen, Richard E., and Brian Friel, "Yes, They Can . . . Govern?" *National Journal*, July 12, 2008, 26.

Cusack, Bob., J. Taylor Rushing, and Hugo Gurdon, "I Don't Work for Obama," *The Hill*, January 7, 2009, 1.

Davidson, Joe. "GAO Details a Bloated Budget for Government Contracts," *The Washington Post*, January 23, 2009, 4(D).

Dionne, E. J. "Back from the Dead: Neoprogressivism in the '90s," *American Prospect* (September-October 1996), p. 25.

______. "The Unavoidable Issues," *The Washington Post*, August 5, 2008, A19.

Edsall, Thomas B. "Clinton and Blair Envision a 'Third Way' International Movement," *The Washington Post*, June 28, 1998, 24(A).

Feldstein, Martin. "An $800 Billion Mistake," *The Washington Post*, January 29, 2009, 19(A).

Fisher, Richard W. *Congressional Record*, January 6, 2009: E13.

Frank, Barney. *Congressional Record*, July 13, 2006: H5212.

Galston, William A. "The Right Bite," *Wilson Quarterly*, Winter 2009: 50-54.

Gribben, August. "540 U.S. Statutes Changed the World for the Better, Brookings Study Says," *The Washington Times*, December 21, 2000, 4(A).

Hallard, Vic. "In Defense of Legislatures," *The Council of State Governments*, February 1996: 9.

Harris, Shane. "Explaining FISA," *National Journal*, July 19, 2008, 66–70.

Heifetz, Stephen R. "The Risks of Too Much Oversight," *New York Times*, July 21, 2008, 21(A).

Herszenhorn, David M. "Stimulus Plan Ensures Boom Sector: Oversight," *New York Times*, February 20, 2009, 16(A).

Hollings, Ernest. *Congressional Record*, November 5, 1997: S11737.

Hook, Janet. "Obama's Budget Is the End of an Era, *Los Angeles Times*, February 27, 2009.

———. "Barney Frank," *Los Angeles Times*, April 4, 1999, 3(M).

Ives, Benton, and Alan K. Ota. "Financial Rescue Becomes Law," *CQ Today*, October 6, 2008, 2692.

Javers, Eamon, and Jim VanDeHei, "The 'Do-Nothing Crowd' Says: Who Needs It?" *Politico*, January 28, 2009, 1.

Kuttner, Robert. "The 'Deficit Hawks' Attack on Our Entitlements," *The Washington Post*, February 23, 2009, 19(A).

Lambro, Donald. "Don't Kill Job Creation," *The Washington Times*, February 16, 2009, 21(A).

Lee, Jeannette J. "Show Me the Money," *National Journal*, February 21, 2009, 52.

Light, Paul. "A Ray of Hope in a Dark Moment," *Government Executive*, October 2001, 74.

———. *The True Size of Government*. Washington, DC: Brookings Institution Press, 1990.

———."The True Size of Government," *Government Executive*, January 1999, 20.

Lindeman, Ralph. "OMB Issues Guidance to Agencies on Disclosures Under Stimulus Bill," *Daily Report for Executives*, February 19, 2009.

MacGillis, Alex. "Government Gets Chance to Prove It Can Work," *The Washington Post*, February 23, 2009, 1(A) and 3(A).

Mahler, Jonathan. "After the Imperial Presidency," *The New York Times Magazine*, November 9, 2008, 42-49, 58, 60, 62.

McPike, Erin. "Both Parties Seeing Advantage in Their Stimulus Positions," *National Journal's CongressDaily/AM*, February 12, 2009, 11.

———. "Bulked Up Machine Pushes GOP Message," *National Journal's CongressDailyAM*, February 25, 2009, 1, 9.

Miller, Greg. "Global Economic Crisis Called Biggest U.S. Security Threat," *Los Angeles Times*, February 13, 2009.

Miller, S. A. "Democrats Pursue Ambitious Agenda on Hill," *The Washington Times*, January 5, 2009, 11(A).

Nakashima, Ellen. "Pentagon Hires Out More Than In," *The Washington Post*, April 3, 2001, 13 (A).

Nather, David. "Congress as Watchdog: Asleep on the Job?" *CQ Weekly*, May 22, 2004, 1190.

Norquist, Grover. Interview on "The Morning Edition." Bob Edwards, host. National Public Radio, May 25, 2001.

Obama, Barack. *Congressional Record*. February 26, 2009: S2557.

O'Neill, Thomas P. *Workshop on Congressional Oversight and Investigations*. Washington, DC: U.S. Government Printing Office, 1979.

Parker, Richard. "Government Beyond Obama?" *The New York Review of Books*, March 12, 2009, 38.

Power, Stephen, and Neil King, Jr. "Next Challenge on Stimulus: Spending All That Money," *Wall Street Journal*, February 13, 2009, 6(A).

Richardson, James D. *A Compilation of the Messages and Papers of the Presidents* 1. New York: Bureau of National Literature, Inc., 1897.

Rohatyn, Felix "Big Government Is Best in a Crisis," *Financial Times*, December 14, 2001, 19.

Rucker, Philip. "At Meeting, Governors Share Plans for Stimulus Funds," Philip Rucker, *The Washington Post*, February 22, 2009, 2(A).

Russell Chaddock, Gail. "Will Obama 'Deimperalize' the Presidency?" *Christian Science Monitor*, January 2, 2009, 3.

———. "New Congress to Toughen Oversight," *Christian Science Monitor*, December 21, 2006, 2.

Sands, David R., and Stephen Dinan. "Spending the Windfall Won't Be Easy," *The Washington Times*, February 18, 2009, 6(A).

Sanger, David. "U.S. Bank And Trust?" *New York Times*, January 26, 2009, 1(A).

Schlesinger, Arthur M., Jr., and Roger Burns, eds., *Congress Investigates: A Documented History, 1792-1974*, 1. New York: Chelsea House, 1975.

Schmidt, Susan. "Policing TARP Proves Tricky," *Wall Street Journal*, February 20, 2009, 4(A).

Shipan, Charles R. "Congress and the Bureaucracy." Pp. 437 in *The Legislative Branch*, edited by Paul Quirk and Sarah Binder. New York: Oxford University Press, 2005.

Stiglitz, Joseph. "Do Not Squander America's Stimulus on Tax Cuts," *Financial Times*, January 16, 2009, 9.

Starks, Tim. "Bush Signs FISA Rewrite into Law," *CQ Weekly*, July 14, 2008, 1900–1902.

Stencel, Mark. "Information Underload," *CQ Weekly*, February 16, 2009, 342.

Stolberg, Sheryl Gay. "Cutting Slack Is So Old School," *New York Times*, February 22, 2009, 4(E).

Stokes, Bruce. "The New 'N' Word," *National Journal's CongressDaily/AM*, January 29, 2009, 5.

Stokes, Bruce and Corine Hegland, "Running the Rescue," *National Journal*, October 11, 2008, 16–23.

Thrush, Glenn. "Pelosi Draws Her Lines With Obama," *Politico*, January 21, 2009, 1.

———. "With the 111th, The Age of Pelosi Dawns," *Politico*, January 6, 2009, 16.

U.S. News & World Report, December 14, 1981, p. 65.

Victor, Kirk and Brian Friel. "Post-Partisan Blues," *National Journal*, February 21, 209, 35.

Walzer, Michael. "The Popular Patron," *The New Republic*, April 9, 1984, 35.

Ward, Jon, and John Solomon, "Cheney Defends Morality of War on Terror," *The Washington Times*, December 18, 2008, 1(A).

Washington Post, January 29, 2009, 15(A).

Wilson, Woodrow. *Congressional Government.* Boston: Houghton Mifflin, 1885.

Wolf, Richard. "Summit Looks At How to Halve Deficit," *USA Today*, February 24, 2009, 5(A).

Wolfensberger, Don. "Fiscal Oversight Directive a Welcome Breath of Spring Air," *Roll Call*, March 2, 2009, 6.

Wolfram, Gary. "Obama, Central Planning, and the Constitution," *The Examiner*, February 27, 2009, 18.

Oversight Panel Summary

John D. Marvel*

Presenter: *Walter J. Oleszek*, Congressional Research Service and American University

Discussants: *Congressman Jim McGovern* (D–MA, 3rd Congressional District)

Congressman David Price (D–NC, 4th Congressional District)

Congresswoman Connie Morella (R–MD, 8th Congressional District, January 3, 1987–January 3, 2003)

Moderator: *James Thurber*, Professor of Government and Director, Center for Congressional and Presidential Studies, American University

Introduction

What do we expect from our government? Two prominent schools of thought, which Walter Oleszek summarizes in his piece, "Transition Time at the National Level: The Government, Congress, and Party Leaders," offer opposing answers to this question. The Jeffersonian school, so named for its intellectual progenitor—Thomas Jefferson—propounds limited government. In this view, government should do what is necessary to maintain social order, but otherwise stay out of society's way. According to Jefferson, "That government governs best that governs least." The Hamiltonian school, in contrast, champions vigorous government—government that should be equal to any task. As Alexander Hamilton, the originator of this school of thought, wrote in *Federalist* No. 31, "A government ought to contain in itself every power requisite to the full accomplishment of the objects committed to its care." In answer to this

* Ph.D. Student, School of Public Affairs, American University.

volume's overriding question, then, the Jeffersonian school would say that we should not expect much from our government, while the Hamiltonian school would say that we should expect a good deal from it.

In reality, as Walter Oleszek points out, the Hamiltonian school has triumphed over the Jeffersonian school. Today, the United States government's size and the scope of its actions are both considerable. The federal government's reaction to the country's current economic crisis provides a vivid illustration of its reach. In February 2009, Congress approved a fiscal stimulus package of almost $800 billion (the American Recovery and Reinvestment Act) to bolster a floundering national economy. Whether one subscribes to a Jeffersonian or Hamiltonian perspective, it is undeniable that this $800 billion stimulus package is the mark of an interventionist government.

How do American citizens feel about this state of affairs? What is the proper role of government in a free society? Having passed the American Recovery and Reinvestment Act, what are Congress's consequent responsibilities? More generally, what are Congress's responsibilities with respect to all of the laws it enacts, and what role should the legislative branch play in promoting effective, accountable public policy? Members of the panel on Congressional Oversight addressed these and other questions facing the 111th Congress with a particular eye on the changes ushered in by the Obama election. A short question and answer session followed the formal discussion. This essay summarizes the proceedings and highlights a few of the themes that emerged.

During Crises, We Expect the Government to Help Us

A majority of the panelists, including McGovern, Price, and Oleszek, agreed that national crises justify aggressive government interventions. In his remarks, Congressman McGovern asserted that "We're a big country; we've got big problems; we're going to need some big government to solve them." Walter Oleszek concurred, stating that "Unprecedented crises demand a big response from both the President and the Congress." Moreover, as Oleszek notes in his essay, citizens tend to look to government for solutions during crises, justifying government intervention.

That citizens turn to government during trying times is proof of former Secretary of Defense William Cohen's observation that "The government is the enemy until you need a friend." Walter Oleszek referenced Cohen's words in his piece, and Former Congresswoman Morella mentioned them in her remarks. Cohen's quotation pithily captures American citizens' tendency to be, as Oleszek notes, "ideologically conservative but operationally liberal." Congressman McGovern shared an anecdote that illustrated this tendency, relating how at a town hall meeting, one constituent railed against big government one moment and told him to "protect my Social Security and Medicare" the next. Political scientists have long known that American citizens' political belief systems are riddled with inconsistencies (see, e.g., Converse 1964). In general, as Congressman McGovern asserted, "People rely on government and expect more of government while they're also demanding a smaller government." In light of this conversation and the recent history of the Bush Administration—widely recognized as growing the size of the federal bureaucracy while espousing a conservative, anti-government rhetoric—one wonders whether how much value remains in the 'big vs. small/activist v. laissez-faire' debate.

Congressional Oversight—Its Many Definitions

In addition to addressing the public's expectations for government, the panelists discussed the topic of congressional oversight, which Oleszek defined as the "member and committee review of the administration of our laws." Oleszek allowed that congressional oversight might be more broadly defined—and impactful—than anything else Congress does vis-à-vis the executive branch. This breadth of authority gives the legislative branch a true check on executive power and a legitimate means to assert its institutional values on public policy. Congressman McGovern implied that an important facet of congressional oversight is program evaluation, saying that "whether you are on the education committee or the transportation committee or whatever committee, the fact is your job is not only to pass legislation, but then to do the oversight to make sure that what you did is actually a good thing." In this view, Congress's responsibilities do not end with the passing of legislation; rather, members have an obligation to follow a program's implementation in order to ensure that a policy framework is generating positive, 'real world' benefits.

In contrast, Congressman Price argued that oversight should occur before legislation is enacted. Specifically, he asserted that an important part of oversight is cost-benefit analysis, wherein members weigh the economic pros and cons of competing legislative proposals before making a final decision. More generally, he argued that any proposal should be studied with "due diligence" before it is enacted as law; that is, all the implications of a given project (e.g., its financial and environmental ramifications) should be weighed, and outside sources should be consulted in the process of doing so. As Congressman Price observed, it is Congress's responsibility to provide "justifications and analysis before we release huge amounts of money."

The panelists' separate attempts to define oversight suggest two things. First, legislative oversight encompasses a broad array of activities. As the panelists' remarks indicate, these include program evaluation and cost-benefit analysis, each of which occurs at a distinct stage of the legislative process—the former before legislation is enacted and the latter typically following formal implementation. Second, there is no consensus on what oversight is, or on what the most important facets of oversight are. Though there is power in definitional breadth, it stands to wonder whether the lack of consensus on what sound oversight actually entails may serve to blunt the effects of this vital accountability mechanism. Nevertheless, Congressman McGovern offered a definition of oversight that most American citizens would probably agree with: "Oversight is about truth; it's about getting to the truth."

What Goes into Effective Oversight?

Though the panelists did not agree on a definition of oversight, they did agree on what makes oversight, in any form, effective. All mentioned the importance of bipartisanship to effective oversight, and all stressed that political axe-grinding is a barrier to good oversight. Congressman Price and former Congresswoman Morella both observed that oversight works when committee members focus on "issues" and do not get bogged down in partisan sniping. Likewise, Congressman McGovern said that "oversight doesn't work when it becomes a political or partisan weapon," and emphasized that oversight works when members cooperate to get to the truth. Of course, in politics 'the truth' is inherently subjective, which may make reaching bipartisan consensus on the proper approach to oversight quite difficult. It could also increase the likelihood—and the effectiveness—of an accusation that one party or another is 'playing politics' by pursuing robust oversight. This is especially true in the case of high-profile policy efforts driven by one party and opposed by the other. The 2009 federal stimulus package is a recent example of a law that polarized congress and the public while creating incredibly complex public policy. In other words, just the type of program most in need of persistent, aggressive oversight.

All of the panelists also pointed to the "power of the purse" as a requisite for effective oversight, where effective oversight means Congress's ability to get executive branch agencies to do what it wants them to do. Former Congresswoman Morella, for instance, observed, "if you don't have the power to do something, you just look at that money, and you cut it off, or maybe you add money." Similarly, Congressman Price noted that the annual appropriations process "is the best oversight I know of in the Congress, and it's moreover oversight that has some teeth, some bite, because it's tied to the power of the purse." As these statements suggest, Congress's control of the federal purse strings is probably the institution's most effective means of overseeing and controlling executive branch agencies.

Vigorous Governmental Action Requires Vigorous Oversight

Another theme the panelists highlighted was the increased importance of oversight following aggressive government action. This was especially evident in the panelists' comments on the struggling national economy, the $800 billion American Recovery and Reinvestment Act (ARRA), and the Troubled Asset Relief Program (TARP). Congressman McGovern remarked that with "an unprecedented crisis, and an unprecedented response in terms of government, there is going to be an unprecedented need for oversight." In the same spirit, Congressman Price stated that "the fact that they are so huge and that they were done under such extraordinary pressures . . . that in some ways increases the stakes in having very careful oversight." As the Congressmen's statements suggest, governmental actions that involve large sums of money require heightened Congressional vigilance.

Again, this discussion raised important questions for the relationship between politics and public policy and efforts to bring together the unique values that drive the legislative and executive branches. Strict oversight of the TARP program, for instance, may require enduring criticism from the Obama administration and accusations that congressional hearings and legislative investigation are hindering program implementation and slowing its effects on economic recovery. In theory, members of congress value their oversight responsibilities, but there is some evidence to suggest that pursuing robust accountability may come at some personal and institutional political cost. These issues date to the country's founding and will no doubt endure as long as the tripartite system of government exists in the United States.

Conclusion—From Bush to Obama

Will oversight be different during the Obama years? James Thurber opened the question and answer session with this query, noting, "some would argue that . . . under the Bush administration they went a little light on oversight." The increased vigilance which Congressmen Price and McGovern emphasized in their remarks about the Troubled Asset Relief Program and the American Recovery and Reinvestment Act suggests that Congressional Democrats will go heavier on oversight than their Republican counterparts did during the Bush years. Whereas during the Bush years, as Walter Oleszek stated, Congressional Republicans were wary of "turning over rocks" for fear of what lurked beneath—and so assented to many of the Bush administration's wishes without protest—Congressional Democrats have vowed to be more assertive. Senate Majority Leader Harry Reid (D-NV), for one, has declared, "I don't work for Obama."

The panelists' comments suggested that a commitment to increased oversight is something that the American public will welcome. Former Congresswoman Morella observed that more oversight will lead to more accountability—something that is especially important to citizens when their government is spending large sums of taxpayer money. Congressmen Price and McGovern also stressed that citizens want more accountability. In answer to the 75th Anniversary Conference's guiding question, then, we can answer that citizens expect a lot from their government. They expect to benefit from government programs like Medicaid, Medicare, and Social Security. They also expect Congress to oversee the administration of those programs with a watchful eye.

Chapter 8

What Do We Expect from Our Elections?

David A. Dulio*

To address the question of what we expect from our elections, it is instructive to consider the language of James Madison. In *Federalist* No. 39 Madison began to lay out his argument for "the execution" of the plan created at the Constitutional Convention. More importantly for our purposes here, Madison also tried to distinguish between a democracy and a republic saying about the latter, "we may define a republic to be, or at least may bestow that name on, a government which derives all its powers directly or indirectly from the great body of the people, and is administered by persons holding their offices during pleasure, for a limited period, or during good behavior." It is appropriate to return to Madison and the Framers, and this passage in particular, because it helps make two important points. First, the question of what we expect from our elections is one with which the Framers also struggled. And second, the passage contains language that is still relevant to what we expect of our elections today.

This paper is designed to make us think about what we expect out of our electoral process. Because of the seemingly omnipresent nature of elections in the United States with over 500,000 elected officials today, I will limit my remarks to federal elections. Yes, the framers thought about this question too. But this question of electoral expectations was different at and immediately after the founding for at least two reasons. First, there were simply fewer elections to worry about. There were fewer elected officials because government was not as vast and because at the federal level, the framers limited the number of officials directly impacted by citizens voting. As we all know, senators were not directly

* Associate Professor of Political Science, Oakland University

elected until 1913, and popular votes were not envisioned to be a part of the Electoral College system, which they are today. In short, the framers expected much less of the electoral system because it was not as large a part of our government.

In addition, the question of expectations was probably a much simpler inquiry in 1787 for another important reason—there was much less cynicism about the electoral process than exists today. One way to think about the question of expectations would be with sarcasm and cynicism. For instance, if we approach the question from this view, and a candidate for office, say, ran a so-called negative ad against his or her opponent, a possible response from the citizenry might be: "Typical politicians. I should have expected that." While many in the United States might think this way, I choose not to approach the question this way. Another way to approach this question is from an unrealistic perspective—by thinking of it from an idealistic point of view. One who approaches the question in this manner might do so with the following statement: "I expect U.S. elections to be conducted without any negative ads or private donations to candidates." In our system this is simply impractical and unrealistic, for many reasons that are beyond the scope of this paper.[1]

Rather than approach the question in an emotional manner, I tackle it from an analytical yet practical approach by considering what we can realistically expect from our elections. Given the candidate-centered nature of our elections, as well as our mass-media dominated, communication-rich, federalist system, what can we expect of our elections? In addition, I see this question as being broken down into two parts: what we expect from our elections as they are taking place, and what we expect from our elections after the votes have been counted. In other words, what we expect when elections are being contested is wholly different from what we expect our elections to produce. I will consider each of these in turn, offering several expectations in each set as well as thoughts on how we are doing in terms of meeting each. In addition, at the end of the paper I offer a recap of how we are doing in meeting these expectations as a whole. Before I begin, let me say that I make no claims that the following set of expectations is an exhaustive list. Rather, it is a starting point for discussion that will certainly yield spirited debate either because I have left something out that others feel is a central expectation or because I simply describe expectations differently than someone else might. But, in a democracy like ours, this is healthy.

Election Cycle Expectations

I can think of few better ways to start a discussion of expectations for a democratic electoral process than by looking to Robert Dahl, one of the great modern political theorists. In one of his more recent works, *On Democracy*, Dahl argues there are several political institutions that large-scale democracies require. One of these is "free, fair and frequent" elections (1998: 85). Free and fair elections get at something that has been at the heart of American democracy since the beginning—political equality. Certainly, we have fallen short of equality at numerous and various points of our history, whether it be the exclusion of anyone who was not a white, land-owning male from casting a ballot in the first elections to the scourge of slavery. However, political equality remains an important tenet of the liberal political tradition on which our nation was founded. More importantly, free elections are clearly something that Americans today expect their government to provide. This translates into elections that are contested without bias, without regard to, race, gender, ethnicity, social standing, or any one of a number of additional characteristics, and where the principle of one person one vote applies.

Most of the time equality of this nature is measured by the ability of a citizen to cast a ballot. As I have noted, if our modern expectations were applied to this principle when the nation was founded, those expectations would not have been met. Huge segments of the American population were forbidden by law from casting a vote, and this issue was not fully addressed from a legal standpoint until constitutional amendments granted the franchise to African Americans (the Fifteenth) and women (the Nineteenth). Of course, the nation continued to fail to meet this expectation after the ratification of those amendments as literacy tests and poll taxes remained.

A case can be made, even today, that we do not meet the expectation of equality when we consider that the act of voting is administered with different standards across the nation. Some of these are simple differences of preference across states—poll closing times, for instance—but others are more troubling—different voting mechanisms and ballots, different voter registration requirements, and even voter intimidation. We have made strides here, however, from the days of the party machine when voters got their ballot from the party boss who made sure voters filled them out correctly, mainly by issuing colored ballots with only that party's candidates listed.

In some respects, free and fair elections may refer to similar principles. However, fairness goes further in that it can encompass expectations related to more than voters casting a ballot and into how an election is contested by candidates, political parties, interest groups, and other players including individual citizens. Here, fairness translates into the idea of a level playing field for those competing for elective office. In other words, we would expect that there are no inherent advantages for one side or the other. Here again, our expectations are likely not met, even today, if we impose even a modest standard. I do not mean to suggest that there is an expectation that every electoral actor is in exactly the same condition as their counterparts. This is unrealistic in our market-based society, but there is, I think, still an expectation that one candidate, for example, is not guaranteed victory because of some inherent advantage.

Those competing in today's elections are rarely, if ever, on the same footing. This comes in many forms, but many of these differences can be boiled down to one factor—resources. In most electoral contests, especially at the federal level, there is a vast gulf between the candidates in terms of resources. For instance, during the 2008 congressional elections incumbents running to keep their seats in the House of Representatives raised, on average, over $1.3 million compared to only $300,000 for challengers; in Senate races these numbers ballooned to nearly $9 million for the average incumbent compared to over $1 million for the average challenger (Center for Responsive Politics, 2009a). Is this fair?

The same question can be asked of parties and organized interests. While the U.S. electoral system is dominated by two parties, there are dozens more that exist but usually fail to win elective office.[2] These minor parties certainly lack the funding that Democrats and Republicans enjoy, both of which raised nearly $1 billion over the course of the 2008 cycle (Center for Responsive Politics, 2009b), but they also face the larger problem of ballot access. In many places around the nation, minor parties simply find that they cannot get their candidates on the ballot because of the rules put in place, usually by the Democrats and Republicans they would be running against. Is this fair?

Organized interest groups serve an important function in our system as they share information with elected officials that help shape policy.[3] In fact, lobbying is, at its core, the constitutionally protected right to petition the government for redress of grievances granted to every citizen in the First Amendment. Moreover, while the theory of pluralism may not fully reflect the way in which our system works, important lessons and criticisms of it are central to the question of electoral fairness, specifically with respect to how organized interests pursue their agendas. According to E. E. Schattschneider (1960), "The flaw in the pluralist heaven is that the heavenly chorus sings with a strong upper-class accent." According to the Federal Election Commission, there were over 5,000 political action committees (PACs) active in the 2006 election cycle; in total these groups raised over $1 billion. However, there are many more than 5,000 organized interests active in the United States. What is more, of the millions donated by PACs during an election cycle, the vast majority of those come from an even more select group; in 2004, for instance, 63 percent of all PAC money came from only 296 groups. Is it fair that only a small portion of them are active in elections?

There is also the question of whether or not it is fair that some individual citizens can impact elections more than others with the use of their personal wealth. Is it fair that some citizens can use their fortune to influence elections while others are unable to do so? Take for instance, some of the top donors to Democratic and Republican parties and interests. In 2004, financier George Soros and Progressive Insurance company chairman Peter Lewis both gave over $23 million each to different political groups that exist solely to influence elections; in 2006 Bob Perry gave nearly $10 million to a handful of groups to impact the congressional races. Does the one-person-one-vote standard still apply? Is this fair?

In addition, candidates are rarely created equal. Some have built-in advantages, with the clearest example being the incumbency advantage that exists today which helps sitting officeholders get reelected at sometimes alarming rates.[4] Incumbents have the advantage of: being able to deliver benefits for their constituents, both on an individual basis in the form of casework and district-wide in the form of pork; the funding advantage over their challengers note above; and the franking privilege, which amounts to taxpayer-funded mail they can use to boast about their accomplishments. Certainly, incumbents and the candidates that challenger them are not on equal footing. As Gary C. Jacobson (2008) notes: "incumbency remains a conspicuous factor in congressional elections from almost any perspective . . . and everyone involved in politics knows it" (27). Is this fair?

This brings us to another expectation that many Americans likely have about our elections—competitiveness. Many of the elections that take place are not competitive—to the point where some incumbents do not even face opposition from a member of the other party. And even when there is a full complement of candidates on the ballot there may only be token competition for the incumbent. Taking the U.S. Congress as an example, in 2006 fifty-five House members faced no competition, and this was down from prior years like 2002 in which seventy-eight incumbents did not have a challenger and 1998 when that number was ninety-four (over 20 percent of all House seats). U.S. Senate elections are more likely to be competitive. For instance, in the last twenty years when there have been uncontested seats it has only been one senator running unopposed (this is with two exceptions—1990 and 2002—when five and four senators, respectively, ran unchallenged).

Taking a larger view of competitiveness, however, shows cause for even more concern here. According to Paul S. Herrnson (2008), incumbents who are "shoo-ins" for reelection make up about one-third of the candidates seeking reelection in the House and about a quarter of all Senate incumbents; these figures have been relatively stable over the last two decades. Those incumbents who are "in jeopardy" make up a much smaller share of candidates seeking reelection—over the last twenty years only about one in ten House members fell into this category compared to roughly 20 percent of senators. These small percentages exist even though Herrnson categorizes those who are "in jeopardy" as having won by 20 percent or less (i.e., beating their last opponent by an outcome of 60 percent to 40 percent or less); if we used a more strict standard, we would find even fewer incumbents who were in serious trouble. Of course this is nothing new. Even as early as the 1970s David Mayhew noticed that the number of marginal seats—Herrnson's shoo-ins—was declining. Before 1966, 61 percent of House members seeking reelection won with more than 60 percent of the vote; between 1968 and 1982, that figure jumped to 73 percent. These changes got Mayhew's attention and led him to write his important piece on the "vanishing marginals" in 1974.

Incumbent officeholders make it difficult for challengers to unseat them because of the power they have at their fingertips in Washington, their state capitals, their city hall, or wherever they are making decisions. The incumbency advantage noted above certainly plays a major part in the lack of competitiveness in many races today. The perks that come with incumbency help increase incumbents' vote share. Using Andrew Gelman and Gary King's (1990) measurement, Gary Jacobson (2008) finds that, on average, incumbency itself means an extra 10.6 percent for those running for reelection.

There are other reasons for the lack of competitiveness, however. One that gets a good deal of attention is the redistricting process. A broad discussion of this phenomenon is outside the scope of this paper, but suffice it to say that a process that is controlled by partisan elected officials in the states (state legislators and governors) will likely produce a partisan process designed to help their fellow partisans. Many scholars have blamed the redistricting process for helping create uncompetitive elections, but on several occasions when voters have been given the choice to take the power away from elected officials with an interest in the outcome of the process, each one has failed (however, a measure on the ballot in California during 2008 was adopted taking the control of state legislative districts only out of the hands of the legislature, leaving it in control of deciding the congressional district boundaries). Incumbency and redistricting are two structural factors that lead to a lack of competitiveness.

It seems rather commonsensical to say that we expect our elections to be informative. After all, how can one vote when not informed about the choices before them? According to the popular model of democracy, an informed electorate (presumably through the campaign process) is not only an expectation, but a necessity. But, even if we side with those who argue for the responsible model of democracy which says that individuals do not need to be exceptionally well informed because citizens vote retrospectively, campaigns need to be informative at least to the point where voters can judge whether the incumbent officeholder or party has done a good enough job to be put back into office. In other words, the public needs to have information on how the officeholder has voted on particular issues of concern to the district or state, whether they have been a productive member of the government, whether they have fulfilled promises from the last campaign, among a host of other pieces of information that will help voters make a judgment.

The issues about which our elections inform citizens, one probably expects, would be those that are important to the polity. The expectation that our campaigns and elections would inform individuals about issues that they care about is also fairly reasonable. To this point, it may be seen that the expectations I have laid out are not being met. On this point, however, there is clear evidence that our elections meet or even exceed this expectation. There is little doubt that candidates, parties, and interest groups are rational actors during the election cycle. They are engaging in the electoral process with a particular goal—to win the election—and will pursue that goal with clear strategies and tactics. The issues discussed during an election are part of this strategy.

The cynical view of expectations in our elections I noted at the outset may appear if we think about candidates and the issues they discuss during a campaign as simply pandering to voters. Much of this is driven by the criticism of candidates being "poll driven." In short, this is the view that candidates simply take a poll and regurgitate the issue positions favored by a majority of the electorate. This view of candidates (and their campaign teams) using polling data to drive their campaign message is simplistic and wrong. Candidates do use polling, but they do not use it to find which positions to take on important issues.[5] Rather, it is part of a more complex process that is actually well grounded in theory. Stephen Medvic (2001) has developed a theory of "deliberate priming" which details how campaigns select the issues on which to focus during the election. Medvic's theory basically states that campaigns (candidates and their consultants) use polling to select *issues* (not *positions*) to emphasize that are 1) most important to the public and 2) on which the candidate has an advantage over their opponent. In short, candidates want to prime voters to use issues that favor them when making their candidate choice on election day. As noted, those issues can be found in polling data during an individual campaign, but the idea has deeper theoretical roots. John Petrocik noted this with respect to presidential candidates in his theory of issue ownership, where there are certain issues the public views one party or the other to be better able to "handle." According to Petrocik (1996), Democrats have an advantage on issues such as civil liberties and social welfare (i.e., entitlements), while Republicans have an advantage on issues such as crime and defense (see also, Petrocik, et al., 2004).

When candidates (or other campaign actors) select issues to feature in a campaign that the public cares about it is good for everyone. It would serve no purpose if candidates discussed issues of no concern to anyone. It does little to help them get elected and it does not help voters understand what the candidates think of the important issues of the day.

If candidates and others involved in our elections stress issues that the public cares about during the election season, what impact does this have on the electorate? After all, candidates spend millions upon millions of the dollars they raise for their campaigns communicating with voters via mail and other print materials, radio ads, television commercials, and the Internet. One telling signal of this impact is that while campaign communications inundate citizens during the election the public often quickly tires of seeing television commercials and receiving political mail. Whether the public uses these communications in a meaningful way, however, is another question. In other words, we expect elections to be informative, but are they?

A distressing finding of early empirical political science research was the lack of sophistication present in the average American's thinking about politics, which may mean that all the effort candidates' campaigns put into creating and distributing their messages could be for naught. "The democratic citizen is expected to be well informed about political affairs. He [*sic*] is supposed to know what the issues are, what their history is, what the relevant facts are, what alternatives are proposed, what the party stands for, what the likely consequences are" (Berelson et al., 1954: 308). In truth, however, scholars have consistently found that voters do not meet this ideal. Rather, classic works such as *The American Voter* by Angus Campbell, Philip E. Converse, Warren E. Miller, and Donald E. Stokes, as well as others that followed, illustrate that the American public is not very sophisticated in terms of political knowledge. In fact, according to Larry Bartels (1996), "The political ignorance of the American voter is one of the best-documented features of contemporary politics" (194). The conclusion is fairly consistent: "ordinary citizens tend to pay attention to politics only fitfully, and possess in consequence a thin, rather than thick, knowledge of it."[6] Some in the literature, including Norman Nie, Sidney Verba, and John Petrocik, have challenged this idea (see, Nie et al., 1979), but recent research "has hammered away at the Nie argument, confirming the continuing validity of the image of citizens as 'low involvement' spectators of politics" (Sniderman, 1993: 220). Even in the face of the modern scholarship that illustrates a more positive assessment of the electorate, "most voters . . . still fall short of the standards of classic democratic theory" (Dalton and Wattenberg, 1993: 196).

A final expectation for our elections prior to election day could have been connected to the issue of fairness discussed above. I have chosen, however, to keep the issue of ethics separate because of the importance of this topic to AU's Center for Congressional and Presidential Studies (CCPS) and the seven-year, multi-million dollar grant CCPS and its Campaign Management Institute undertook in the late 1990s and the early 2000s. Ethics can be a touchy subject since what is ethical to one person is unethical to another. This, however, is important in our discussion of expectations because of the close connection between ethics and morals, and ethics and the law.[7]

Work done by CCPS has addressed the issue of ethics in our elections by examining it in both a practical and theoretical manner, much of which is found in *Shades of Gray: Perspectives on Campaign Ethics*, a collection of essays by scholars and practitioners on the state of ethics in our elections (Nelson et al., 2002). Data reported in this volume indirectly indicate the importance that Americans place on ethics in their elections. First, the general attitude of the public as it relates to the behavior of candidates is reflected in data showing 59 percent of the public believed that "all or most" candidates twist the truth during an election, 39 percent reported that they felt candidates tell outright lies during a campaign, and 55 percent said that elections had gotten worse with respect to "ethics and values" since the 1970s (Rourke, 2002). In addition, according to a survey of the general public conducted by CCPS just before the 2000 election, seven in ten Americans supported the idea of candidates signing a code of ethics during their run for office.[8] These figures are in addition to the voluminous data which shows that the public continues to have less and less trust in government over time. Clearly the electorate is disappointed.

Some of this disappointment may come from the expectations the public places on electoral actors. How we think about ethics is important to this discussion. Also in *Shades of Gray*, Dale Miller and Stephen Medvic propose two ways of approaching the question of ethics. They argue there are two models of campaign ethics—the civic responsibility model and the self interest model. Under the latter, "beyond following universal moral rules that apply to everyone in nearly all situations, individuals and groups are obligated to only advocate on behalf of their own interests in the campaign" while in the former, "campaign actors have a duty to enhance democracy" (Dulio et al., 2002: 8). These two models may seem to reflect the two approaches I said at the outset that I would not use in this paper. The civic responsibility model may seem like pie-in-the-sky, idealistic thinking about how campaign actors will behave, while behavior under the self interest model is likely to elicit thoughts of "well, imagine that, John Smith is only going to do what helps him get elected." This may be the case for some, but because of the inherent difficulty in defining what is and is not ethical, it is not necessarily so. We can have a discussion about what is and is not ethical, but no one can tell another person what that actually is. What is, I think, indisputable, is that the public wants and expects more of its electoral actors.

How our elections are meeting the ethical expectation is up in the air depending on how one defines ethics. What is and is not ethical is impossible to define universally; it is also beyond the scope of this paper. However, some recent events during election cycles at least has to make one wonder how our elections are doing on this front. During the 2004 presidential election we had the infamous "RATS ad" created by the Republican National Committee, the NAACP's "James Byrd" ad, as well as an ad run against Max Cleland (D-GA), a Vietnam veteran who lost three limbs during his service, linking him to Osama bin Laden. We also saw some disputable claims by both George W. Bush and John F. Kerry—Kerry saying Bush wanted to reinstate the draft and Bush saying that Kerry's health care plan would be "government run" when both candidates knew their claims to be false. There are also advertisements from the past that have raised ethical questions—the Johnson campaign's "Daisy Girl" spot from 1964 and the National Security PAC's ad in 1988 against Michael Dukakis featuring Willie Horton. There are literally dozens of events that can cause one to wonder about the ethical state of our elections. One plus, however, is that in 2008 there seemed to be fewer instances that made cynics shake their heads. This is not to say that nothing happened during the most recent election cycle that could be considered unethical. There certainly were events during 2008 that were questionable in terms of ethics, with a couple at the top of the list; for instance, John McCain's use of Rev. Jeremiah Wright and William Ayers, and Barack Obama saying McCain was "losing his bearings" or that he was "erratic," which could be construed as a veiled attempt to make an issue of McCain's age. These are neither the only two events of 2008 that could fit in this category, nor are they clear violations of ethical standards, which illustrates the difficulty of establishing the nature of our campaign ethics.

Expectations Post-Election Day

To this point, it is a fair point to say that many of the expectations I have identified are debatable. As we turn our attention to what we expect from our elections after election day, the picture becomes much clearer. In short, we expect our elections to simply produce results. We expect them to produce representative government, good leaders, and most importantly good public policy.

The questions of representation and leadership are again ones with which the framers struggled. In the late 1780s, the Federalists and Anti-federalists engaged in a debate that dates back to Edmund Burke—should elections produce delegates or trustees? Without going into too much detail, generally Madison and the Federalists were expecting legislators in the House (again the only branch of the federal government directly elected at the time) to be trustees while Melancton Smith and other Anti-federalists thought delegates should be produced.

The Federalists' expectation was one where representatives would "filter" the masses' views and "refine and enlarge the public views by passing them through the medium of a chosen body of citizens whose wisdom may best discern the true interest of their country" (quoted in Kramnick, 1987: 126). In *Federalist* No. 10 Madison noted that in a large republic the electoral process would reject "unworthy candidates," select "men who possess the most attractive merit," and would lead to "the substitution of representatives whose enlightened views and virtuous sentiments render them superior to local prejudices and schemes of injustice" (Kramnick: 127, 128). These clearly reflect the expectation (and desire) that elections produce representatives who would use their own talents and judgments to make decisions on behalf of those who selected them.

The Anti-federalists, however, disagreed and thought it better for elections to produce delegates who would act as if those who had chosen them were at their side while making a decision. Patrick Henry, for instance, told the Virginia ratifying convention that "the Constitution . . . presupposes that the chosen few who go to Congress will have more upright hearts and more enlightened minds" (quoted in Moore, 1857: 35.) Rather than filter the public's desires, the Anti-Federalists thought elections should produce a group of representatives that mirrored the public. The aforementioned Melancton Smith argued at the New York ratifying convention that representatives should "*resemble* those they represent. They should be a true picture of the people, possess a knowledge of their constituents and their wants, sympathize in all their distress, and be disposed to seek their true interests" (quoted in Manin, 1997: 110). In contrast to the Federalist view, Smith argued that citizens should not look for "brilliant talents" in their representatives, but rather find "a sameness, as to residence and interests, between the representative and his constituents."

I mention these historical expectations not only because they illustrate the fact that this question has been around since the founding, but also because they provide a point of comparison for today's expectations. Certainly the delegate and trustee models are both legitimate forms of representation. However, it is clear that today's expectations for our representatives favor one over the other. According to Roger Davidson, Walter Oleszek and Frances Lee, writing in *Congress and Its Members*, "Today's voters prefer . . . instructed delegates rather than lawmakers who exercise too much independent judgment" (2008: 136).

This desire on the part of citizens translates into one of the cornerstones of representation—being responsive to constituent demands (Pitkin, 1967). This responsiveness can take many forms, as elected officials can represent the policy (national or local) concerns of their district or state, provide services to constituents, or deliver benefits to the district or state.[9] Indeed, this heterogeneity in expectations is found in the attitudes of the public. "Some citizens desire assistance in dealing with government; others want their representative to focus on national policy concerns. Still others want their member to devote most of their time to local policy concerns" (Toobin and Rudolph, 2004: 442). In a recent study that examined what citizens expected their member of Congress to spend time on, working on local issues was ranked by over 45 percent of survey respondents as the most important issue followed by working on national issues (nearly 39 percent) and helping people with government (over 15 percent) (435-36).

"Few voters anywhere are averse to pressuring their congressman to bring home the bacon. Nor is the average congressman liable to any great compulsion, personal, political, or otherwise, to resist" (Cavanaugh, 1982: 126). This is the problem of the much-lamented practice of pork-barrel spending. Most citizens do not like pork, except when it is for their district and their representatives are the ones bringing it home. And as has been shown by some of the great congressional scholars, members of Congress who are effective in securing federal money for their district or state (and most are) do very well at reelection time.[10]

Interestingly, our elected officials may not be as firm in their beliefs about acting as delegates as their constituents might like. Several studies over time (Whalke et al., 1962; Davidson, 1969; Cavanaugh, 1982) have shown that members of Congress assume the role of both delegate and trustee. Roger H. Davidson found that only about one quarter of members he studied in the 1960s could be described as either delegates or trustees with nearly half saying they took on both roles; "Many congressmen observe that their problem is one of balancing the one role against the other" (Davidson, 1969: 119). Thomas Cavanaugh (1982), updating the earlier studies, during the 1980s found members of the House of Representatives took several factors into consideration, but concluded that, "In practice . . . members generally accede to district sentiments on distributive issues, while they tend to follow their own personal beliefs on issues of social morality, legal rights, and foreign and defense policy" (124).

One expectation that is necessary for elections to produce both good leaders and good policy is a legitimate government in which the public has confidence regarding how the winners were decided. In some ways, this question of legitimacy is tied to the issue of ethics discussed at the end of the last section. If a campaign is not waged in an appropriate manner that is befitting the office being pursued, questions can arise as to whether the victorious candidate is actually a legitimate officeholder. If a winning candidate is seen to have been engaging in underhanded and deceitful practices during the campaign, the legitimacy of the results may be called into question. If elected officials are going to produce good public policy and represent their constituents, their victories must be viewed as legitimate.

Rightly or wrongly, the question of legitimacy plagued George W. Bush throughout his eight years in office. After the disputed recount in Florida and the Supreme Court decision in *Bush v. Gore* many Americans were left wondering whether the right candidate was inaugurated. As Jack Balkin (2002) notes in an essay devoted to the topic, "It is very difficult for people living in a proud and long-standing democracy like the United States to accept that they are ruled by persons who have no right to their office" (215). This hampered Bush's efforts in dealing with the public as well as the Congress, and certainly meant he was less successful than he might otherwise had been. Even Karl Rove, Bush's top political strategist for six of his eight years in office noticed this. Recently reflecting on the Bush presidency, Rove said: "There were people who never accepted the legitimacy of George W. Bush and acted accordingly" (Herman, 2008). It is next to impossible for a public official to deliver on promises made during a campaign if that same official is under some cloud of doubt on the question of whether he or she holds the office legitimately.

The Bush example is an ironic one because of the office involved—the presidency—and the mechanism used to pick the winner—the Electoral College. Many aspects of the Electoral College are debatable, and those debates were certainly rekindled after 2000. However, one of the supposed benefits of this system is the conveyance of legitimacy to the winner. Yes, one of the benefits of the Electoral College is an added amount of legitimacy to the winner. This certainly seems hard to believe after the 2000 race; much of this comes from the fact that Al Gore garnered 500,000 more popular votes than did George W. Bush.

However, many other examples illustrate the point clearly. In 1992, Bill Clinton won the presidency with roughly 43 percent of the popular vote; he won the votes in the Electoral College with 69 percent. There was no question who the president of the United States was after election day in 1992 even though 57 percent of the voters cast a vote for a candidate other than Bill Clinton. In many other instances through history candidates with very small margins in the popular vote were seen as very legitimate victors because of their much larger Electoral College victories. In 1960, John F. Kennedy beat Richard Nixon by 0.2 percent of the popular vote but won by eighty-four electoral votes. Grover Cleveland defeated James Blaine in 1884 by thirty-seven electoral votes and only 0.7 percent of the popular vote. Similarly, in 1844 James K. Polk defeated Henry Clay by sixty-five electoral votes but only 1.4 percent of the popular vote. In 1880 James Garfield won the presidency over Winfield Hancock by fifty-nine Electoral Votes despite winning the popular vote by only 0.1 percent. Even the 2004 race where George W. Bush beat John Kerry could fall into this category—Bush won the popular vote by 2.4 percent but won by thirty-five electoral votes. In each instance, there was little doubt which candidate would be sworn in on inauguration day, despite the fact that each won by a small, and in some cases, the slimmest of margins.

Americans need to have confidence in election returns so they know that they are being represented by a legitimate government. Does this happen each and every time? Of course not—the Bush vs. Gore fiasco certainly reminds us of how the system can misfire, but so do other instances such as the 2008 race between Norm Coleman and Al Franken for the right to represent Minnesota in the U.S. Senate.

A final expectation is one that many Americans likely take for granted—a peaceful transfer of power after an election where a candidate of one party replaces an elected official of the other. As Americans we simply assume that this will be the case. In fact, it has been the case in every transfer of power at the federal level since the founding. Even in more recent years when the level of partisanship has been ratcheted up before and during each election cycle, after the votes have been counted, the transition from one official to the next has been peaceful. The most extreme case recently was in January 2001 when George W. Bush was inaugurated after the disputed election and a fierce battle in the courts. The 2000 election was also on the heels of the highly partisan impeachment of President Clinton roughly two years before. In another, less stable democracy inauguration day may have turned out much differently. But our expectations, and the resulting transfer itself, were for something much different. Even in instances such as the aftermath of the 1994 and 2006 congressional elections when control of the House of Representatives changed hands, there were no guns in the streets, only the handing over of the gavel from one Speaker of the House to another. Have there been times when one office holder had trouble handing power over to another? Certainly.[11] However, these are very few and far between and do not come close to what has sometimes occurred in other nations. Here, we have met this expectation very well.

Concluding Thoughts

If I were to sum up the expectations for our elections it would be with two simple words: a lot. Americans expect a great deal from the processes that ultimately forms their representative government, as well they should. I have separated these many expectations into two categories—those that are centered on the campaigns that lead up to election day, and those that are focused on the aftermath of the elections. In general, the evidence is mixed on whether these expectations are being met. In short, our elections do not meet many of the expectations we might place on our campaigns. While we have made many strides in assuring that the principle of "one person one vote" is realized, there are still many instances where fairness can be questioned in our elections. Many of our elections for seats in state legislatures and in Congress are not competitive which results in one party having a lock on those seats. While candidates, parties and interest groups collectively spend hundreds of millions of dollars each election cycle communicating with voters, those same voters are not very well informed about issues. And, our elections always seem to feature some example of behavior that is questionable in terms of its ethics; of course this is the easiest criticism to dispute because of the subjective nature of ethics.

I do, however, believe our elections do a much better job of meeting the expectations we have after election day has passed. It is difficult to argue with the results of our elections when the United States has been and continues to be the most stable democracy in the world since the founding. While there are going to be disagreements about whether our leaders produce good policy—Republicans will complain about President Obama's $800 billion stimulus plan, his ideas for health care reform, and planed tax increases, just as Democrats did not like much of anything George W. Bush did while in office—we can say with some confidence that in terms of responsiveness our elected officials score highly.

Moreover, our elections do a fairly good job of producing good leaders. Yes, we can always point to individuals such as Randy "Duke" Cunningham, William Jefferson, Ted Stephens, Rod Blagojevich, or one of the others in the handful of politicians perceived to be corrupt. But the vast majority of individuals who devote time to public service are good leaders who want simply to make public policy that improves the quality of life for their constituents. More importantly, we achieve these results even in the face of the fact that the average citizen is not that well informed. This is an important caveat to the related point above. While most Americans do not have a full complement of information at their disposal, this does not mean that they cannot make good decisions and choices on election day. Indeed, "individuals can make reasonable decisions . . . without perfect information" (Carpini and Keeter, 1991; Dalton and Wattenberg, 1993: 196). Moreover, some recent research has painted a more optimistic picture of the American electorate, arguing that citizens do have what they need to make sense of politics and campaigns even though they are not fully informed (Popkin, 1991; Sniderman, et al. 1991). The reason for this optimism is that scholars have seen that voters can, and do, use information shortcuts or their own individual reasoning to make a decision on election day (Neuman, 1986).

As I have noted above, our elections also score well on measures of representativeness (through responsiveness) and producing a legitimate government that takes power peacefully. Are the outcomes always perfect? Certainly not. But on balance do our elections produce what we expect? That answer is more complex. It certainly depends on the standards one uses and the expectations one sees as most important. In the end, I believe our elections meet our expectations fairly well, given the number of demands we place on our electoral system. Could we do better? Most definitely. And as we move forward, questions must be asked and answered with respect to how we improve our system so it not only meets, but ultimately exceeds our expectations.

Notes

1. One main reason this is unrealistic, however, is the First Amendment to the Constitution. Freedom of speech not only applies to citizens, but candidates and it allows them to say nasty things about their opponents. Thanks to *Buckley v. Valeo* (1976) it also allows a free flow of money into the electoral system. The First Amendment also stands in the way of other "wishes" such as a shorter campaign season.

2. The Green Party is an exception in that its candidates have had some minimal successes, usually at lower level races like city council and mayor in small towns. A full listing of the Green Party's electoral successes can be found at www.gp.org.

3. The appropriateness of this fact is an entirely different question.

4. Members of Congress, for instance, have been getting reelected at rates of between 80 and 90 percent for more than two decades.

5. Does this happen sometimes? Certainly. But does it represent the vast majority of candidates? No.

6. For a review of this literature, see Paul M. Sniderman. "The New Look in Public Opinion Research," in *Political Science: The State of the Discipline II,* ed. Ada W. Finifter (Washington, D.C.: American Political Science Association, 1993), 219.

7. For a discussion of the relationship between ethics and both morality and law, see Dale E. Miller and Stephen K. Medvic. "Campaign Ethics: Civic Responsibility or Self Interest," in *Shades of Gray: Perspectives on Campaign Ethics*, eds. Candice J. Nelson, David A. Dulio and Stephen K. Medvic (Washington, D.C.: Brookings Institution Press, 2002).

8. Survey details can be found at: http://spa.american.edu/ccps/getpdf.php?table =publications&ID=2 (accessed February 21, 2009).

9. On policy concerns see Richard L. Hall, *Participation in Congress* (New Haven: Yale University Press, 1996), and Warren E. Miller and Donald E. Stokes, "Constituency Influence in Congress," *American Political Science Review*, 57 (1963): 45–56; on providing services, see Bruce Cain, John Ferejohn, and Morris P. Fiorina, *The Personal Vote: Constituency Service and Electoral Independence* (Cambridge: Harvard University Press, 1987), and John Hibbing, *Congressional Careers: Contours of Life in the United States House of Representatives* (Chapel Hill: University of North Carolina Press, 1991); on benefits see Morris P. Fiorina, *Congress: Keystone of the Washington Establishment* (New Haven: Yale University Press, 1989).

10. Only two of the many studies illustrating this point are: David R. Mayhew, *Congress: The Electoral Connection* (New Haven: Yale University Press, 1974); Morris

P. Fiorina, *Congress: Keystone of the Washington Establishment* (New Haven: Yale University Press, 1978).

11. One recent example of an example of a less-than-typical transfer of power was after a 2006 House contest where Melissa Bean beat incumbent Phil Crane by only 4 points. After the election, Crane's behavior led the Almanac of American Politics to call him "an unusually bitter loser, refusing to speak to Bean or to arrange for the usually routine post-election transfer of district cases and other office files." Michael Barone and Richard E. Cohen, *The Almanac of American Politics*, 2006 Edition (Washington, DC: National Journal, 2005): pp. 580-81.

References

Balkin, Jack M. "Legitimacy and the 2000 Election." Pp. 215 in *Bush V. Gore: The Question of Legitimacy*, edited by Bruce A. Ackerman. New Haven: Yale University Press, 2002.

Bartels, Larry M. "Uninformed Votes: Information Effects in Presidential Elections." *American Journal of Political Science* 40 (1996): 194.

Berelson, Bernard R., Paul F. Lazarsfeld, and William N. McPhee. *Voting: A Study of Opinion Formation in a Presidential Campaign*. Chicago: University of Chicago Press, 1954.

Buckley v. Valeo, 424 U.S. 1 (1976).

Cain, Bruce, John Ferejohn, and Morris P. Fiorina. *The Personal Vote: Constituency Service and Electoral Independence*. Cambridge. MA: Harvard University Press, 1987.

Cavanaugh, Thomas E. "The Calculus of Representation: A Congressional Perspective." *Western Political Quarterly* 35, 1 (1982): 126.

Center for Responsive Politics. "Incumbency Advantage, Politicians and Elections, 2010 Overview." February 2010. www.opensecrets.org/overview/incumbs.php (accessed February 13, 2009).

Center for Responsive Politics. "Political Parties Overview." February 2010. www.opensecrets.org/parties/index.php.

Cohen, Richard E. *The Almanac of American Politics*, 2006 Edition. Washington, DC: National Journal, 2005.

Dahl, Robert. *On Democracy*. New Haven: Yale University Press, 1998.

Dalton, Russel J., and Martin P. Wattenberg. "The Not So Simple Act of Voting" Pp. 196 in *Political Science: The State of the Discipline II,* edited by Ada W. Finifter. Washington, DC: American Political Science Association, 1993.

Davidson, Roger H. *The Role of the Congressman*. Indianapolis: Pegasus, 1969.

Davidson, Roger H., Walter J. Oleszek, and Frances E. Lee. *Congress and Its Members,* 11th ed. Washington, DC: CQ Press, 2008.

Delli Carpini, Michael X., and Scott Keeter. "Stability and Change in the U.S. Public's Knowledge of Politics." *Public Opinion Quarterly* 55, 4 (1991): 583–612.

Dulio, David A., Stephen K. Medvic, and Candice J. Nelson. "Campaign Ethics: Approaching the Issue." Pp. 8 in *Shades of Gray: Perspectives on Campaign Ethics,* edited by Candice J. Nelson, David A. Dulio, and Stephen K. Medvic. Washington, DC: Brookings Institution Press, 2002.

Fiorina, Morris P. *Congress: Keystone of the Washington Establishment*. New Haven: Yale University Press, 1989.

Gelman, Andrew, and Gary King. "Measuring Incumbency without Bias." *American Journal of Political Science* 34 (1990): 1142 –1164.

Green Party of the United States. General Website. www.gp.org.

Hall, Richard L. *Participation in Congress*. New Haven: Yale University Press, 1996.

Herman, Ken. "Bush Insiders Reflect on President's Legacy," *The Austin American Statesmen*, December 07, 2008. www.statesman.com/news/content/news/stories/nation/12/07/1207bushinside.html (accessed February 22, 2009).

Herrnson, Paul S. *Congressional Elections: Campaigning at Home and in Washington.* 5th ed. Washington DC: CQ Press, 2007.

Hibbing, John. *Congressional Careers: Contours of Life in the United States House of Representatives*. Chapel Hill: University of North Carolina Press, 1991.

Jacobson, Gary C. *The Politics of Congressional Elections*. 7th ed. New York: Longman, 2008.

Madison, James. "Federalist 10." Pp. 126 in *James Madison, Alexander Hamilton, and John Jay: The Federalist Papers*, edited by Isaac Kramnick. New York: Penguin Books, 1987.

Manin, Bernard. *The Principles of Representative Government*, New York: Cambridge University Press. 1997.

Mayhew, David R. *Congress: The Electoral Connection*. New Haven: Yale University Press, 1974.

Mayhew, David R. "Congressional Elections: The Case of the Vanishing Marginals." *Polity* 6 (1974): 295–317.

Medvic, Stephen K. *Political Consultants in U.S. Congressional Elections*. Columbus, OH: The Ohio State University Press, 2001.

Miller, Dale E., and Stephen K. Medvic. "Campaign Ethics: Civic Responsibility or Self Interest." in *Shades of Gray: Perspectives on Campaign Ethics,* edited by Candice J. Nelson, David A. Dulio, and Stephen K. Medvic. Washington, DC: Brookings Institution Press, 2002.

Miller, Warren E., and Donald E. Stokes. "Constituency Influence in Congress." *American Political Science Review* 57 (1963): 45–56.

Moore, Frank. *American Eloquence: A Collection of Speeches and Addresses by the Most Eminent Orators of America*. New York: Appleton, 1857.

Nelson, Candice J., David A. Dulio, and Stephen K. Medvic, eds. *Shades of Gray: Perspectives on Campaign Ethics*. Washington, DC: Brookings Institution Press, 2002.

Nie, Norman H., Sidney Verba, and John R. Petrocik. *The Changing American Voter.* Cambridge: Harvard University Press, 1979.

Neuman, W. Russell. *The Paradox of Mass Politics: Knowledge and Opinion in the American Electorate*. Cambridge: Harvard University Press, 1986.

Petrocik, John R. "Issue Ownership in Presidential Elections, with a 1980 Case Study." *American Journal of Political Science* 40 (1996): 825–50.

Petrocik, John R., William L. Benoit, and Glenn J. Hansen. "Issue Ownership and Presidential Campaigning, 1952-2000." *Political Science Quarterly* 118 (2004) 599–626.

Pitkin, Hanna. *The Concept of Representation*. Berkeley, CA: University of California Press, 1967.

Popkin, Samuel L. *The Reasoning Voter: Communication and Persuasion in Presidential Campaigns*. Chicago: University of Chicago Press, 1991.

Rourke, Brad. "The Citizenry: More than Voting" in *Shades of Gray: Perspectives on Campaign Ethics*, edited by Candice J. Nelson, David A. Dulio, and Stephen K. Medvic. Washington, DC: Brookings Institution Press, 2002.

Schattschneider, E. E. *The Semi-Sovereign People*. New York: Holt, Rinehart and Winston, 1960.

Sniderman, Paul M. "The New Look in Public Opinion Research." Pp. 219 in *Political Science: The State of the Discipline II*, edited by Ada W. Finifter. Washington, DC: American Political Science Association, 1993.

Sniderman, Paul M., Richard A. Brody, and Philip E. Tetlock. *Reasoning and Choice: Explorations in Political Psychology*. New York: Cambridge University Press, 1991.

Tobin, Grant, J., and Thomas J. Rudolph. "The Job of Representation in Congress: Public Expectations and Representative Approval." *Legislative Studies Quarterly* 29, 3 (2004): 442.

Whalke, John C., Heinz Eulau, William Buchanan, and LeRoy C. Ferguson. *The Legislative System: Explorations in Legislative Behavior*. New York: Wiley, 1962.

Elections and Campaigns Panel Summary

William L. Harder[*]

Presenter: *David Dulio*, Associate Professor of Political Science, Oakland University

Discussants: *Rob Engel*, Project Director, National Committee for an Effective Congress

David Winston, President and Founder, Winston Group

Anne Caprara, Chief of Staff, Office of Congresswoman Betsy Markey, 4th District of Colorado

Moderator: *Candice Nelson*, Associate Professor of Government, School of Public Affairs and Director of the Campaign Management Institute, American University

Introduction

The process of reaching public office is arguably of more importance today than it has been at any other point in history. Public opinion polls are ubiquitous and increasingly influential; some political operatives double as policy staff, with the ability to directly affect substantive legislative and executive decisions; and the length of the election cycle increases every year. With more than 500,000 elected officials in the U.S., and the evolution of a state of permanent campaigns, elections are a vital component of American representative democracy.

[*] Ph.D. Student, School of Public Affairs, American University.

Against this backdrop and in the shadow of the historic election of President Barack Obama, members of the panel on campaigns and elections addressed several wide-ranging issues, including the peaceful transfer of power, expectations of the electorate both before and after Election Day, and the relationship between elections and governance. David Dulio's piece, "What Do We Expect from Our Elections?," framed the discussion. Following his remarks, a panel of campaign practitioners offered their perspective on the issue.

David Dulio

According to Dulio, there are several ways to approach the magnitude of the public's expectations for elections. At one end of the spectrum are sarcasm and cynicism; idealism and unrealistic goals are at the other. Rather than framing his discussion around what are clearly emotional responses, Dulio chose to address the question analytically and practically. In order to best conceptualize the issue Dulio divided the public's expectations into two groups: those occurring before Election Day and those occurring after.

Dulio began by arguing that the public has at least five distinct expectations of the pre-Election Day campaign process: They want equal access to the voting booth, a fair process for all candidates, and a process characterized by good competition and an informative, ethical discourse.

Even these basic expectations, according to Dulio, are often not met. Inequality between candidates is often a function of asymmetric resources, which takes many forms in the electoral process: the incumbency advantage, major party advantages over third parties, disparate influence of wealthy interest groups, and lopsided PAC money distribution, to name a few. Further, the candidates themselves are rarely equal, with an incumbent running either unopposed or against token opposition being an example. Without any sort of robust challenge to his or her seat, an incumbent is not forced to engage with the issues and the voters in any real way. If complacency sets in, the quality of representation may suffer, and with it the very function of our democratic process.

Even hotly contested elections are not always as informative as voters expect them to be. One potential problem may be a disconnect between the candidate's message and what the voter wants or needs to hear. From the substance of a candidate's message, to the clarity and tone used to deliver the message, many of these problems are self-inflicted. There is also the potential for the candidate's message to be overwhelmed by the vast amount of external information available to the voter, a problem that has become much more salient in the internet age: The public's final pre-election-day expectation is for sound campaign ethics. While the level of ethically questionable actions varies from campaign to campaign, Dulio suggests that it is difficult to find one without any incident.

Moving past Election Day, Dulio made clear that he believes the public's expectations for governance are simple: good results. More specifically, this includes expecting good leaders, good policies, and good representation. According to Dulio, these expectations are met more often than those related to the campaign process. The public expects its representatives to be responsive and effective, and to produce results that are both legitimate and confidence-inspiring. Relatedly, Dulio highlighted the importance of an expectation often overlooked: the peaceful transition of power. Though inequalities still plague the electoral process, though the conversation between candidate and voting public is neither as informative or as ethical as many desire, Dulio argued that the stability and quality of government after Election Day consistently meets expectations.

Rob Engel

In his response to Dulio, Rob Engel addressed the issue from the perspective of a campaign manager, emphasizing the importance of one question, "Who is responsible?" According to Engel, Dulio placed the onus on the voters, arguing that it is the responsibility of the voter to become educated and engaged in the process. Engel disagreed, arguing instead that it is the candidates and their staff that should be seen as the responsible parties. Elections, for Engel, are about choices, and campaigns are about definitions. It is the responsibility of candidates and their staff to actively create and define the choices put before the voter. When candidates approach an individual to ask for their vote, the request must be specific in order to be effective. At minimum, the candidate must be able to explain in some detail how the voter's interests will be represented. It is the responsibility of the candidate to ensure that when the individual is in the voting booth, they have the information necessary to make an informed decision. This is an expectation, like several of Dulio's other expectations, which often is not met. And when it is not met, at least according to Engel, it is the candidate, not the voter who should be held accountable.

Engel also described the six principles that define how he approaches elections:

1. Stay focused.
2. Never underestimate the intelligence of the voter, but don't overestimate their interest in the American political process.
3. Campaigns are about choices and elections are about definitions.
4. The greatest determinant of electoral behavior is electoral history.
5. Less is more.
6. Stay focused.

The list begins and ends with command to "stay focused." Engel's second point, one that was echoed by every other member of the panel, is to avoid underestimating the intelligence of the voter, without overestimating their interest in the American political process. Achieving this balanced perspective is imperative for a candidate who competes every day with the voters' preoccupation with the details of their own lives. This preoccupation drives Engel's belief that political operatives, whose job revolves around knowing the details of the campaign, should be packaging and providing the voter with easily digestible information. It is unrealistic to expect that individual voters, many of whom face several competing interests in their own lives, will proactively seek out their own campaign-related information.

Engel returned to his assertion that campaigns are about choices and elections are about definitions, reiterating that it is the responsibility of the candidate and staff to define and drive those choices. Next, Engel turned to the importance of history as a predictor of voting behavior. In his experience, districts don't often shift their voting patterns, which suggests that past behavior is the most accurate predictor. His fifth campaign principle is "less is more," which is Engel's way of emphasizing the importance of the first three principles.

Ultimately, Engel described the electoral process in very rational terms: an election is a zero-sum game and the candidate who most artfully manages the process ends up representing the district. Elections are won by those who can package information into digestible sound bites, simplified dichotomous 'choices,' not those willing to acknowledge the complexity of public policy and engage the voter in a genuine conversation about the issues of the day.

David Winston

In response to both Dulio and Engel, Winston focused on the implications of distinguishing the process of campaigning from that of governing. Though he agrees with Engel's contention that a successful candidate must present a choice to voters, Winston sees trouble in the fact that winning an election is the only value motivating how those choices are framed.

In making his case, Winston began by referencing David Cameron, leader of the Conservative Party in Britain. Mr. Cameron views the purpose of political parties as platform for proving to voters that a candidate is ready to govern effectively, not simply skilled at winning elections. Parties in the United States, according to Winston, lack this perspective and deny this approach to politics, as illustrated by the emphasis placed by campaigns on developing an understanding of electoral history, acquiring external funding, creating get out the vote programs, and so on, in an effort to defeat the opponent. Noticeably absent from this equation, however, is a focus on the issues. To Winston's mind, a campaign that fails to address substantive issues, necessarily places a mystery candidate into office. It is this disconnect—between winning elections and governance—that has created much of America's cynicism toward politics. Because a candidate's views on governing have been so efficiently removed from the campaign discourse, Winston believes the public has lost all trust in both the electoral process and the government it renders.

Winston sees two critical issues when discussing the concept of fairness in elections: redistricting and resources. Winston managed the 1990 redistricting process for the RNC, and describes a process where incumbents choose the people who will vote for them and then draw the lines accordingly. He considers the technological ability to select people with a remarkable level of precision one of the main reasons that really competitive districts are disappearing from the electoral landscape. The ability to know how a district will vote for the next decade results in political parties moving away from center and toward their ideological extremes. This move towards extreme positions is a way of insulating a candidate from primary challengers. In contrast to Dulio, Winston believes that the threat to fairness in electoral politics posed by resources is overblown. They are important, but if a campaign is without a message, then it could have limitless resources but go nowhere. To make his point, Winston used the example of the 2008 Republican presidential primary, where the candidates with the most money—Mitt Romney and Rudy Giuliani among them—had very little effect. In Winston's view, McCain was the best candidate, even when he had relatively little money; once he became better funded, he was on track to win the nomination.

Though Winston disagreed with Dulio's assertion that individuals focus on national rather than local issues when determining how to vote, he did admit that national elections can hinge on key national issues, especially as a means of distinguishing candidates during a primary campaign. For example, despite the effectiveness of his local-level grass roots efforts, if Obama had been for the war in Iraq, he would have lost in the Democratic primary.

Anne Caprara

Caprara used her remarks to draw on her recent experience managing Congresswoman Betsy Markey's campaign to represent Colorado's 4th District in the House of Representatives. She noted that there is no such thing as a safe seat in Congress anymore. Some seats however are safer than others, owing primarily to redistricting efforts. Caprara stressed that timing and the constituency's present sentiment as well as a number of other situational factors all played major roles in each election.

Caprara argued that campaign finance has become a dominant issue in political campaigns. She noted that, while not everyone is pleased with the amount of money required to run a campaign, most acknowledge that the ability to raise money has become a necessity in order to prove a candidate's viability. Caprara pins much of the blame for this new reality squarely on the media: Fundraising amounts are easy ways for the media to quantify a race and serve well as an early-stage measuring stick. The result in many cases is a vicious circle for candidates. Without solid funding, a candidate appears less competitive, which may translate into lower levels of attendance at campaign events and less favorable coverage from the media. And so on.

Caprara also believes that the 2008 presidential election—particularly the Democratic primary—represented a sea change in campaign finance and electoral strategy. In many respects, the race pitted the old, classic style of campaign finance—Hillary Clinton's traditional, well-connected fundraising network—against Barack Obama's 21st century internet-based funding machine. In Caprara's mind, Obama's model was successful largely because its focus on small contributions from many donors facilitated a strong local level of ownership of the campaign.

Toward the end of her remarks, Caprara attempted to link the electoral process with the business of governing by returning to the organizing theme of the Conference.

How do campaigns and elections relate to the public's expectations for their government more broadly? Caprara believes that while the national issues may play a large role in the election, local issues are what drives individual voters and that casework is what defines a constituent's view of their representative. She did not discount the ability of key issues to frame the terms of a campaign. Drawing on her experience in the 2008 congressional race, she described how the incumbent candidate's almost singular focus on an opposition to gay marriage created an opportunity for Caprara and her candidate to shift the terms of the debate. Instead of engaging with Marilyn Musgrave on the gay marriage issue, Caprara and Markey focused on Markey's economic plan, an issue that resonated with voters in Colorado.

Questions from the Audience

The first question from the audience was directed to Winston. In light of his earlier remarks on redistricting, how does one break the cycle of a majority-controlled system? Winston responded that the only way to do so was to take the pen out of the hand of political operatives. Proposals like establishing non-partisan boards are not realistic. Instead, Winston recommended developing a system of unified standards that would govern the process. Allowing partisan individuals to draw plans to their benefit and interest will only serve to perpetuate the system. In Winston's view, establishing such a standards-based system would require action by the Supreme Court. As currently constructed, the Court sees nothing unconstitutional about the current system, owing to the belief that redistricting is fundamentally a political process. Winston believes that only a shift in the Court's thinking would be able to unlock the existing approach to redistricting, which continues to negatively affect the American system of representative democracy.

The second question addressed a perceived dearth of election-specific training in public affairs schools around the country. Candice Nelson responded that American University's School of Public Affairs is contemplating a certificate program in election administration. Dulio commented that the nature of a federalist system and the varied rules between states could be a hindrance to training election officials. Relatedly, Caprara lauded the creation of "election protection systems"—developed by both political parties in the wake of the contested presidential election of 2000—to ensure that federal, state, and local election laws are strictly adhered to on Election Day.

A third audience question dealt with misinformation and lying during campaigns, wondering whether the high stakes of elections justified unethical behavior like lying. The entire panel agreed that there is a clear ethical standard against lying during a campaign. Engel and Caprara both commented that tactics like lying are simply too irrational for campaigns to use. The risk is too great, and the tolerance for such behavior is too low.

Chapter 9

Restoring Public Protections: Regulatory Challenges Confronting President Obama and the 111th Congress

Rick Melberth*

"Starting today, we must pick ourselves up, dust ourselves off, and begin again the work of remaking America. For everywhere we look, there is work to be done."

President Barack Obama
January 20, 2009

Introduction

Following this statement in his inaugural address, President Obama recounted the work that needs to be done, including the need to "transform our schools and colleges and universities to meet the demands of a new age." Our colleges and universities can play an important role in helping to rebuild the capacity of government at all levels because few institutions in society can address the range of

* Director of Regulatory Policy, OMB Watch

policy issues that need work. One of the biggest challenges facing this new administration and all of American society is the restoration of government's ability to protect the public.

Political scientists, economists, and legal scholars who generally focus on administrative law produce most of the literature on public protections. These writings reflect the battle in Washington over whether federal agencies regulate too much or too little, or whether federal regulations cost too much or are insufficient. Empirical studies of regulation, however, are few and thus the disputes about what approaches work best and whether there is need for regulatory reform continue (Copeland, 2004: CRS 3). Efforts to evaluate regulatory effectiveness and understand the real costs of rulemaking in agencies are hindered by lack of data and by too few resources for agencies to undertake these efforts in concert with their public protection missions.[1]

This paper presents a range of challenges that the new administration and Congress face. Section II describes the importance of public protections, gives a brief history of our recent attitude towards government's role, and describes the context in which the new president and Congress find themselves. Section III outlines some major questions confronting the administration in its efforts to reform our regulatory process.

Why Regulations are Important

Regulations are critical components for implementing public policy. They provide protections that we take for granted every day from our toothpaste to transportation, from our food to children's toys. Especially now, improving the federal regulatory system has become an urgent issue.

History

Regulations are not just legal implementations done by federal, state, or local bureaucrats even though their implementation is often fought out in the courts. They are the expressions of a very public legislative process at the heart of government. Without a mandate to develop standards of safety for public health, consumer products, and the workplace, or to protect our financial transactions, this legislative process is powerless. And yet, despite their impacts and importance, regulations have been attacked as burdens, stifling innovation and causing businesses unnecessary costs. In the 20th century, these attacks occurred as far back as 1906 when Upton Sinclair published *The Jungle.* Public outrage and President Theodore Roosevelt's lobbying against the deplorable working conditions Sinclair described led to the creation of the U.S. Food and Drug Administration (FDA)—but not without overcoming considerable opposition from meat packers.[2]

The current structure of federal regulatory agencies largely grew out of a range of environmental, civil rights, and banking crises during the 1960s and 1970s (Croley, 2008: 3). For example, the Environmental Protection Agency (EPA) was created in 1970, the Occupational Safety and Health Administration

(OSHA) in 1971, and the Consumer Product Safety Commission (CPSC) in 1973.

But there has been a three decades-long backlash against the regulatory state. In President Ronald Reagan's 1981 inaugural address, he cataloged the rise of inflation, unemployment, and the burden of taxes on citizens, but he argued that those problems paled in comparison with the "pace of public spending." To address this "present crisis," he called for reducing the size of government and the burdens it places on individual freedom. He cited the burden of bureaucratic red tape on businesses to highlight the problems of the regulatory state. His now famous phrase that "government is not the solution to our problem; government is the problem" has been the banner behind which subsequent presidents have marched. The revolution President Reagan started led to one of the longest periods of deregulatory activity in U.S. history.

President Bill Clinton told the American people in his 1996 State of the Union address that "The era of big government is over." George W. Bush's presidency only differed from preceding attacks on the role of government in its degree of vitriol aimed at agencies and the strategies employed to limit regulations. The impacts of his deregulatory approach across a wide range of issues are well-documented.[3] President Bush cut agency budgets, appointed industry leaders to run the agencies that had recently regulated their businesses, rolled back protective standards, suppressed and distorted scientific information used in regulatory decision making, refused to regulate or put in place voluntary standards, and preempted states' ability to regulate and provide legal remedies when consumers were harmed by defective products.

As this list of strategies illustrates, the attacks on public protections over these decades have been both substantive and procedural. To the basic legal framework for developing regulations set out in the Administrative Procedure Act (APA) of 1946, presidents and Congress since the 1980s have added components through executive orders, legislation, and administrative directives. These additions have created a process fraught with delays and obstacles agencies must overcome at multiple points for a rulemaking to proceed.

With each additional obstacle, it takes agencies longer and requires more public resources to promulgate a regulation. The process, as Professor Thomas McGarity noted, has become ossified.[4] Although estimates vary, it now takes years to complete a regulation.[5] For some agencies, like OSHA, it now takes nearly a decade to complete a rule.

This delay has serious implications for the public, agencies, and presidential administrations. Delays in solving public health, safety, and environmental problems potentially threaten the public and frustrate federal and state regulators. It is possible that a president could serve an entire four-year term without seeing a major rule initiated and completed in some agencies before he leaves office.

The Impact

The procedural delays, the lack of safety standards, and standards compromised for political purposes have real impacts. Although declining, the number of people who die on our nation's highways each year is more than 37,000 (National Highway Transportation Administration, 2009). Food-borne illnesses kill an estimated 5,000 and sicken seventy-six million (Center for Science in the Public Interest, 2009). The 2008 incidence of salmonella-related deaths and illnesses from food produced at peanut-processing facilities killed nine people and sickened 637 across the country (Martin, 2009). More than 5500 workers die each year as a result of injury on the job (Bureau of Labor Statistics, 2009) with an additional 50,000 to 60,000 killed by occupational disease (AFL-CIO, 2008). And asthma—linked to air pollution—is rising dramatically, afflicting twenty million, including five million children (Asthma and Allergy Foundation of American, 2008). Changes in natural cycles are causing more Katrina-like events and more flooding, loss of cropland and fisheries, and contamination of drinking water aquifers. The government's response to these natural and man-made accidents and events has been inadequate, which breeds further distrust and dissatisfaction with the federal government.

The current financial crisis, caused in part by inept banking and financial regulators and the lack of regulations governing the trading of increasingly exotic products like credit default swaps, is bringing the country to economic depths not seen since the Great Depression. Unemployment in July 2009 rose to 9.4 percent, to 14.5 million unemployed, and payroll jobs across nearly all sectors of the economy have declined by 6.7 million since the current recession started in December 2007, according to the Bureau of Labor Statistics (2009). Most economists expect these trends to get worse before they get better.

Demonstrations targeting bankers and auctioneers are occurring across the country as foreclosed homes are being auctioned off. Home foreclosures in the US are happening at a rate of one foreclosure every thirteen seconds, according to the Center for Responsible Lending (Fears, 2009). Clearly, the country faces regulatory crises that stretch across both financial and social sectors.

Not surprisingly, the sustained attack on regulations has influenced attitudes towards government's role in protecting the public. The majority of the public expects our government to ensure that the food we eat, the water we drink, the air we breathe, the items we buy, and the places we work are safe.[6] Yet survey respondents complain about excessive regulation and support the notion of personal responsibility.

The current crises have begun to shift these attitudes, at least with regard to financial regulation. In the 2008 presidential campaign, both candidates forecasted a change in the role of government regarding both financial and social regulation (Calmes, 2008). Recent polling conducted for the Coalition for an Accountable Recovery (2009) indicates that 58 percent of Americans support the economic stimulus plan President Obama has proposed, and that support reaches across regional and demographic divides.

A December 2008 Harris poll found that attitudes towards government's role are shifting in other policy areas as well. The survey "finds that public support for government services is substantially higher than it was in 2005." Although support differs across policy areas, Harris notes:

> The changes between December 2005 and December 2008 are very striking. We believe that they reflect a more positive attitude to government in general now compared to three years ago. A major reason for this change is surely a decline in the belief that "government is the problem" and a stronger belief that "government is part of the solution" —as a result of the economic and financial crisis, and discussion of government plans to "bail out" or "rescue" the banks and the auto industry, and of the need for a government stimulus program to generate economic recovery. (Harris Poll, 2009)

As President Obama said in his inaugural address:

> The question we ask today is not whether our government is too big or too small, but whether it works—whether it helps families find jobs at a decent wage, care they can afford, a retirement that is dignified. Where the answer is yes, we intend to move forward. Where the answer is no, programs will end. Those of us who manage the public's dollars will be held to account—to spend wisely, reform bad habits, and do our business in the light of day—because only then can we restore the vital trust between a people and their government. (2009)

President Obama and the 111th Congress took the stage at a point in U.S. history when our regulatory system was failing, presidential powers continued to expand at the expense of the legislative branch and federal agencies, and scarce federal resources were stretched to the limit. Still, government has to function. Rebuilding our regulatory structures is an important part of the work that needs to be done. "And to ensure that a crisis of this magnitude never happens again," the president told Congress in his February 24th address on the state of the economy, "I ask Congress to move quickly on legislation that will finally reform our outdated regulatory system. It is time to put in place tough, new commonsense rules of the road so that our financial market rewards drive and innovation, and punishes short-cuts and abuse" (2009).

Setting Regulatory Priorities

In addition to the current problems facing the country, the long-standing negative attitudes toward public protections, and dysfunctional regulatory processes, the president and Congress face new problems requiring new approaches. These current and emerging problems will likely require them to make very difficult policy choices.

Substantively, these new issues are daunting: financial reform, reorganizing and restoring government to provide basic protections like food and product safety, national security issues like chemical security, and climate change, among others. Many observers believe that these problems require new thinking and reformulating existing organizational and management approaches. Solutions to these problems might lead to dramatically different ways of thinking about public policy and administration to say nothing of the changes that may result in our economic system. For an issue as complex and far-reaching as climate change, for example, do we need a new regulatory architecture to consider all the implications of this problem?

Procedurally, we need new approaches for government accountability. President Obama's decision to create White House czars to address crosscutting issues may help rationalize policy across government. His choice to lead the office that currently oversees most agency regulations, law professor Cass Sunstein, has argued that regulatory decision making should be further centralized and coordinated in the White House.[7]

What are the risks and rewards of further centralizing policy and regulatory decisions in the White House? Are there implications for the role of agencies in setting public health and safety, consumer protection, and environmental standards? What are the implications for transparency and government accountability with more centralized executive power? Or is this the right approach to take for an increasingly complex government with overlapping agency jurisdictions?

Also, how can we use new information technology to create greater accountability? How can we meet the expectations of an increasingly electronic world for access, openness, and transparency? New websites like Recovery.gov, created to track federal stimulus spending, and USAspending.gov, which tracks grants and contracts spending, may be prototypes for a new era of government transparency and accountability.

A recent American Bar Association study called for reconceptualizing the current online regulatory system, Regulations.gov, to allow the public to participate in and follow the development of individual regulations more easily (2008). How will technological changes like e-rulemaking factor into regulatory decision making? If we develop systems to increase public participation and government transparency while policy decisions are increasingly centralized, will policymakers become aware of public comments even with enhanced information management capability? Is increased openness a partial antidote for increasingly centralized decision making?

President Obama and Congress are faced with a daunting series of crises and new issues. The policy challenges are, in some instances, unlike any that the federal government has had to address. So are the regulatory challenges. As government leaders sort out the policy priorities, so too, must they address the regulatory priorities. The following section outlines some important questions regarding government's regulatory function that should be addressed if the country is to rise to the challenges before it.

Major Regulatory Issues Facing the President and Congress

The scholarship on regulation that we see in our work has real gaps. Most of the literature advances explicit viewpoints or policy positions. Much of the scholarship comes from think tanks funded by businesses and their associations. The academic literature also appears more heavily tilted toward business interests like discussions of which market mechanisms seem to work, the deficiencies of regulatory agencies, and how to make regulations more efficient (Croley, 2008: 1-3).

The discussion below raises some questions that policy specialists can answer to provide greater evidence of what works and what does not in regulatory government. What can we learn from mistakes and/or incidents that point to regulatory failures? How can we achieve better regulatory outcomes?

In April 2007, OMB Watch initiated a project to address the pressing need to reform the regulatory process. Seventeen regulatory and policy experts convened to examine issues and make reform recommendations to the next president and Congress (Bass et al, 2008). The group represented very different perspectives on the problems with the process but all recognized that the process is broken. The project report, *Advancing the Public Interest through Regulatory Reform* (the *Regulatory Reform* report), contains 49 recommendations of varying size and scope, but there are a few issues that clearly become higher priorities than others.

The four major questions outlined below are important ones debated by the project participants and by other students of the regulatory process. They reflect issues and debates that have occurred during the last half of the 20th century over the proper role of regulations. These questions are based on the assumption that the current regulatory system is in need of serious repair. They are among the questions the new administration faces as it begins to address the very difficult task of reforming our regulatory structures in order to produce more effective policy outcomes.

What Are the Proper Roles for Government Regulatory Organizations?

In 1980, Congress created an office within the Office of Management and Budget (OMB) to achieve certain paperwork reduction goals, review agencies' information collection and management activities, and develop improvements in federal information policy.[8] President Reagan also assigned to this office, the Office of Information and Regulatory Affairs (OIRA), the duty to review agencies' regulatory proposals and especially the economic costs and benefits of regulations.[9] OIRA has reviewed agency regulations since Reagan's executive orders outlining its functions. President Clinton replaced the Reagan orders with one of his own.[10] President George W. Bush amended the Clinton executive order.[11] President Obama rescinded the Bush orders in January, leaving in place and effect President Clinton's order (E.O. 12866).[12] All of these changes solidified this review function for OIRA and the reliance on cost-benefit analysis as an important criterion for determining whether a rule meets with OIRA's approval. What this means practically is that agencies do not issue significant regulations unless those regulations have been approved by OIRA.[13]

There has been considerable controversy over OIRA's role as the gatekeeper for agency regulations. Because regulations have been viewed so negatively in recent decades, OIRA has had political support for adding procedural obstacles to the rulemaking process like guidance document review and government-wide cost-benefit analysis guidelines. The office has also tried to control the information—technical, scientific, economic, and social information—used in formulating rules in order to achieve regulatory outcomes it wants. These procedures have led to delay, deregulation, or no regulation in some areas where agencies have been directed by Congress to regulate.

Conflict between the White House and Federal Agencies

On January 30, 2009, President Obama issued a memorandum to the heads of executive departments and agencies asking for recommendations to help develop a new regulatory executive order.[14] On February 27, OMB published a notice that it would accept public comment on a new regulatory executive order.[15] As the president begins this process of overlaying the legal framework for rulemaking set out in the APA with his own process for governing regulatory policy through a new executive order, one of the critical issues he faces is defining the relationship between OIRA and the agencies. What should OIRA's role be in reviewing agency regulations?

The president has a right to ensure that the substance of agency decisions is consistent with his administration's priorities and to manage the agencies in order to enhance their effectiveness. Most legislation directs agency heads to develop regulations implementing congressional wishes. The president already exerts control over regulatory outcomes by his constitutional power to appoint and remove these agency heads. On the other hand, agencies have the technical knowledge and experience in the disciplines and issues to address the legislative mandate they have been given by Congress. OIRA, by contrast, is a small office of about 55 employees, mostly economists and policy analysts. These employees do not have the technical and scientific knowledge to assess the quality of the complex information upon which regulatory standards are based. Therefore, should they be deciding which regulations should be approved and which should be rejected?

Alternatively, if OIRA retains this review of individual regulations, should it duplicate the expertise of the agencies even at a somewhat smaller scale than the agencies? How would this expansion of OIRA change the relationship between OIRA and the agencies? How would the roles of agencies change in the presence of an extra-regulatory body that maintains the final say over decisions—would the agencies have only enforcement duties similar to the role of states in our federal system?

President Obama has already created a system of interagency managers and policy advisors above agency heads—"czars" in media terms—to oversee cross-cutting and government-wide policy initiatives. This system of "czars" could result in other power centers within the White House which might compete with OIRA, expanded or not, and with agency regulatory activity. How will this new dynamic affect regulatory decision making?

For example, as EPA moves ahead with regulating vehicle emissions and greenhouse gases under the Clean Air Act, to what extent will the agency act independently (i.e., in the normal regulatory process that the agency would pursue) versus in a coordinated manner with Carol Browner who heads the White House Office of Energy and Climate Change Policy? How will regulatory decisions be made among EPA, OIRA, and this new policy office if OIRA has the responsibility to review and approve each regulation? If OIRA's role is redefined, where then does the locus of regulatory decision making rest, within the policy advisor's office or within the agency mandated to promulgate regulations? The management and policy challenges this institutional arrangement creates could be significant during the Obama administration and impact future administrations if these institutional changes last for four or eight years.

The president's decision to appoint a series of policy advisors has already come under fire. Sen. Robert Byrd (D-WV) criticized President Obama's use of the "czars" as a threat to the system of checks and balances. He is quoted as saying, "the rapid and easy accumulation of power by White House staff can threaten the Constitutional system of checks and balances. At the worst, White House staff have taken direction and control of programmatic areas that are the statutory responsibility of Senate-confirmed officials." If these advisors are not confirmed by the Senate, it is too easy to hide information and decision making, Byrd argued (Congress Daily PM, 2009).

The *Regulatory Reform* project made its recommendations regarding the role of OIRA and the agencies before the Obama administration announced its plans to use advisors to oversee crosscutting policies. Project members struggled with how to reform the relationship between OIRA and the agencies, but agreed that OIRA's review of agency rules should be done differently than during the last three decades. First, this relationship should recognize the expertise and statutory obligations of federal agencies; this recognition would result in a greater deference to agency decisions than currently exists.

Second, OIRA's penchant for creating one-size-fits-all approaches to the use of regulatory tools, such as cost-benefit-analysis and risk assessment, needs to stop. Federal agencies are far too diverse in their missions and statutory obligations to have standardized requirements for the use of such tools. These two changes alone should result in a different review process even if OIRA continues to review each significant rule.

If these two recommendations for change raised by the *Regulatory Reform* report are heeded in combination with the Obama administration's new institutional arrangements, the likely result will be a very different executive order than E.O. 12866 which has governed this review process since 1993.

There are many who disagree with the changes in OIRA's role suggested by the *Regulatory Reform* project. Business interests want a strong and active OIRA to counteract strong environmental legislation, for example, and to restrain allegedly overzealous agencies. Others argue executive control over agencies should extend to independent agencies. We need evidence to support or refute the impact of OIRA's review process. Has the system created by President Reagan produced better regulations or just fewer? How can we determine if regulations are qualitatively better?

Conflict between the White House and Congress

Historian Arthur M. Schlesinger traced the growth of presidential power to Franklin Roosevelt's creation of the Executive Office of the President in 1939.[16] This power has continued to grow throughout the 20th century. Two recent books explore the rise of President George W. Bush's further expansion of executive branch powers especially in matters of foreign intelligence and the use of presidential signing statements in which President Bush set aside portions of laws that administration officials thought infringed too greatly on presidential power.[17]

In the regulatory arena, the expansion of presidential power parallel's the growth of the regulatory state and presidents' use of executive orders for governing the review of agency rulemaking. As noted above, President Reagan's executive orders assigned to OIRA the responsibility for reviewing regulations. Subsequent presidents have followed that lead even while amending the mechanics of the process. President Clinton ordered OIRA to review only significant regulations instead of all regulations. President Bush issued one significant order that further centralized OIRA's power and represented "a clear expansion of presidential authority over rulemaking agencies" (Copeland, 2007) consistent with the expansive view of presidential power reflected in other aspects of the Bush presidency.

Layered on top of these orders are other mechanisms that helped presidents control regulatory outcomes. Whether through orders, directives from OIRA, information manipulation, or budget constraints on agencies, the executive expanded power over the process. Congress was complicit by abdicating its regulatory responsibilities such as oversight, reducing funding and resources for agencies, and passing a series of laws that made it harder to promulgate regulations by building in delays or creating hurdles for agencies (Copeland, 2004). Congressional impetus to reign in regulations are often framed as efforts to free small businesses from the burdens of regulation just as President Reagan argued in his inaugural address. This argument is difficult for elected officials to fight. As a result, agencies sometimes only regulate in the face of a crisis.

Is there a need today for Congress to reassert itself in regulatory matters? In what ways can Congress reassert its role or at least check the continued expansion of presidential control? Do the current crises in financial and social regulatory systems suggest instead that presidential power should be expanded and Congress should get out of the way?

Congressional efforts either to check the executive or to reassert Congress's role were few during the Bush administration. In the circumstances in which both the legislative and executive branches are controlled by one political party, or where Congress has little chance of overriding a presidential veto of legislation aimed at changing some aspect of the president's power, little change will occur in this balance of power. For example, Congress tried to defund OIRA after President Bush issued E.O. 13422 further centralizing power in OIRA. The appropriations language that passed in the House, aimed at stopping the order from being implemented, was eliminated when Congress passed a continuing resolution to fund the government for FY 2008 (OMB Watch, 2007).

Congress has attempted over the years to amend OIRA's responsibilities and/or change its funding and staffing. Some students of the regulatory process have argued that independent agencies such as the Securities and Exchange Commission, whose rules are not subject to review by OIRA, should have their rules reviewed just like other regulatory agencies. The justification for including independent agencies in the review process is that other laws implemented by OIRA, for example the Paperwork Reduction Act's paperwork clearance, apply to independent agencies now and it is only a logical extension to review the rules.[18]

Proposals for a congressional review office, greater analysis of agency rules by the Government Accountability Office (GAO) at the request of committee chairs, and regulatory budgets and reporting requirements are all examples of ways in which there might be greater congressional checks on agencies and presidents (not without bringing their own consequences). While various proposals to change the congressional role have been debated, it is likely the process will be driven largely by presidential executive orders. The result is more likely to be continued expansion of presidential power.

Who Do Agencies Serve? The Public or the Regulated?

Conventional wisdom holds that under Republican presidents agencies tend to work more cooperatively with regulated interests and are more anti-regulatory, and under Democratic administrations agencies cooperate less and are more forceful and aggressive in their approach to regulating. No doubt there is some truth in this generalization especially in some agencies.

There is research that indicates, however, that the swing in agency approaches to regulation between administrations is not as great as this generalization would have us believe. For example, although the data for many agencies are difficult to obtain and analyze, some agencies have had their budgets and/or staff cut over the last three decades.[19] Presidents have been generally slow to initiate rules early in their administrations but increase the number of proposed and final rules initiated at the end of their terms in office (O'Connell, 2009). Moreover, there is evidence that the total number of rules proposed and finalized is decreasing (Lubbers, 2008). These studies at least suggest that there are not large swings between administrations.

The larger points here are 1) that there is little empirical data to help us understand the effectiveness and efficiency of agencies' rulemaking activities, and 2) the current regulatory process relies heavily on regulated interests supplying information of all kinds to the agencies. This information includes regulatory strategies employed by different businesses, cost estimates of new regulatory requirements (before actual costs are known), and scientific and technical information. Agencies generally work with violators, especially first time violators, to mitigate practices that lead to noncompliance with regulatory requirements, and rely on sanctions and penalties as a last resort.

What we do know about who agencies serve comes from examinations of individual agencies. Based on recent reports one can conclude that agencies have done a far better job of serving the regulated communities than protecting the public if only because they have not been able to meet their missions. This may not be intentional since agencies' resources are so scarce and their capacities diminished. For example, recent reports indicate widespread problems at the Food and Drug Administration (FDA) with regulating medical devices, domestic and international food products, and national security because the agency has such diminished scientific and technical capacities.[20] An FDA report, *FDA Science and Mission at Risk,* concluded "the Agency suffers from serious scientific deficiencies and is not positioned to meet current or emerging regulatory responsibilities" (2007). As noted in Section II, these deficiencies have real impacts on our health and safety.

News reports and congressional hearings showed how the Federal Aviation Administration (FAA) had such a cozy relationship with some airlines that inspectors allowed airlines to skip safety inspections that would have resulted in grounding planes (Wolfe, 2008). CPSC, which regulates thousands of consumer products, struggled to respond to the dangerous exposure to lead in toys and other products that resulted in extensive recalls over the last few years (OMB Watch, 2007).

These widespread problems are the inevitable result of both three decades of viewing public protections as burdens on businesses and of a concerted, eight-year-long deregulatory effort by the Bush administration. The result is that even many businesses have begun to recognize the damage done by dismantling regulatory agencies after supporting the hands-off approach the Bush administration championed (Lipton and Harris 2007). From cigarettes to toys to cars to mortgages, industry groups have begun to work with Congress and agencies to regulate harmful market practices.

Companies often suffer substantial losses when these harmful practices and regulatory gaps result in product recalls and food safety scares. A recent study of the impacts of the toy industry recalls that occurred in 2007 is illustrative. Christmas sales that year of toys in product categories that were recalled dropped 30 percent; the entire industry experienced the spillover effects of the recalls and stock values declined significantly.[21]

Food product recalls were similarly damaging to industry. The salmonella contamination of peanut products made by the Peanut Corporation of America (PCA) in 2008 led to the Kellogg company recalling 7 million cases of its products at a cost of \$65-70 million.[22] Clearly, there are substantial costs to businesses in not regulating effectively.

One of the important themes underlying the recommendations in the *Regulatory Reform* report, and recommendations from many others who are concerned about public health, safety, and the environment, is the dire need to increase resources so that agencies can fulfill their organizational missions and meet their statutory obligations. While the public and businesses may be wary of regulations, the current crises provide opportunities to establish a more effective balance between supporting business and protecting the public. Rebuilding agencies' capacities is a long-term project but a critical one.

How Do We Restore Resources to Regulatory Agencies?

Agencies have responsibilities for more than promulgating regulations. They also monitor, inspect, and enforce compliance with regulations. Most agencies have experienced a drain of agency expertise—scientists, lawyers, engineers, inspectors, and safety officials. In many instances as noted above, agencies cannot meet their current mandates and will fall further behind as they are presented with new responsibilities for issues like climate change or creating new financial regulatory mechanisms.

How do we begin to rebuild these agencies? As some scholars have noted, there is very little data on the effectiveness of administrative agencies.[23] The lack of resources at agencies makes it very difficult for them to plan their regulatory agendas and enforcement programs, examine the effectiveness of regulations and programs, or even determine the costs of their rulemaking activities. In short, not only is there poor information about agency budgets over time, but there are few methods for evaluating individual regulations (GAO, 2007). As the *Regulatory Reform* report noted, "Without sufficient financial and human resources, clear enforcement goals, and sound evaluation tools, the problems identified and addressed in law cannot effectively be solved" (Bass et al, 2008).

The report suggested some ideas for how agencies can begin to build comprehensive regulatory initiatives. Some of the recommendations included:

- Agencies should work with small businesses and state and local governments (which often have substantial responsibilities under federal regulations) to create or improve compliance programs.
- These programs should include a mix of compliance assistance initiatives (programs by which agencies work with regulated entities to build compliance), sound enforcement, and clear sanctions such as increased civil and criminal penalties.
- Agencies should examine and experiment with a range of enforcement tools such as allowing citizen suits with fee-shifting components and new technological tools for monitoring compliance.
- Once new or revised compliance programs and approaches are developed, agencies should reflect in their budget requests to OMB and Congress sufficient funding to carry out these programs. (2008)

Lastly, the report recommends that Congress "[f]und an historical assessment of regulatory agency budgets and resource needs" (2008). This recommendation is aimed at gathering budget and staffing information into a consistent format to determine historical trends within agencies of their resources. These data should then be compared to the array of statutes each agency is charged with implementing. This historical assessment can assist Congress in allocating resources more efficiently as Congress and the administration face difficult budgetary decisions in the current environment.

Would conducting and using an assessment like this help insulate agencies from political and administrative swings within and between presidential administrations? Are there models, at the state level, for example, for assessing comprehensively the growth of statutory regulatory responsibilities compared to available resources? Agencies are caught in a Catch-22 of having to develop, plan, and enforce multi-year programs while their budgets are determined in an annual appropriations process in Congress. Are there appropriations mechanisms to better synchronize multi-year implementation of congressionally-mandated programs with annual appropriations?

What Kinds of Regulatory Tools and Information Are Needed?

Government accountability and effective public protections in complex policy areas require data, studies, evidence, and analysis to be duly considered. All types of information—economic, scientific, technical, and social—are used in regulatory decision making. This information is collected and analyzed using a range of tools critical to setting regulatory standards. In undertaking this task, agencies are often caught in a conflict between statutes and governance. One of the clearest examples of this conflict is the debate over the appropriate use of cost-benefit analysis (CBA).

Conflicts between Authorizing Statutes and Regulatory Tools

Tools like risk assessment and CBA are used by agency experts to determine the feasibility, effectiveness, and efficiency of regulations. As regulations have become more heavily influenced and/or determined by OIRA, the number of analytical requirements in the regulatory process have increased.

The use of CBA is most illustrative. Congress passed many laws establishing as the highest priorities public health, workplace safety, and environmental quality, not the cost of achieving those protections.[24] Conflicts between the statutes and a president's approach to governing arise when executive orders and directives require agencies to consider and analyze the economic impacts of rules. Those analyses are then used by OIRA to judge the acceptability of the rules even if there are clear legislative prohibitions to considering costs and legislative directions to use a standard such as an adequate margin of safety. If there is not an express legal prohibition against using CBA, it becomes an overlay on top of the legislative requirements Congress established. (Even when CBA is expressly prohibited by statute agencies must still expend considerable time and effort developing cost-benefit analyses before submitting draft and final rules to OIRA.) The use of this cost versus benefit calculation narrows the criteria by which standards are set. Agency rulemaking increasingly becomes a game of regulation-by-numbers.

Quantitative analyses are useful and sometimes essential to producing quality regulatory standards. They should be only part of the consideration in decision making when other criteria, such as establishing a clear margin of safety, are established in statute. In addition, the quantitative analyses are conducted by making certain assumptions. For example, the costs of meeting air and water quality standards may depend on the application of specific technological fixes (e.g., air pollution controls). In a CBA, assumptions are made about, for example, pollution dispersal rates, in calculating the estimated costs of compliance. These cost estimates are provided to the agency by the regulated industries who have an interest in overestimating the costs of compliance. The industry-generated estimates are used in the CBA. Agencies seldom, if ever, gather actual costs from regulated entities after new regulations have been in effect.

Benefits, meanwhile, are also estimated—when they can be quantified. Many benefits cannot be quantified and, therefore, are excluded from consideration or assigned a value of zero (i.e., no benefit) in the current method of conducting a CBA.

Over the last three decades, CBA has become a nearly determinative factor in many of OIRA's regulatory decisions, and these decisions have often conflicted with the statutes mandating agency action. The *Regulatory Reform* report contains recommendations to help counter this trend toward quantification (at the expense of qualitative considerations) in regulatory decision making. The report contains basic principles for the use of CBA (Bass et al 2008: 24). The principles rest on the basic premise of allowing agencies to decide when and how to use CBA based on the statutory mandate under which agencies operate.

One of the important tasks to undertake in the course of reforming the regulatory process is to determine the right tools for analyzing and proposing policy options. Is there a need to develop alternatives to the current use of CBA, risk assessment, peer review, and environmental impact statements? Do current analytical tools just need to be used differently and fairly? If so, how do we determine those practices and protect them from political interference? Does cost-benefit analysis lead to better regulations? There is one recent study to indicate that CBA is not done well and does not lead to substantially better outcomes.[25] New and complex policy areas may well require different methods for determining effective and efficient regulations. What are the right tools to meet these new regulatory challenges?

Conflicts between Statutes and Transparency of Information

President Obama has indicated that transparency is an important principle in his administration. New technologies make this easier than ever. There may be conflicts, however, between regulatory statutes (or their intent) and a president's approach to governing which may impact the extent to which government actions should be transparent. For example, the Administrative Procedure Act creates the basic statutory framework for the regulatory process. Its requirements are rather minimal, allowing agencies flexibility to develop their own internal procedures for creating rules. The procedural approach generally used by agencies, known as "informal rulemaking" in the APA, requires an agency to 1) publish a notice of proposed rulemaking in the *Federal Register,* 2) seek public comments through a notice-and-comment process, 3) consider public comments and information in formulating the final rule, and 4) publish in the *Federal Register* the final rule at least 30 days before the rule goes into effect.

The *Federal Register* publication of proposed rules is the first opportunity for the public to see the content of new rules even though there are many more ways to make the rule development process more transparent. (Regulations.gov is another public venue for learning about rules, but the information is not always posted in a timely manner and can be difficult to access.) With so much of the substance of regulations decided before an agency publishes a notice of proposed rulemaking, the public is largely shut out of the process until a rule has been drafted and ready for review at OIRA and publication in the *Federal Register.* A process based on a presumption of openness is important to achieving accountability in the stage where rules are developed prior to their publication.

There are a variety of additional procedural requirements overlaid on this APA process by executive orders, administrative directives, and legislation. While many of these additions have laudable policy goals, the cumulative effect is to create a cumbersome regulatory process and to delay the promulgation of important public protections. From a transparency perspective, much of the information generated by these additional requirements is not available to the public. For example, unless an agency chooses to make public communications between OIRA and the agency as a rule is being developed, those communications are not available to the public.

The lack of transparency at OIRA has been an issue to which John Graham, President George W. Bush's first OIRA administrator, was somewhat responsive when recommendations were suggested in a 2003 GAO report; he limited new disclosure policies, however, to the period in which rules are under review at OIRA, not to the period before rules are submitted. It is in the period before review where OIRA has its greatest impact on shaping agency rules (GAO, 2003).

The *Regulatory Reform* report urged the administration to create a commission to review the procedures added to the basic framework of the APA and to recommend changes to the structural components, including, if necessary, removing some to achieve a more effective process. Similarly, an American Bar Association (ABA) report also suggested the president and Congress undergo a process to "rationalize and streamline" the process (2008). A thorough review should result in a list of changes that can lead to more timely and effective regulations. Accomplishing this would be a considerable regulatory legacy.

Both of these reports also addressed the issue of transparency and government accountability. The *Regulatory Reform* report contained several recommendations about how to make the communications between OIRA and agencies open to the public, among other transparency recommendations. Likewise, the ABA report recommended a general emphasis on increased transparency of the review of regulations.

Technology also allows opportunities for increased public participation. Experimenting with new approaches that provide the public a greater voice in the regulatory process should enhance civic engagement and a better understanding of government. Agencies may benefit from enhanced participation as well. The public includes experts from many areas and people who have real world experience with the issues raised in rulemakings. New communication channels may lead to a process that is open, informative, and interactive. Agencies may gain better insight into the issues addressed in rules than the current closed and largely formal process.

What kind of interactive technologies can be applied to the regulatory process to achieve new levels of transparency and participation that President Obama supports? The European Union has created an interactive website, Your Voice in Europe, to allow the public to participate in policy decisions.[26] What is the experience with this approach and is it a useful model for the U.S.?

Conclusions

President Obama and the 111th Congress took office at a time of deep national crisis. The financial and social challenges they face are enormous and the American people expect government to play a large role in solving these problems. From the banking system to health care and consumer safety to national security, government must find solutions and competently implement them.

Part of this challenge is rebuilding our regulatory structures. They are critical to protecting the public, restoring normalcy, and rebuilding trust in government. We need to know more about how to make government work effectively after facing a generation in which government was viewed as the problem. Agencies have withered to ineffectiveness and yet they are responsible for implementing present and future policy solutions. This paper raises only a few questions about the kinds of information and answers society needs to begin addressing these challenges.

As Professor Freeman told Congress, "Given the importance and power of federal agencies, it is surprising how little we know about them" (2007). The scholars that dominate regulatory studies are mostly legal scholars and economists. Policy specialists need to be contributing to the field because public protections are far more broadly about governing than they are about legal or economic components, as important as those are.

For such an important topic that affects all of us each day, there is little scholarship on the process by which these protections are developed and managed, and few places to learn about this critical governmental function. American University's School of Public Affairs (SPA) was founded with the mission of preparing public servants and based partly on Franklin Roosevelt's notion of "practical idealism." It is one of the few schools and universities that can use Washington, D.C. as its laboratory. The Center for the Study of Rulemaking

(CSR) is one of the few places in the country that focuses on this process. President Kerwin's 2007 report, *The Management of Regulation Development: Out of the Shadows,* helps explain why this function is hidden "in the shadows of public administration:"

> The reasons for this imbalance of interest between the content of regulation and how that content is created are many. They range from the obvious (regulatory processes are difficult to understand and inherently dull) to the highly technical (cross-agency comparisons of management techniques require sophisticated research designs, data collection protocols, and nuanced analysis). Causes notwithstanding, the current state of knowledge of the architecture of regulation development should be a matter for deep academic and professional concern. (2007)

This paper is, in part, a plea for our educational institutions to do their part in recognizing and teaching the importance of government's role in protecting the public. We need a new generation of scholars to address these issues. We have a rich arena in which to do this work because 1) we are likely to experience a major restructuring of regulatory processes and agencies due to various crises facing the country, and 2) President Obama's promise of increased government transparency and accountability and use of information technology in ways other administrations have never done may provide a unique opportunity to study the workings of government agencies.

All of us have a responsibility to help rebuild society. As noted in the introduction, educational institutions can play a unique role. Evaluating which policy solutions work and which do not, proposing new ideas to address complex societal issues, and teaching about the importance of government's role—in conjunction with teaching about the responsibilities of other sectors—are tasks colleges and universities can and do undertake to "meet the demands of a new age." Our current challenges provide opportunities to start again and experiment with new approaches to rebuild the regulatory architecture of government.

Notes

1. See Jeffrey S. Lubbers, "The Transformation of the U.S. Rulemaking Process—For Better or Worse," *Ohio Northern University Law Review* 34 (2008): 469, 472-73; reeman, Jody. Testimony from Hearing on: H.R. 3564, the "Regulatory Improvement Act of 2007." Subcommittee on Commercial and Administrative Law, House Committee on the Judiciary. September 19, 2007. http://judiciary.house.gov/hearings/September2007/hear_091907_2.html; and Government Accountability Office, *Reexamining Regulations: Opportunities Exist to Improve Effectiveness and Transparency of Retrospective Reviews,* July 16, 2007, available at http://www.gao.gov/new.items/d07791.pdf, GAO-07-791.

2. For a brief history of 20th century regulation, see Osha Gray Davidson, *The Bush Legacy: An Assault on Public Protection,* (Washington, DC: OMB Watch, January 2009), available at www.ombwatch.org/node/3877.

3. See generally, for example, Davidson, *The Bush Legacy*; Charlie Savage, *Takeover: The Return of the Imperial Presidency and the Subversion of Democracy* (New York: Little, Brown, 2007); Frederick Schwarz and Aziz Z. Hug, *Unchecked and Unbalanced: Presidential Power in a Time of Terror* (New York: The New Press, 2007); Mark Zandi, *Financial Shock: A 360° Look at the Subprime Mortgage Implosion, and How to Avoid the Next Financial Crisis* (Upper Saddle River, New Jersey: FT Press, 2009); and Reece Rushing, *Special Interest Takeover: The Bush Administration and the Dismantling of Public Safeguards* (Washington, DC: Center for American Progress and OMB Watch, 2004).

4. Thomas O. McGarity, "Some Thoughts on 'Deossifying' the Rulemaking Process," *Duke Law Journal*, vol. 41 (1992), pp. 1385, 1385-86. Four years later, during debate over the Contract with America, McGarity makes the "paralysis by analysis" argument in Thomas O. McGarity, "The Expanded Debate Over the Future of the Regulatory State," *University of Chicago Law Review*, vol. 63 (1996), pp. 1463, 1523.

5. Government Accountability Office, *Federal Rulemaking: Improvements Needed to Monitoring and Evaluation of Rules as Well as to the Transparency of OMB Regulatory Review*, April 20, 2009, available at www.gao.gov/new.items/d09205.pdf, GAO-09-205. GAO's study showed wide variations among agencies in the length of time required to complete the rules evaluated. The average time was 4 years but the range for the rules in the study was 1 to 14 years.

6. See, for example, a nationwide Harris poll of adults taken October 16-23, 2007 found 53 percent believed there was too little government regulation around environmental protection; only 21 percent thought there was too much regulation. In another Harris poll of adults, from October 9-15, 2007, a majority of Americans believed oil, drug, and health insurance companies should be more regulated. At least 41 percent wanted more regulation of HMOs, gas and electric utilities, and tobacco.

7. See generally Cass Sunstein and Robert Hahn, "A New Executive Order for Improving Federal Regulation? Deeper and Wider Cost-Benefit Analysis," *University of Pennsylvania Law Review* 150 (May 2002).

8. Paperwork Reduction Act (44 U.S.C. 3501 *et seq*).

9. See Executive orders 12291 (issued in February 1981) and 12498 (issued January 1985).

10. See Executive order 12866 (issued September 1993).

11. See Executive orders 13258 (issued February 2002) and 13422 (issued January 2007).

12. See Executive order 13497 (issued February 4, 2009).

13. Under E.O. 12866, OIRA does have to approve regulations before they can be published by agencies. The review process consists of OIRA desk officers reviewing agencies' rules and supporting documents. The rules are either sent back to the agencies for further consideration or OIRA labels the rules "consistent with change" if revisions have occurred or "consistent with no change" if the rule has not been revised during the review process.

14. Memorandum for the Heads of Executive Departments and Agencies, January 30, 2009, available at http://edocket.access.gpo.gov/2009/pdf/E9-2434.pdf.

15. *Federal Register*, "Federal Regulatory Review," Vol. 74, No. 37, Thursday, February 26, 2009, available at http://edocket.access.gpo.gov/2009/pdf/E9-4080.pdf.

16. Arthur M. Schlesinger, *The Imperial Presidency* (Boston: Houghton Mifflin, 1973).

17. See Charlie Savage, *Takeover* (New York: Little, Brown and Company, 2007); and Frederick A. O. Schwarz, Jr. and Aziz Z. Huq, *Unchecked and Unbalanced.* (New York: New Press, 2007).

18. See Curtis W. Copeland, "The Role of the Office of Information and Regulatory Affairs in Federal Rulemaking," *Fordham Urban Law Journal* 33 (May 2006), for a description of these legislative issues.

19. See the series of articles by OMB Watch entitled *Bankrupting Government,* articles available at www.ombwatch.org.

20. See Government Accountability Office, *Medical Devices: FDA Should Take Steps to Ensure that High-Risk Device Types are Approved through the Most Stringent Premarket Review Process,* GAO-09-190, January 2009, available at http://www.gao.gov/new.items/d09190.pdf; and Food and Drug Administration Subcommittee on Science and Technology, *FDA Science and Mission at Risk*, November 2007, available at www.fda.gov/ohrms/dockets/ac/08/briefing/2008-4365b1_02_04z Subcommittee%20Report%20on%20Science%20and%20Technol.pdf.

21. Seth Freedman, Melissa Kearney, and Mara Lederman, "Product recalls, Imperfect Information, and Spillover Effects: Lessons from the Consumer Response to the 2007 Toy Recalls," National Bureau of Economic Research Working Paper No. 15183, July 2009, available at http://papers.ssrn.com/sol3/Determine_Quantity.cfm?nber_id=w15183.

22. Statement of A. D. David Mackay, President & Chief Executive Officer Kellogg Company before the Subcommittee on Oversight and Investigations, House Committee on Energy and Commerce, Hearing on "The Salmonella Outbreak: The Role of Industry in Protecting the Nation's Food Supply," March 19, 2009, available at http://energycommerce.house.gov/Press_111/20090319/testimony_mackay.pdf.

23. See again Jeffrey Lubbers, "The Transformation of the U.S. Rulemaking Process" and Freeman's testimony before the Subcommittee on Commercial and Administrative Law.

24. See, for example, the Clean Air Act, the Clean Water Act, the Occupational Safety and Health Act, the Mine Safety and Health Act, the Transportation and Motor Vehicle Safety Act, the Consumer Product Safety Act, the Comprehensive Environmental Response, Compensation, and Liability Act (Superfund), the Toxic Substances Control Act, and the Resource Conservation and Recovery Act.

25. Robert W. Hahn and Paul C. Tetlock, *Has Economic Analysis Improved Regulatory Decisions?* AEI-Brookings Joint Center for Regulatory Studies, Working Paper 07-08 April 2007.

26. The European Union's Your Voice in Europe site is available at http://ec.europa.eu/yourvoice/index_en.htm.

References

AFL-CIO. *Death on the Job: The Toll of Neglect,* 17th ed. April 2008. www.aflcio.org/issues/safety/memorial/doj_2008.cfm.

American Bar Association, Committee on the Status and Future of Federal e-Rulemaking. "Achieving the Potential: The Future of Federal e-Rulemaking." November 2008. http://ceri.law.cornell.edu/erm-comm.php.

American Bar Association, "Improving the Administrative Process: A Report to the President-Elect of the United States." 2008.www.abanet.org/adminlaw/Report%20to%20the%20President-Elect%20Oct%202008%20Final.pdf.

Asthma and Allergy Foundation of America. *Asthma Facts and Figures.* http://www.aafa.org/display.cfm?id=8&sub=42. (accessed September 9, 2008).

Bass, Gary D., Michael Byrd, and Caroline Smith DeWaal. *Advancing the Public Interest through Regulatory Reform: Recommendations for President-Elect Obama and the 11th Congress.* (Washington, DC: OMB Watch, November 2008).

Bureau of Labor Statistics. *Census of Fatal Occupational Injuries, All Charts.* 2009.

Bureau of Labor Statistics, *Employment Situation Summary News Release,* August 7, 2009.

Calmes, Jackie. "Both Sides of the Aisle See More Regulation," *New York Times*, October 14, 2008. Online Edition. www.nytimes.com/2008/10/14/business/economy/14regulate.html?scp=30&sq=%22Jackie%20Calmes%22&st=cse.

Center for Science in the Public Interest. "Hot Issues: Safe Produce." Food Safety Outbreak Alert. http://www.cspinet.org/foodsafety/hotissues.html. (accessed February 24, 2009).

Clinton, William J. *State of the Union Address*, January 23, 1996. The National Archives. http://clinton4.nara.gov/WH/New/other/sotu.html.

Coalition for an Accountable Recovery. "New Poll Shows Broad Support for Economic Recovery Package and Tough Government Accountability Measures," Press Release. Feb. 1, 2009.www.ombwatch.org/files/budgetstimulustransparencypollresults.pdf.

CongressDaily/PM. "Byrd Calls on Obama to Stop Naming Czars," National Journal. February 25, 2009.

Copeland, Curtis W. "Federal Regulatory Reform: An Overview," Congressional Research Service Report RL32356. April 20, 2004.

———. "The Law: Executive Order 13422: An Expansion of Presidential Influence in the Rulemaking Process." *Presidential Studies Quarterly* 37, 2 (September 1, 2007).

Croley, Steven P., *Regulation and the Public Interest: The Possibility of Good Regulatory Government.* Princeton: Princeton University Press, 2008.

Fears, Darryl. "Foreclosure Protests at D.C. Offices Reflect Trend," *Washington Post,* February 11, 2009, 1(B).

Freeman, Jody. Testimony from Hearing on: H.R. 3564, the "Regulatory Improvement Act of 2007." Subcommittee on Commercial and Administrative Law, House Committee on the Judiciary. September 19, 2007. http://judiciary.house.gov/hearings/September 2007/hear_091907_2.html

Food and Drug Administration, Subcommittee on Science and Technology. "FDA Science and Mission at Risk." November 2007. www.fda.gov/ohrms/dockets/ac/08/briefing/20084365b1_02_Subcommittee%20Report%20onScience%20and%20Technol.pdf

General Accounting Office. "OMB's Role in Reviews of Agencies' Draft Rules and the Transparency of Those Reviews." GAO-03-929. September 2003. www.gao.gov/

Government Accountability Office. "Reexamining Regulations: Opportunities Exist to Improve Effectiveness and Transparency of Retrospective Reviews". GAO-07-791. July 2007.

Joseph O'Connell, Anne. *Cleaning Up and Launching Ahead: What President Obama can Learn from Previous Administrations in Establishing his Regulatory Agenda.* Center for American Progress, January 2009. www.americanprogress.org/issues/2009/01/cleaning_up.html.

Kerwin, Cornelius M. *The Management of Regulation Development: Out of the Shadow.* Washington, DC: IBM Center for The Business of Government, 2007.

Lipton, Eric, and Gardiner Harris. "In Turnaround, Industries Seek U.S. Regulations," *New York Times,* September 16, 2007. www.nytimes.com/2007/09/16/washington/16regulate.html?_r=1&scp=2&sq=%22Eric%20Lipton%20and%20Gardiner%20Harris%22&st=cse.

Lubbers, Jeffrey S. "The Transformation of the U.S. Rulemaking Process—For Better or Worse," *Ohio Northern University Law Review* 34, (2008): 469, 472–73.

Martin, Andrew. "Peanut Corporation of America to Liquidate," *New York Times*, February 14, 2009, 2(B).

National Highway Transportation Administration, *Traffic Safety Facts: 2008 Traffic Safety Annual Assessment - Highlights*, June 2009. www-nrd.nhtsa.dot.gov/Pubs/811172.pdf. REF

OMB Watch. "A Year for Failure: Regulatory Policy News in 2007." December 18, 2007. http://www.ombwatch.org/node/3571.

OMB Watch. "Congress Hears Pleas for Expanded Authority and Resources at CPSC." September 25, 2007. www.ombwatch.org/node/3439.

Reagan, Ronald. *Inaugural Address*, January 20, 1981. www.presidency.ucsb.edu/ws/?pid=43130.

The Harris Poll. "Support for Government Services is Substantially Higher than It Was in 2005," Press Release. Jan. 13, 2009. www.harrisinteractive.com/harris_poll/pubs/Harris_Poll_2009_01_13.pdf.

Wolfe, Kathryn A. "Inspectors Suggest FAA Slipping on Airline Safety," *CQPolitics,* April 3, 2008. www.cqpolitics.com/wmspage.cfm?parm1=5&docID=news-000002696789.

Regulation Panel Summary

William G. Resh*

Presenter: *Rick Melberth*, Director of Federal Regulatory Policy, OMB Watch

Discussants: *Mark Greenwood*, Partner, Ropes and Gray LLP, and former senior member of the Environmental Protection Agency's (EPA) Office of General Counsel

Kathy Rest, Executive Director, Union of Concerned Scientists

Moderator: *Beryl Radin*, Scholar in Residence, School of Public Affairs, American University

Introduction

Few recognize how central the notion of regulation is to the function of government in American society. Regulation is at once a vehicle for addressing the size and orientation of the state and the utility of private markets, and tends to function as an ideological Rorschach test. Set against the backdrop of the 2008 election and the ongoing economic crisis, members of the panel on regulation dissected the process of developing and implementing effective rules, and debated the utility of government intervention for a society grappling with economic turmoil and environmental degradation.

Beryl Radin introduced the session with a quote from a *New York Times* editorial to frame the problems facing the country and the place of regulation in the Obama administration's agenda:

* Ph.D. Student, School of Public Affairs, American University.

> [The financial crisis] is rooted in the refusal of regulators, lawmakers, and executive branch officials to heed warnings about risk in the system and to use their powers to head them off. It is the result of antiregulatory bias and deregulatory zeal ascendant over the last three decades, but especially prevalent in the last ten years, that has eclipsed not only rules and regulations, but the very will to regulate." (*New York Times*, March 18, 2009: A30)

Radin went on to argue that even though such sentiments focused on financial sector reforms, the crisis may extend to the Bush administration's approach to social regulations as well. Thus, with the pervasive policy debates over reforms in federal spending, financial regulations, and health care policy, the Obama administration's social regulatory regime was in many ways being pursued under the public's radar, and through administrative means.

Rick Melberth

Undeniably, as Melberth stated later in the panel's discussion, "this is not a topic that everyone is drawn to." Yet, the importance of procedural reform for social and environmental regulations was not lost on the public interest groups and reformers who invested considerable energy in scrutinizing both the Obama and McCain campaigns. These activists expected substantive changes in regulatory policies and substantial procedural changes in executive oversight of administrative rulemaking. Among these groups, OMB Watch led the charge for increased transparency and statutory integrity in the rulemaking process. Melberth framed his remarks around four questions that he stressed must be answered to meet the current regulatory challenges: (1) under what oversight structure, (2) for whom, and (3) with what tools and (4) what information does government regulate private interests?

Melberth admitted that the current challenges facing the Obama administration and Congress were enormous. It was also his assertion that the American people "expect government to play a large role in solving these problems." Melberth continued by addressing the potential role for universities to play along those lines, with special emphasis for public affairs scholars and students. He lamented the fact that "the scholars that dominate regulatory studies are mostly legal scholars and economists," arguing that the contributions of policy specialists had been undermined in regulatory development. "Public protections," he explained, "are far more about governing than they are about legal or economic components (as important as those components are)." Finally, Melberth pleaded for American educational institutions

> to do their part in recognizing and teaching the importance of government's role in protecting the public. We need a new generation of scholars to address these new issues. Evaluating which policy solutions work and which do not, proposing new ideas to address complex societal issues, and teaching about the importance of government's role are tasks that colleges and universities can undertake to meet the demands of a new age.

To meet the current challenges, he argued, it was not the place of universities to merely teach about the current regulatory architecture of government, but "to start again and experiment with new approaches" to build it anew.

Mark Greenwood

Mark Greenwood addressed the panel with an explicit recommendation on how the regulatory regime could start again with an emphasis on correcting the substantial delay that accompanies most regulations that are now promulgated. As he recounted his days as an EPA administrator, Greenwood noted that at the EPA of the 1970s, "it was possible to do a rulemaking in a matter of two years." He argued that this was a reasonable timeframe, even for the challenging substantive issues and strict procedural mandates that faced the Agency in the 1970s. Yet, he argued that it now takes five to ten years for rules with the same or even less economic and societal impact to be produced. The reasons are many, according to Greenwood.

Certainly, he admitted, rules sometimes take a long time to be developed "because they should": "Any rule we have on climate change, for instance, will be very complex—moving up to billions of dollars . . . with a lot of societal effects." However, there were three other factors that Greenwood claimed led to delay in rulemaking that often get much less attention: data collection, analytical efforts, and the process itself.

Consonant with Melberth's description of information asymmetries between agencies and regulated industries, Greenwood claimed industries often do not understand the questions agencies pose to them when seeking information related to regulation. The lack of clarity about what information agencies need may lead to a back-and-forth that could extend the data collection time considerably. In addition to delays created by the requisite cost-benefit analysis (CBA), negotiations between federal and state governments, as well as an agency's internal analytical requirements may also add to the time needed to promulgate regulations.

Finally, Greenwood noted that some of the delay is owed to the process itself which may include "notice-and-comment, responding to public comment, the interactions between the agency and the Office of Management and Budget (OMB), expert consultation, peer review, etc." Greenwood's primary concern is "the pressure to have more process before the rule is proposed," which he believes makes the business of instituting government regulation "unwieldy."

While agreeing with Melberth's concern that OMB is part of the problem, Greenwood's emphasis was on what he termed the "bottleneck problem" that occurs within agencies themselves. Greenwood argues that there is a tendency within regulatory agencies to impose unnecessary layers of internal review at the regulatory development stage. These additional layers of review act, in effect, like a death of a million "little cuts" on the efficient and effective development of regulations.

By way of remedying this problem, Greenwood emphasizes the need for "real-time transparency of rulemaking." He argues many of things that are "held back before a rule is proposed" should be made available in the public domain. Traditionally, following the rulemaking process through the *Federal Register* could traditionally carry prohibitive time and information costs to resource-strapped stakeholders in different policy domains, especially individual citizens. Therefore, the onus was formerly placed upon the agencies to seek the information necessary to inform proposed regulations. President George W. Bush's "eRulemaking Initiative" (eRI) was created to decrease these costs. Started in 2003, the intention of eRI is to "provide the public with one-stop Web access to all proposed federal regulations and to give the public the ability to electronically submit comments on all federal agencies' rulemakings."[1]

eRI provides a centralized, online platform for all potential stakeholders from which rules issued by any and all federal agencies can be reviewed and commented on during the notice-and-comment stage. The web site (www.regulations.gov) provides opportunities for stakeholders to navigate agency rulemaking activities using dockets that hold all materials related to an issued rule (e.g., the proposed rule, supplementary materials and analysis, other stakeholder comments). Though the initiative was not yet fully implemented at the time the panel convened, agencies had been migrating to the new centralized platform incrementally over the previous five years. [Full implementation across the federal government was completed on September 30, 2009.]

Greenwood stressed that there is no reason why e-dockets published through *Regulations.gov* cannot be used to put documents into a "docket pre-rule." Rather than relying on agencies to send unsolicited information to constituencies they think are interested, Greenwood sees the e-docket platform and associated RSS feeds[2] as an opportunity to switch the burden to consumers by "push[ing] that information out . . . so [agencies] can notify people when something important went out in that docket." Greenwood believes that norms must be changed within agencies so that managers can create "an obligation among staff to put this information into an e-docket in a timely manner." He stressed that doing so would mean "getting away from the notion that we are investigating every fact that's interesting and getting to specific questions that you need answer to and what information helps answer them." To create a more efficient process, agencies should rely on the expert discretion of the agency staff to determine when certain forms of analysis are really necessary rather than simply adhering to one-size-fits-all rules applied regardless of case-specific facts.

Greenwood closed by addressing how important both staffing and management can be for promoting effective regulatory regimes. Rather than focusing on creating efficiencies through outsourcing, as advocated by some scholars, Greenwood argued that government needs to reinvest in career government employees, not contractors: "Agencies do not have the critical mass for things like enforcement and inspections. They don't have the skills that you need in a very complex, technological world. And, there is a wonderful skill called 'project management' that is terribly important in agencies that is completely undervalued and doesn't receive the attention and resources it deserves."

Kathy Rest

In her remarks, Kathy Rest attempted to expand the discussion from micro-level process matters to a "broader and more transformational vision for regulation." She began by describing the role regulation can play in promoting technological and scientific innovation. Taking a more provocative stance on reform, she focused on two points:

> (1) the potential for regulations to drive innovation, more fundamental change, and sustainable transformations—the things that we really need to address the complex problems of today and tomorrow, and the innovations we need to ensure that our country remains a vital and productive leader in the world; and (2) what all this may imply to the education of our future policymakers and regulators.

Rest argued that most environmental health and safety regulations have focused "rather narrowly or singly" on controlling pollution or hazards or waste in specific media like the air, water, or land. Product or worker safety regulations, she stressed, looked too narrowly at specific environments rather than addressing the true complexity of the problems at issue. In her view, "the time may be right to adopt, promote, and pursue a broader role for regulation—one that drives technological change and innovation, one that could be win-win-win for health, safety, and the environment." Doing so would enhance economic growth and increase societal wellbeing, she asserted: "Regulation can be a really potent motivator and stimulus of change, change that is more than incremental, to cleaner, inherently safer and energy-efficient technologies."

Rest called for a transformative regulatory scheme that goes beyond controlling pollution or risky technologies and products. To her, it is the moral imposition that gives government regulation the potential to be "a really potent motivator and stimulus of change . . . regulations generally send the clearest, the sharpest, and the loudest and most direct signal that something has to change." She advocated the use of technology-forcing regulation, noting the tool's past success in bringing about innovative technologies and pushing industry to new frontiers. The "win-win" to Rest is that a progressive and aggressive technology-forcing regulatory architecture will protect our citizenship and our economy, while helping to "ensure our global leadership in science and technology as well."

She went on to call for a multi-disciplinary, integrative approach to regulatory development, one that is not constrained to "one discipline's interpretation of a problem or proposed solution." Like Rick Melberth, she recognized the importance of legal and economic expertise to the development of government regulation. Rest argued that regulation will succeed in shifting private behavior and changing public institutions only when law and economics are supplemented by public policy and political science expertise. Additionally, she stressed the need "to add another lens to public policy, one that involves science and technology." Rest believes that both policymakers and scientists need to make each other literate to their particular discourse. "We need people who not only understand the importance of dialogue across disciplines, but have a basic understanding of those disciplines enough to harness the contributions of the different disciplines and to recognize their limitations."

Like most institutions, Rest admits, academic institutions are siloed. She sees little effort to promote cross-disciplinary dialogue through seminars, conferences, and community building within our universities. Rest argued that a cross-disciplinary dialogue is necessary if we want more than single-purpose solutions to today's complex policy problems. "Economics is too important to leave to economists . . . the law is too important to leave to lawyers . . . public policy is too important to leave to policymakers and public administrators . . . and science and technology are too important to leave just to the technical experts," Rest assures the panel. She warns that we not "miss the forest for the trees" and to explore more broadly, more deeply, and with the creativity that can only be developed with such a vision of the academy that seem to be missing.

Questions from the Audience

This panel offered the audience both a micro-level view of the some of the procedural changes that have been scrutinized by advocates for regulatory reform and a macro-level view of the societal changes regulation can purportedly achieve. During the question and answer period, the audience expressed a mixed reaction to Rest's appeal. The first question, addressed directly to Rest, noted that contrary to her argument, environmentally protective innovations have occurred within the private sector without the coercive guidance of government. Rest responded by noting that such advancements were not necessarily of the transformative nature she sees as being made possible through government regulation. Greenwood noted that centering a regulatory framework on both public and private disclosure and information-sharing might help to avoid combativeness between the business community and government and could simultaneously drive competition and consumption in the marketplace.

When asked if the recent transition to the *Regulations.gov* platform has helped increase transparency, Greenwood thought that information is being shared more frequently, and *Regulations.gov* is being used much more. Melberth was hesitant to admit much progress. He noted that *Regulations.gov* has been roundly criticized, has not been very effective, and it is "certainly very difficult to use, although there are improvements all the time." As evidence, he cited an American Bar Association (ABA) report recommending that *Regulations.gov* be revamped considerably, and changed in ways that would allow the core system to be maintained. According to Melberth, many of these early problems were a function of growing pains. For example, he noted that it was still the regular practice of stakeholders to go directly to the agencies and not to *Regulations.gov* for information about proposed rules. This initial reluctance resulted in navigation problems under the new centralized platform and had the effect of reducing rather than enhancing transparency. Consequently, Melberth agreed with many of the ABA recommendations and advocated for a more integrative platform.

Finally, Melberth admitted that the perceived assumption of the panel was that the use of regulation will have public support. However, he pointed to the importance of how regulatory policy is framed. Recalling the results of focus group analysis by OMB Watch, Melberth noted that the word "regulation" did not test very well. Rather, the word "protection" presented a more acceptable frame. Thus, the transformative nature that Rest advocates must be accompanied by a winning frame that assures public support for progressive action.

Notes

1. Available at www.regulations.gov/search/about.jsp#. (accessed October 14, 2008).

2. RSS, or "Really Simple Syndication" is any web feed format used "to publish frequently updated works—such as blog entries, news headlines, audio, and video—in a standardized format." An RSS document "includes full or summarized text, plus metadata such as publishing dates and authorship." Available at http://en.wikipedia.org/wiki/RSS. (accessed September 26, 2009).

List of Figures

List of Tables

About the Editors

Beryl A. Radin is a Scholar in Residence in the Department of Public Administration and Policy in the School of Public Affairs at American University. She is a fellow in the National Academy of Public Administration and the author of a range of books and articles dealing with public administration, policy analysis, intergovernmental management, and federal management. She was the chair of the 75th anniversary conference that served as the basis for this volume. She received the 2009 H. George Frederickson Award given by the Public Management Research Association for lifetime achievement and continuous contributions to public management research over an extended career.

Joshua M. Chanin is a Ph.D. candidate in Public Administration and Justice, Law, and Society. His dissertation, "Negotiated Justice? The Legal, Administrative, and Policy Implications of 'Pattern or Practice' Police Misconduct Reform," uses three analytical lenses to examine the implementation and institutionalization of reform in police departments found in systematic violation of constitutional law. Recent publications include, "What Every Public Manager Should Know About the Constitution" (with David H. Rosenbloom) and an edited volume titled *Federal Government Reorganization: A Policy and Management Perspective* (with Beryl A. Radin). The third edition of *Public Administration and Law*, written with David H. Rosenbloom and Rosemary O'Leary, will be published in 2010. In addition to his work at the School of Public Affairs, Josh is a Research Assistant at the National Institute of Justice and an adjunct instructor in George Washington University's Program on Security and Safety Leadership. He holds JD and MPA degrees from Indiana University – Bloomington.

Conference Information

The following organizations joined American University in celebrating SPA's 75th Anniversary:

American Political Science Association
American Society of Criminology
American Society of Public Administration
Association of Public Policy Analysis and Management
National Academy of Public Administration
National Association of Schools of Public Affairs and Public Administration

SPA Advisory Council

Pamela Deese, Chair
Gina Adams
Steven Albert
Ken C. Biberaj
L. Thomas Block
John Boyer
Theodore N. Carter
Stephen M. Daoust
Barbara Dyer
Robert Engel
S. David Fineman
Betsey Fischer
Jefferson Gill
Edward Goldberg
Charles P. Griffin
Elizabeth Kellar
Anita McBride
Warren L. Miller
Steven Nesmith
Anthony Pajunas
Samantha Sackin
Susan Spagna
Gwen Sykes
Nancy E. Tate

SPA 75th Anniversary Planning Committee

Beryl A. Radin, Chair
Richard R. Bennett
Dierdre Golash
Jacqueline M. Linde
Howard E. McCurdy
Candice J. Nelson
Margaret A. Weekes
Gamze Zeytinci

SPA Staff Assistance

Sarah Ammar
Torrey Androski
Matt Bourdon
Alison Brooks
Shree Chauhan
Mylinda Garrett
Amanda Girth
Bill Harder
Teri King
My-Lien Le
John Marvel
Kelley Moult
Bill Resh
Laura Lloyd
Allison Williams

Breinigsville, PA USA
11 August 2010
243379BV00003BA/2/P